Doing Justice to Mercy

STUDIES IN RELIGION AND CULTURE

Frank Burch Brown, Gary L. Ebersole,

and Edith Wyschogrod, Editors

Edited by Jonathan Rothchild
Matthew Myer Boulton
and Kevin Jung

Doing Justice
to
Mercy

Religion, Law, and
Criminal Justice

UNIVERSITY OF VIRGINIA PRESS

Charlottesville & London

University of Virginia Press
© 2007 by the Rector and Visitors of the University of Virginia
Printed in the United States of America on acid-free paper
First published 2007

9 8 7 6 5 4 3 2 1

Library of Congress Cataloging-in-Publication Data
Doing justice to mercy : religion, law, and criminal justice /
edited by Jonathan Rothchild, Matthew Myer Boulton, and
Kevin Jung.
　　　　p.　　cm. — (Studies in religion and culture)
Includes bibliographical references and index.
ISBN 978-0-8139-2642-1 (cloth : alk. paper) —
ISBN 978-0-8139-2643-8 (pbk. : alk. paper)
　　　1. Religion and justice. 2. Mercy. 3. Religion and law.
I. Rothchild, Jonathan. II. Boulton, Matthew Myer, 1970–
III. Jung, Kevin, 1970–
BL65.J87D65 2007
201'.764—dc22

2007008228

To my two sons, Kenny and Ryan
　—K.J.

*To all those working for more
humane, just, merciful institutions
of criminal justice*
　—M.M.B.

*With thanks to my parents, sister
and brother-in-law, and, in particular,
my wife, Charlotte Radler*
　—J.R.

Contents

PART II. APPROACHES TO JUSTICE AND MERCY

Preface

This is a book about the relationship of mercy to justice in systems of criminal justice. The contributors are, in the main, scholars and professionals in the fields of law and religion, and one might make the facile assumption that the lawyers were assigned the topic of justice while the theologians took the concept of mercy under consideration. This, however, would be a mistake. Codes of law and principles of just conduct abound in the world's religions, and the scriptures of Judaism and Christianity, by attributing ultimate justice and mercy to God, make the relationship of justice to mercy an essential, if often mysterious, feature of existence. Legal procedure, meanwhile, draws back from too simply identifying justice with retribution and asks whether mercy may introduce a more humane dimension to judicial decisions, sentencing, and imprisonment.

But, if both law and religion concern themselves with the relation of mercy to justice, do they mean the same things by the terms and do they relate them to one another in analogous ways? The contributors to this book propose that a discussion of such questions will be illuminating for law and religion alike. The contributors are also mindful that, since the 1970s, the United States has massively expanded its prison system in ways that raise fundamental questions about the purposes of the criminal justice system as a whole.

The book grew out of a three-day conference sponsored by the Martin Marty Center, the institute for the advanced study of religion at the University of Chicago Divinity School, with additional support from the University of Chicago Law School. A central purpose of the Marty Center is to identify critical issues in the academic study of religion that also engage other academic disciplines, the professions, and a significant segment of the wider public. In this case, we asked participants to consider the relationship of justice to mercy in some aspect of the criminal justice system. The conference examined the relation of mercy to justice at both theoretical and practical levels and in domestic and international contexts. The conference emphasized the necessity of approaching complex issues from multiple perspectives and included persons actively engaged in jurisprudence and public advocacy as well as scholars of law, religion, and ethics. We think that the resulting book chapters nicely cohere around the relationship of justice to mercy in criminal justice and, in so doing, also cast fresh light on both legal and religious studies.

On behalf of the Marty Center, I thank the conference organizers—Matthew Boulton, Kevin Jung, and Jonathan Rothchild—for conceiving the project and bringing it to fruition.

W. Clark Gilpin
University of Chicago Divinity School

Acknowledgments

Many hands have helped develop this book, along the way sharing their time, resources, and wisdom. Richard Rosengarten, Dean of the University of Chicago Divinity School, and W. Clark Gilpin, former director of the Martin Marty Center, the University of Chicago Divinity School, provided both institutional and personal support during the original conference that gave rise to these essays. Other members of the Divinity School, including Winnifred Fallers Sullivan and Jean Bethke Elshtain, helped facilitate and enrich the discussion. William Schweiker offered tireless encouragement and guidance in developing the project into a book. Finally, Cathie Brettschneider has been an exceptional editor, both supporting and sharpening our vision.

We thank Blackwell Publishing for granting permission rights for Marc Mauer's essay, which originally appeared as "Race, Class, and the Development of Criminal Justice Policy" in *Review of Policy Research* 21 (2004): 79–92.

Doing Justice to Mercy

Introduction

The Purpose of the Book

Breaches of law and the challenges of administering justice pervade and inform everyday human life. From domestic violence to corporate corruption, senseless hate crimes to the carnage of ethnic cleansing, a local homicide to an act of international terrorism—issues of crime and punishment deeply touch the lives of victims, offenders, and the rest of society.

Recent events on both domestic and international fronts have underscored how pressing issues of crime and punishment are reawakening awareness and discussion, from the dinner table to the highest centers of government. The September 11 attacks and the subsequent war on terror and war in Afghanistan and Iraq have indelibly shaped conceptions of order, security, and the rule of law; they have also provoked enormous debates on the constitutional and moral limits of government power in seeking this order and security. The execution of the one-thousandth person since the reinstatement of the death penalty in the United States in 1976 has reignited debates about the efficacy of the death penalty as a deterrent to crime. Others point to the falling crime rate, particularly with respect to violent crime, as evidence that mandatory sentencing has effectively reduced crime. In confronting these realities, tougher language of punishment has emerged and gained some momentum, intensifying questions about proper modes of administering punishment and protecting human rights.

Beyond the different discourses and high emotions surrounding these issues, there are also a number of undeniable facts that demand attention and make the subject matter of this volume all the more pressing. As contributors to this volume repeatedly note, in recent decades the number of people incarcerated in the United States has increased at a breathtaking rate to an unprecedented level in world history, quadrupling since 1980. There are now in excess of 2 million people incarcerated, including more than 1.4 million people of color, some 70 percent of the whole.

These numbers alone, implicating as they do not only the lives of the imprisoned but also the lives of their families, children, neighborhoods, and wider communities, call for renewed attention to questions of crime and punishment in the United States. Moreover, both contributing to this trend and constituting a trend of its own, sentencing in the United States has become increasingly punitive, as mandatory sentencing, "three-strikes-and-you're-out" policies, and longer sentences for nonviolent offenders increasingly dominate the penal and political landscape. Further, as grave concerns about terrorism and homeland security now appear as permanent and determining fixtures in American life, new questions arise as to just how far state power may or should go in the alleged interest of national defense, and accordingly, how far civil liberties may or should be compromised in the process.

In light of these contemporary issues and growing public concerns, a comprehensive public discourse on the relationship between "justice" and "mercy" vis-à-vis criminal justice systems seems necessary, not only to clarify the issues at stake but also to generate critically ideas and frameworks for reshaping current institutional patterns. The purpose of this book is to help convene just such a conversation. Because issues of criminal justice are theoretically and practically complex, an interdisciplinary approach seems to us most promising. This approach engages diverse realms of expertise, methodology, and terminology. Accordingly, the contributors to this volume are eminent scholars representing diverse fields—jurisprudence, theology, ethics, public policy, public defense, and social activism—as well as distinct subdisciplines within these fields: constitutional law, criminal law, international law, theological ethics, philosophical and social ethics, and political theology. As these contributors demonstrate, issues of mercy and justice do not conform to received dichotomies between religious convictions and legal obligations; rather, the complexity of these terms warrants capacious modes of thinking that embrace diverse conceptual frameworks.

Principal themes considered by these contributors include the place of mercy within the criminal justice system with reference to purposes of justice (e.g., deterrence, retribution, rehabilitation, and restoration); various grounds for practices of mercy (e.g., legal, philosophical, theological dimensions); and practical aspects of implementation. The volume is intended to demonstrate that, despite common misconceptions, the conversation between law and religion on these themes can be complementary and provocatively constructive for each other. It is often assumed that religion and ethics articulate complex systems of norms and justifications of mercy as constitutive of a proper standard of conduct and moral transformation, while law conceives of the rational limits of mercy and the inner dynamics of procedural structures, and frames questions of justice and mercy through statistical data and practical public policy concerns. Yet, as this volume illustrates, there is a nexus between law and religion that requires more critical attention. Despite unique vocabularies and sensibilities, the discourses of law and religion and ethics resonate in deep concerns about the nature and relationship of justice and mercy.

Imagining Justice and Mercy: A Brief History

Debates regarding justice and mercy lie entrenched within the legal, theological, and literary imaginations. Sophocles' brilliant portrayal of Antigone, who must weigh her familial duty to bury her treasonous brother Polyneices against the state-mandated prohibition against such burials, captures the tensions between civil order and authority (or justice that governs the polis) and religious and moral convictions (or mercy that privileges and exempts one from absolute rules). In response to Creon's claims for uniformity, Antigone cautions:

> Yes it was not Zeus that made the proclamation;
> nor did Justice, which lives with those below, enact
> such laws as that, for mankind. I did not believe
> your proclamation has such power to enable
> one who will someday die to override
> God's ordinances, unwritten and secure.
> *They* are not of today and yesterday;
> they live forever; none know when first they were.[1]

Questions of justice and mercy are equally important in the Hebrew Scriptures. The Torah requires adherence to the law in the form of the covenant. The two tables of the Decalogue integrate righteousness and justice within the community. Disavowing the covenant eviscerates righteousness and justice, or, as the prophet Amos put it, "Ah, you that turn justice to wormwood, and bring righteousness to the ground!" (Amos 5:7). Fidelity to the covenant necessitates awareness of the rights and duties derivative from mercy *and* justice and attending to those who stand outside the community (e.g., Exodus 23:9: "You shall not oppress a resident alien; you know the heart of an alien, for you were aliens in the land of Egypt"). Cultivating justice and mercy is to engage in *imitatio Dei*, that is, to imitate divine justice (e.g., the proportionality mandated by Exodus 21:23–25) and divine mercy (e.g., God's sparing of the murderer Cain in Genesis 4:15).

The New Testament and early Christian practices similarly seek to discern the moral duties entailed in and through *imitatio Christi*. Similar to the treatment of widows, orphans, and other outsiders in Exodus that transcends equality as the sole basis for justice, Jesus identifies moral obligations that extend moral boundaries (the Beatitudes), undertake the healing and welcoming of social pariahs and the unclean (the tasks of discipleship), and reveal the inscrutable character of sacrifice and transformation (the paschal mystery). Jesus challenges social structures and presuppositions, and his vision of love reinscribes the claims of justice (mutuality, reciprocity, and legal duties) in terms of the loving commitment to God and neighbor. The forgiveness preached by Jesus does not, as noted by Miroslav Volf, substitute for, but rather enthrones justice.[2] Several essays in this book appropriate the model of Jesus as crucial for understanding the relationship between justice and mercy today.

Additionally, many of the essays in this book probe the voices of theological tradition that reconcile justice and mercy. Essays engage theological interlocutors such as, among others, Augustine, Luther, Calvin, Rahner, Reinhold Niebuhr, and the United States Catholic Bishops. These appeals underscore the extent to which theological voices have—and can continue to have—significant influence on discussions of criminal justice in the form of cultural critique. These critiques, however, are developed more critically and constructively through engagement with philosophers (Certeau, Derrida, Foucault, Nussbaum, and Ricoeur), political theorists (Arendt, Biggar, and Kaplan), and legal thinkers (Morris, Murphy, Tonry, and Zimring) as well as with historical and cultural contexts.

There is no one vision of the relationship between justice and mercy embraced by the contributors. In fact, several essays develop typological models of justice and mercy. The common thread within the essays, as mentioned above, is the recognition that old dichotomies between law, theology, and morality are no longer valid. A 2005 Supreme Court case serves as one recent example. In *Roper v. Simmons,* the Court ruled the execution of minors to be unconstitutional. Writing the decision for the majority, Justice Kennedy pointed to a moral framework, the evolving standards of decency, in discerning what constitutes the Eighth Amendment's standard of cruel and unusual punishment: "To implement this framework this Court has established the propriety and affirmed the necessity of referring to 'the evolving standards of decency that mark the progress of a maturing society' to determine which punishments are so disproportionate as to be 'cruel and unusual.'"[3] The essays in this book seek to expand upon Justice Kennedy's vision by fostering conversations between religion, law, and criminal justice.

Two central sections govern the structure of the book: case studies in justice and mercy; and approaches to justice and mercy. Essays in section 1 address the case studies of race and class, domestic violence, the death penalty, sentencing, law and society, and international law (atrocity law). Essays in section 2 discuss approaches to justice and mercy from the standpoint of Scripture, political theology, theological ethics, phenomenology, social ethics, and historical theology.

Case Studies in Justice and Mercy

Marc Mauer, in "Race, Class, and the Development of Criminal Justice Policy," contends that—though it is worthwhile to continue to identify practices and processes that introduce unwarranted racial disparities into criminal justice decision making—a different level of analysis is required as well if we are to understand the ways in which our prisons have become virtually an obligatory stage in the life cycle of young black men (and, increasingly, women). This analysis suggests that both the means by which we choose to respond to crime problems and the vigor with which we do so are racially determined. That is, to the extent that we perceive crime as a "black problem," this both constrains our imagination in addressing the problem and compels us to design "solutions" that exacerbate inequalities in society. In order to explore these possibilities, Mauer argues, we need to remind ourselves that the means by which society develops a response to crime or any other social problem is always subject to a variety of social, cultural, and political dynamics. Appropriating numerous statistics, particularly data pertaining to the incarceration of African American males, Mauer explores the development of policy responses to crime and sentencing disparities vis-à-vis race and class.

Lois Gehr Livezey, in "Complicity or Justice and Mercy? Sexual Violence Challenges, the Criminal Justice System, and the Churches," discusses the culture of impunity and captivity that underlies contemporary perceptions of criminal justice. Concentrating on the issues of sexual and domestic violence, Livezey appropriates legal, historical, and theological frameworks to probe the problems within domestic and international contexts, including staggering statistics: "at least 4 million cases of domestic violence against women are reported every year." In terms of responses to these crimes, she identifies the role of faith communities, which has ranged from complicity to violence to commitments to justice and mercy. Churches, Livezey argues, can make unique contributions toward replacing impunity with justice. To achieve this objective, churches must undertake critical institutional engagements in the public realm, coupled with mercy in the form of hospitality. To accommodate the obligations of justice and the demands of mercy, churches cannot be reticent to investigate the efficacy and perils of power at their various roots. They must retrieve critical theological resources, including integrity and spirit, freedom, covenant, and joy.

Ernie Lewis reflects on twenty years as a state public defender in "Echoes of Grace: From the Prison to the State House." While he notes the abhorrent consequences of crime in individual and communal life, Lewis holds that there are subtle signs of mercy and grace in the present criminal justice system. These signs, however, are muted by the continuing practice of capital punishment. He notes that the operating principle of the current system is to "risk innocent deaths in order to maintain capital punishment." Lewis proposes an alternative vision, one informed by religious convictions but undergirded by judicial and legislative structures and analysis of Supreme Court decisions. He points to Kentucky's passing of the Racial Justice Act and the restoration of the Civil Rights Act as two points of departure for restorative justice. Restorative justice attends to considerations of mercy and presents more adequately the prospects for reflecting grace within criminal justice.

Jonathan Rothchild, in "Recapturing the Good, Not Merely Measuring Harms: Rehabilitation, Restoration, and the Federal Sentencing Guidelines," examines the four putative strategies for incarceration and concentrates on rehabilitation and its recent decline within criminal justice discourse. Conceptualizing rehabilitation as any method "established for purposes of transforming individuals so as to redress harms, restore social relationships, reintegrate offenders into society, repudiate cycles of vengeance, and replenish moral, social, and individual goods," he asks:

To what extent can the current system retrieve rehabilitation as an efficacious vehicle for achieving these objectives? Rothchild begins his answer by undertaking an expository excursus into the rehabilitative models of the United States from the 1800s until today. Rothchild critically analyzes the 1987 Federal Sentencing Guidelines, which created a 258–cell grid that formulates determinate, mandatory minimum sentences predicated on aggregate harms; he argues that these guidelines do redress previous sentencing discrepancies but at the price of attenuating the role of judges and reducing individuals to quantifiable data shorn of life histories. Appropriating resources from restorative models of justice and theological symbols, Rothchild contends that a more capacious vision of rehabilitation—one that attends to relationships between offender, victim, and community—can better accommodate the procedures of justice and the claims of mercy.

In "A Place for Mercy," Albert W. Alschuler assesses mercy and justice with respect to law and society. As he sees it, mercy—as "supererogatory," always "going beyond the requirements of duty"—is permissible only when it "does not undercut the sense of justice or the sense of reciprocity and obligation." To close his response, he considers two examples of what he calls "acts of mercy" in criminal justice proceedings: first, state decisions to dismiss or not pursue prosecution of individuals guilty of theft who are also recent victims of an "evil regime" (e.g., Jewish Holocaust survivors between 1945 and 1948, or emancipated slaves in late nineteenth-century America); and second, victims' decision not to pursue capital punishment.

David Scheffer brings the question of justice and mercy into the crime scenes of massive deaths and lost humanity around the world. His powerfully illustrated essay begins with consideration of what might constitute a proper response to these horrific crimes against humanity. He promotes an argument for recognizing and establishing a new category of international law and court under the concept of *atrocity,* which is meant to provide a more precise meaning and basis for responding to such high crimes. Using this as a case study, Scheffer reconsiders the question of justice and mercy. He claims that the importance of retributive justice cannot be ignored for the sake of restorative justice, at least in the case of atrocity crimes, because forgiveness without accountability not only awards atrocity criminals but also minimizes the seriousness of their crimes. He seems to view forgiveness as a personal act, whereas he defines accountability as a collective social responsibility. Furthermore, he contends that mercy and justice are compatible only when a proper repentance from the offender is obtained prior to the act of forgiveness. In this sense, accountability works both to induce the repentance and to help deter further heinous crimes.

In his response to Scheffer, David Little seeks to clarify Scheffer's overall argument and to understand why Scheffer is reluctant to replace retributive justice with restorative justice. The main context for this revisit is where Scheffer's argument is mostly concentrated, namely, the context of gross human rights violations for which Scheffer proposes atrocity law. While Little recognizes "the inescapability of retributive justice in regard to atrocity crimes," he questions Scheffer as to why the adoption of retributive justice must mean "maximum penalty" for atrocity criminals. In this regard, Little identifies two features of retributive justice: (1) "*forcible restraint*" and (2) "*forcible reversal of advantage*," the implementation of which he claims does not necessarily exclude ways to find "creative and innovative sentencing." Little also notes some points of convergence between forgiveness and justice as he analyzes Scheffer's comments on forgiveness and punishment. Yet he cautions against any quick compatibility between forgiveness and retributive justice, questioning Scheffer's distinction between "judicial" and "nonjudicial" ways of responding to criminal acts.

Approaches to Justice and Mercy

Matthew Myer Boulton, in "Samaritan Justice: A Theology of 'Mercy' and 'Neighborhood,'" provides a theological and Scriptural account of mercy. Boulton contrasts traditionally legal understandings of mercy as lenient remission of deserved punishment with the account of mercy in Luke 10:25–37, including both the framing narrative of Jesus's exchange with "a lawyer" and the framed parable Jesus tells him, the story of the so-called "good Samaritan." These nested narratives, Boulton contends, contain an alternative account of mercy as "the practice of transgressive care, the humane and humanizing work of repair and reconciliation in human life." This care is often "unexpected and extraordinary," "transgressive of customary sociopolitical boundaries," and "restorative for relationships beset by hostility and suspicion." Accordingly, it is a practice persistently attentive to "ushering outsiders 'in'"—including the "outsiders" produced in and through crime and criminal justice practices. This way of conceiving mercy, Boulton argues, not only clears up some conceptual and practical difficulties that arise once mercy is understood primarily as leniency in punishing, it also fruitfully points toward corollary accounts of both justice (as properly "restorative") and neighborhood (as properly restorative "from the 'outside' in"). Boulton spells out these implications to conclude his essay and suggests an agenda for further interdisciplinary work.

In "The Way of the Cross as Theatric of Counterterror," Mark Lewis Taylor makes a provocative case that Christian discipleship—that is, following and participating in Jesus's "way of the cross"—should be reconceived as creative, adversarial, nonviolent resistance to "organized terror" in all its forms, including the terror inflicted by and within the United States criminal justice system. For Taylor, this resistance must be "embedded" in "concrete movements for change in history," confronting organized terror in and through a "theatric" that seeks to engage and upend the theatricality of terror itself. At the heart of his case is an understanding of Jesus—whose entrance into Jerusalem on a donkey, for example, Taylor calls "street theater"—as a political dramaturge challenging Roman imperial power. Accordingly, the arrest, torture, and death of Jesus constitute for Taylor a process of "criminal (in)justice" culminating in a state execution. This execution was intended by the Roman state, Taylor argues, to be a striking bit of political theater, engendering fear among imperial subjects; but Jesus's nonviolent, adversarial approach "upstaged" the Roman drama, reworking it into a catalytic event that "galvanized an audience and set it in motion," inspiring it to carry on its work as a movement of "remembrance and celebration of his life and teachings." To close the essay, Taylor turns to contemporary "sites of struggle" where this "way of the cross" is manifest today, popular movements that actively resist organized terror, including the terrors of police brutality, prison rape, and other grim features of what Taylor calls "lockdown America."

In her response, Sarah Coakley makes four critical points. First, she raises the question of whether Taylor's suggested "performative" strategies promise much success in the face of unjust social structures, and, indeed, whether these strategies—however provisionally "subversive" they may be—actually assume and so contribute to the maintenance of those structures. Related to this first point is Coakley's "challenge" to Taylor to provide some "long-term vision of societal and political change, beyond the delicious subversions of sectarian revolt." Second, Coakley presses Taylor to provide more analysis of the widespread theological commitments supporting and underpinning the "criminal (in)justice" he condemns. In particular, she suggests that "an excerpted misreading of Calvin"—in which Calvin's treatment of the decisive penal and substitutive character of Christ's death is crucially left out—"may be at least partly to blame." Third, Coakley suggests that Taylor has elided a key aspect of criminal justice in the United States, an aspect that distinguishes it from other forms of "terror": namely, "its invisibility." And fourth, Coakley asks whether what she calls Taylor's "language of violence"—for example, his call for "adversarial" theatrics—may lend itself to volatility in the fray of political praxis, and so whether Taylor's case may require not only new rhetorical forms but also accompanying "spiritual disciplines."

William Schweiker, in his "Criminal Justice and Responsible Mercy," attempts to formulate a conception of responsible mercy. Employing resources within the biblical, theological, and philosophical traditions, Schweiker develops a Christian moral philosophy that functions as fully public argument about the validity of its claims. He offers distinctions between clemency, forgiveness, and mercy because their differences carry significant political ramifications. He defines responsible mercy as "non-necessitated action, a forbearance, that enacts or discloses the worth of persons within a system of justice when that system has gone awry and threatens to eradicate or efface human worth." To evaluate the role of responsible mercy, Schweiker undertakes an excursus on mercy and justice in the Judeo-Christian tradition, where he attends in particular to the issue of human wretchedness and the necessity of judgment. He develops a typology—constituted by the classical realist, the amelioristic, and the emancipatory positions—that outlines the main types of responses to human wretchedness in terms of justice and mercy. Schweiker concludes that responsible mercy aims to protect the fundamental worth of humans and to enable the "demands of justice [to] endure within systems of human power, the contexts of responsibility."

Kevin Jung's essay "Fallibility and Fragility: A Reflection on Justice and Mercy" challenges two contemporary theses about justice and mercy: (1) that mercy tampers with or even violates justice; and (2) that mercy should be unconditional in order to escape the economy of justice. In contrast to these views, Jung argues that justice and mercy belong to independent, but systematically related spheres of human action necessitated by the human condition of fallibility. Problematizing firm distinctions between justice and mercy, Jung appeals to the anthropological insights of Paul Ricoeur and Karl Rahner to reconceive justice and mercy as interrelated with respect to two phenomenological aspects, namely, agency and the fragile possibility of good.

Peter J. Paris argues that neither justice nor mercy alone can create a morally good social condition that enhances human flourishing. In Aristotelian terms, he posits that if the purpose of the state is to help individuals to realize their potentialities, the current practices of criminal justice geared toward only deterrence and retribution do not meet this end. One of Paris's important claims is that we should consider and deal with crime as a "societal disease." In this regard, any public crime becomes a public health issue, the solution of which requires a different approach than that of mere punishment. This approach should be more concerned with prevention and rehabilitation in order to help the criminal amend his or her old practices and develop good habits of life. Therefore, Paris finds that rehabilitative systems work best to unite justice and mercy.

W. Clark Gilpin, in his essay entitled "Criminal Justice and the Law of Love: Reflections on the Public Theology of Reinhold Niebuhr," undertakes three interrelated excurses: an exegesis of Reinhold Niebuhr's *An Interpretation of Christian Ethics,* an analysis of the basic tasks of a public theology, and an overview of the United States prison system from 1790 to 1860. Gilpin employs Niebuhr's "fruitful paradox" of the impossible ethical ideal to probe the mutually informative relationship between theological language and broad social issues such as criminal justice. Gilpin's motivation here is to begin to answer, "What can theology contribute to a general analysis of problems in American criminal justice?" As a historically minded theologian, Gilpin considers the penal codes of colonial America to illustrate the influence of class and economics on the administration of justice; he also explores the "Auburn system" of transformation developed in the early 1900s that includes institutionalized solitude. Gilpin juxtaposes these facts with Niebuhr's theology, which promotes both "equality as a principle of criticism" and human solidarity. Gilpin engages Niebuhr's norm of equal justice and his appeal to forgiveness rather than mercy as a vehicle for evaluating the objectives of public theology.

How can one account for the striking discrepancy between the United States and other advanced nations on the statistics of incarceration? Can this be explained sufficiently by the theological language of sin? In his response to W. Clark Gilpin, William C. Placher reexamines the theological merits of Niebuhrian heritage within the context of public theology. While agreeing with Gilpin on the theological relevance of Niebuhr to our contemporary context, Placher expresses concern that Niebuhr's idea of human fallibility and the impossibility of Jesus's ethic—absent Niebuhr's equal emphasis on justice as a means to approximate the ideal of love—may thwart the very efforts of Christians that are necessary for changing the dominating ethos of the criminal justice system in America. At least in contemporary American context, he argues, renewed Christian commitments to and efforts to reform the American criminal justice system are needed.

William Schweiker concludes the volume with a postscript that points to common themes among the essays as well as to conceptual catalysts for future conversations.

Notes

1. Sophocles, *Antigone,* 178 (original emphasis).
2. See Volf, *Exclusion and Embrace,* 123.
3. See *Roper v. Simmons,* 543 U.S. 551 (2005).

PART I

Case Studies in Justice and Mercy

Race, Class, and
the Development of
Criminal Justice Policy

MARC MAUER

The profound racial disparities that permeate the criminal justice system are by now distressingly prevalent and well documented. The unprecedented rise in the prison population over the past three decades—a six-fold increase, leading to the incarceration of more than 2 million Americans—has been accompanied by widespread racial effects. The figures are well known, but shocking nonetheless: one of every eight black males in the 25–34 age group is locked up on any given day, and 32 percent of black males born today can expect to spend time in a state or federal prison if current trends continue.[1]

These disparities have provoked a wide range of studies examining their origins. Broadly speaking, this scholarship has attempted to discern whether the outcomes are primarily a result of greater criminal involvement, and hence imprisonment, among African Americans, or of racially biased decision making within the justice system.

Analyzing these factors turns out to be more complex than one might assume. Gone are the days (for the most part) when a southern judge and jury might blatantly disregard compelling evidence pointing to guilt or innocence, based on the racial dynamics in the courtroom. In most courtrooms and jurisdictions, when disparate sentencing develops, its evolution is considerably more subtle.

The research evidence to date on both the presence and causes of racial disparity is mixed. In the realm of the death penalty, there is compelling evidence that the race of both victim and offender is a key element in the determination of which convicted murderers receive the death penalty. In a review of twenty-eight studies examining these issues, the General

Accounting Office concluded that, "In 82 percent of the studies, race of the victim was found to influence the likelihood of being charged with capital murder or receiving the death penalty; i.e., those who murdered whites were more likely to be sentenced to death than those who murdered blacks."[2]

But in noncapital sentencing, the research findings are somewhat ambiguous. In a study of sentencing outcomes in California, Rand researchers concluded that, for five of the six crimes studied (with the exception of drug offenses), "California courts are making racially equitable sentencing decisions" and that there was "no evidence of racial discrimination in the length of prison term imposed for any of the crimes studied."[3] But other scholars continue to note racial effects at sentencing, albeit sometimes subtle. The work of Cassia Spohn and colleagues has demonstrated that there are often a set of factors that in combination produce racially disparate outcomes. These may include gender, employment, age, income, education, offense, and race of the victim.[4] Spohn warns against considering only the direct effects of race on sentencing outcomes, noting that disparity is rooted in the nexus between race and a host of variables with which it interacts to influence sentencing decisions.

Clearly it is worthwhile to continue to explore these dynamics, with a goal of identifying practices and processes that may introduce unwarranted racial disparities into criminal justice decision making. But a different level of analysis is required as well if we are to understand the ways in which our prisons have become virtually an obligatory stage in the life cycle of young black men (and, increasingly, women). This analysis suggests that both the means by which we choose to respond to crime problems and the vigor with which we do so are racially determined. That is, to the extent that we perceive crime as a "black problem," this both constrains our imagination in addressing the problem and compels us to design "solutions" that exacerbate inequalities in society.

In order to explore these possibilities, we need to remind ourselves that the means by which society develops a response to crime or any other social problem is always subject to a variety of social, cultural, and political dynamics. Broadly speaking, the competing strands of thought for crime policy are represented by prevention and punishment. Prevention responses incorporate both family and community dynamics, and can be thought of as the complex ways in which a society provides support and encouragement for approved behavior. Most families do this rather instinctively, but social policies as developed by various nations are influential as well in this regard. We can think, for example, of the far greater social welfare orientation of the Scandinavian nations, or even most of Europe, in contrast to the market orientation that prevails in the United States.

The other form of response, punishment, is broadly administered by the criminal justice system. As a primarily reactive strategy, criminal justice sanctions would not normally be considered the strategy of choice for controlling crime. After all, by definition they are employed only after some harm has been done. Clearly, however, some significant level of such approaches will always be necessary.

In recent years, the level at which punishment is imposed in the United States has reached unprecedented proportions. By the standards of the industrialized world, American policies are considered quite extreme. The more than three thousand inmates on Death Row nationally have provoked great concern among the European Union and increasingly vocal opposition. Similarly, the growing rate of incarceration in the United States, a level generally five to eight times that of most European nations, stands in sharp contrast to attempts to control prison growth in many industrialized nations.

Thus, policy makers in the United States have consciously embraced a matrix of criminal justice policies that would have been unimaginable just thirty years ago, and have done so while much of the democratic world has remained committed to a far broader vision of the means by which it tries to maintain social order. The question, therefore, is why this particular set of policies and practices has been adopted when a far broader array of options was available.

This essay explores the hypothesis that the racial disparities produced by the punitive orientation of American criminal justice policy were not an unintended byproduct of a well-intended strategy to control crime, but were rather an outcome that was determined by the racial perceptions of the problem and that also could have been foreseen at various times of adoption. Thus, I examine both the framework by which policies have been developed as well as the processes by which they were implemented. I do not contend that a conspiracy has been at work in the development of these policies. While certain elements of intent can be documented at particular junctures, the overall development of policy in many respects represents the product of a willfully ignorant leadership and public that views its policy options from an extremely constrained perspective.

A similar framework has been developed by Jeffrey Reiman in his *Pyrrhic Defeat Theory*. Rather than identifying a single critical point at which discriminatory policy is implemented, Reiman notes that it is the sum of the parts that leads to a race- and class-based enforcement of crime.[5] For Reiman, the culmination of decisions made by legislators, police, prosecutors, judges, and juries adds up to an "implicit identification of crime with the dangerous acts of the poor, an identification amplified by the media."[6]

This analysis will be framed in three parts. First, what are the means by which the national approach to particular crime problems is framed by our racial perceptions?; essentially, under what circumstances do we opt for prevention or punishment as a primary focus of strategy? Second, within the criminal justice system, how is the relative punitiveness of sanctions affected by our race and class perceptions? And, third, what are the mechanisms by which these policies are adopted and implemented?

Developing Policy Responses to Crime

When we think about crime in the abstract, our immediate associations tend to be focused on the criminal justice system. Thus, if our car is vandalized or home broken into, we assume we call 911 and set into motion a series of criminal justice actions. There is nothing inappropriate about this course of action, but if we consider these issues from the point of view of public policy, we would want to consider a different set of options. These would focus on the relative efficacy of various kinds of interventions, both prior to an offender vandalizing a car and in response to that act. For example, to reduce the incidence of car theft, one could explore neighborhood and vehicle security measures or, in a broader sense, the relative availability of public transit. After all, if fewer cars are required, opportunities for auto theft will decline accordingly.

The beginnings of the "get-tough" approach to crime policy in the 1960s and 1970s were framed in a context of the civil rights movement and increasing polarization around racial issues. As criminologist Katherine Beckett has demonstrated, opposition to racial reform has been highly correlated with concerns about crime and support for law and order approaches. She notes that in response to the urban strife of the 1960s, social issues took on increasing prominence in political campaigns and that "beliefs concerning urban unrest, race, and crime had an unmistakable relationship to the vote."[7]

MARC MAUER

Scholars examining the impact of race on the imposition of criminal penalties since that time have noted significant correlations. David Greenberg and Valerie West analyze the rise in prison populations for the period 1971–91 and conclude that the size of a state's black population was an even stronger predictor of the prison population than the rate of violent crime.[8] They suggest that this may be the result of bias within the justice system, harsher sentencing policies, or a greater commitment to prison construction in states with sizable black populations.

A recent study exploring the factors that lead states to adopt the death penalty reached similar conclusions. Sociologists David Jacobs and Jason Carmichael analyzed a range of possible contributors to death penalty legislation from 1970 to 1990.[9] They concluded that rates of violent crime or murder had no influence over a state's adopting the death penalty, but that the proportion of African Americans in the state and income inequality were quite significant. Their results suggest "how important the politics of racial division and the racial foundations of punishment continue to be in the United States."[10]

The race and class dynamics of crime policy can be seen most clearly in the national approach to drugs and drug abuse. While this area of public policy has received much attention in recent years, the racial dynamics of policy making can be traced back a hundred years or more. Historian David Musto, for example, describes the role of racism and xenophobia in the formation of America's antidrug stance. Opium, once deemed a medical miracle due to its use as a powerful anesthetic during the Civil War, fell into disrepute because of its relationship with Chinese immigrants during the late nineteenth century.[11]

Similar patterns can be seen in the development of attitudes toward cocaine. In the context of the Reconstruction era following the Civil War, white southerners had a palpable fear in regard to the flood of recently freed slaves. Cocaine, once touted as a medical cure-all for problems as varied as allergies and alcoholism, soon came to be associated with perceived black violence against whites.[12] Rumors abounded regarding the drug's catalytic properties that led black men to rape white women, as well as making them impervious to smaller-caliber firearms. Dr. Hamilton Wright, in a report submitted to Congress in 1910 as it considered what, if any, regulations should be applied to certain narcotics, concluded that "it has been authoritatively stated that cocaine is often the direct incentive to the crime of rape by the Negroes of the South and other sections of the country."[13]

The history of marijuana policy is instructive as well. For the first several decades of the twentieth century, marijuana was viewed as a drug used primarily by blacks and Mexican Americans. Popular media communicated its presence in jazz clubs and other "racy" parts of town. By the time of the Depression, the presence of Mexican American labor that had previously been sought in the expanding American West was no longer a welcome sight to many Americans.[14] Mexican immigrants in the Southwest came to be seen as prolific marijuana users, and the drug came to be seen as one that led to indolence and vice. C. M. Goethe, the leader of the American Coalition, called for quotas on Mexican immigration in the 1930s: "Marijuana, perhaps now the most insidious of pure narcotics, is a direct by-product of unrestricted Mexican immigration. Mexican peddlers have been caught distributing sample marijuana cigarets [sic] to school children."[15] Whether or not these perceptions were accurate, they no doubt contributed to such legislation as the Boggs Act of the 1950s, which penalized first-time possession of marijuana or heroin with a sentence of two to five years in prison.

By the 1960s, marijuana came to be used widely by white middle-class college students. As reports of the new "counterculture" proliferated, along with increasing arrests of these young people, a reassessment of public attitudes quickly began. Commissions established by Presidents Kennedy and Johnson questioned the prevailing assumption of a direct link between marijuana and violent crime or heroin use. By 1970, federal legislation was passed that distinguished marijuana from other narcotics and lowered federal penalties for possession of small amounts. Calls for outright decriminalization became widespread, and by the mid-1970s, the Carter administration had endorsed decriminalizing possession of small amounts of marijuana.

From the 1930s to the 1960s, virtually nothing about marijuana had changed—except for the public perception of the user. And as this perception evolved from a black and brown hue to a white one, so, too, did the public's preferred policy response evolve from fear-driven punishment to compassionate, benign tolerance.

Overall, drug policy has often been motivated by fear and ignorance, and fueled by an incomplete understanding of cultural differences. This has led legislators to adopt targeted drug laws with a policy objective of preventing the intrusion of certain substances into people of "good homes," despite the fact that the bulk of drug users throughout American history have been white.

In recent years, the racial dynamics of the drug war have played themselves out most prominently in the punishments meted out to crack cocaine offenders. As crack emerged initially in urban areas in the mid-1980s, history began to repeat itself, as a mythology and public hysteria developed around the drug. Without minimizing the real harm caused by the crack trade, we can note the profound distortions and willful ignorance that pervaded public discussion of the new drug. Media and politicians seized upon the crack phenomenon and played up its perceived status as a drug used by poor, minority inner-city dwellers. By the middle of 1986, news magazines like *Time* featured cover stories referring to the crack situation as the "issue of the year," while *Newsweek* called it the biggest news story since Vietnam or Watergate.[16]

Public and policy-maker attention was particularly galvanized in 1986 when University of Maryland basketball star Len Bias died of a drug overdose while celebrating his having just been chosen by the Boston Celtics in the NBA draft. Bias's death was universally described as a crack overdose, thus setting in motion a frenzy of legislative activity in Congress designed to provide harsh penalties for the drug. It was not until the following year that it was revealed that Bias had in fact not died from crack, but from an overdose of powder cocaine. By then, though, the damage had been done, followed in 1988 by additional legislation establishing stiff mandatory penalties for possession or sale of even small amounts of crack.

Even though crack is produced from powder cocaine—just add a baking soda mixture and cook until the water evaporates and the rock "cracks"—the federal legislation established dramatically different penalties for the two forms of the drug. For crack, possession or sale of as little as five grams mandates five years in federal prison, but for cocaine, that penalty is not triggered until the sale of one hundred times that amount, or five hundred grams. The racial disparities that have accompanied the prosecution and sentencing of federal crack offenders have been dramatic, with African Americans constituting 85 percent of defendants each year.

Efforts to scale back the crack penalties and to reduce the sentencing disparity between the two forms of cocaine have been quite unsuccessful to date. Resistance to such change is often accompanied by professions of concern for the harm done to black communities, a plea that loses some potency when one recognizes that virtually all members of the Congressional Black Caucus have been vocal proponents of change. In 2001, Senators Jeff Sessions (R-AL) and Orrin Hatch (R-UT) cosponsored the Drug Sentencing Reform Act of 2001 that would have reduced the 100:1 ratio to a 20:1 ratio by lowering the threshold amount of drugs required to trigger the mandatory sentence for powder cocaine and raising it for crack cocaine. While the bill was not as broad as many reformers would have liked, it was notable in being sponsored by two senior Republican senators, an indication that the disparity issue had achieved considerable attention. The United States Sentencing Commission also held hearings in 2002 on the issue, but despite broad support for reform from diverse constituencies, the Department of Justice made clear that it was opposed to any change, effectively halting the momentum for reform.

Racial dynamics play themselves out in other areas of drug policy. Consider the raft of legislation in various states providing for enhanced penalties for selling drugs near a school zone. Ostensibly designed to protect schoolchildren, these laws are often written in such a way that a drug transaction between two consenting adults near a school at 3 a.m. is treated as if the seller were delivering heroin to a first-grader. Whether intended or not, such laws also inevitably result in vast racial disparities based on geography. Since large sections of urban areas are within one thousand feet of a school zone, arrestees in those areas— disproportionately black and brown—are far more likely to be affected by these penalties than their white suburban counterparts. An examination of juveniles waived to adult court in Chicago for school-zone transactions revealed that fully 99 percent of the cases—390 of 393—were African American and Latino teenagers.[17]

The political hypocrisy enveloped in sentencing policy on drugs becomes particularly evident when it is one of the policy-makers' own who becomes ensnared in these penalties. We saw this when Florida governor Jeb Bush's daughter Noelle was arrested for fraudulently trying to fill a prescription for Xanax, an offense that carries up to a five-year prison sentence. Governor Bush, who had cut funds for drug treatment in the state and expressed opposition to a pending ballot initiative that would divert substance abusers into treatment, immediately became a convert to the efficacy of treatment and the value of family privacy. Acknowledging that "substance abuse is an issue confronting many families across our nation,"

MARC MAUER

he requested that "the public and the media respect our family's privacy during this difficult time so that we can help our daughter." One wonders how many fellow Floridians whose spouses, siblings, and children are incarcerated in state prisons for drug crimes would also have liked to enjoy that same privilege.

But the race and class dynamics of the drug war go well beyond sentencing policy and can be seen most fundamentally in the two-tiered approach employed to deal with the problem. Drug use and abuse cut across race and class lines, but how we address the consequences of those actions depends very much on where we live and what resources we bring with us to the situation. Federal policies for the past twenty years, through both Democratic and Republican administrations, have invested two-thirds of federal antidrug funds into policing and prisons and just one-third into prevention and treatment. As a result, in well-to-do communities, drug abuse is primarily addressed as a social or health problem, and there is no shortage of treatment resources for those with the means to pay; by contrast, in low-income communities, those resources are in limited supply, and a criminal justice response—arrest, prosecution, and incarceration—becomes far more likely.

Ironically, criminal justice reforms of recent years have gone halfway, but only halfway, toward addressing those inequities. The expansion of treatment-oriented drug courts over the past decade has resulted in more than one thousand such systems around the country designed to divert drug-using offenders into treatment rather than incarceration. Judges and others in the court system are generally satisfied with the outcomes of these courts. But given the shortage of treatment slots for *non*offenders, we have now created a situation whereby low-income persons may be more likely to get into a treatment program if they are charged with a crime rather than by their own initiative.

Sentencing Disparities and Issues of Race and Class

In some respects, the development of sentencing policy contains elements of rational deliberation. In recent years, about one-third of the states have developed systems of sentencing guidelines, generally premised on a combined weighting of the seriousness of the current offense and the offender's prior record. Often, these systems represent the product of a several-year deliberative process engaged in by a roundtable of leading criminal justice officials in the state. In 1987, the federal government implemented its own system of guidelines, after undergoing an arduous years-long process.

In sentencing systems that employ more indeterminate structures, the two elements of current offense severity and prior record are still generally the most critical factors taken into account by legislators and judges, although with more room for consideration of aggravating and mitigating circumstances.

But in any of these systems approaches, or in individual sentencing cases, the presumed sentence to be imposed or range to be considered represents nothing more than the prevailing wisdom or current experience. Consider, for example, why a convicted burglar sentenced to prison in England will receive an average sentence of fifteen months, while a similar offender in the United States averages a forty-three-month sentence.[18] Or why a motor vehicle theft in England typically results in a nine-month sentence, compared to twenty-four months in the United States.[19] Similar differentials exist in regard to actual time served in prison as well. Of those incarcerated, an American convicted of burglary or car theft will serve on average eighteen months and just under one year respectively; in England, the comparable figures are six months and three months respectively.[20]

We need not only look abroad to identify significant differences in sentencing patterns. Within the United States, there exists substantial variation in how states sentence offenders as well. In North Carolina, for example, sale of an ounce of cocaine will result in a sentence of 2.9–3.5 years in prison, but in neighboring South Carolina, the same offense produces a sentence of 7–25 years.[21]

To what extent, then, are perceptions of race and class influential in how these determinations are made? Recent research suggests that these considerations are quite germane to the development of public policy. A key study examined the degree of punitiveness expressed by Americans as a function of the extent to which they perceived crime as a "black" problem. That is, if crime is viewed as disproportionately committed by blacks, does that translate into greater support for harsher responses to crime? Among whites, the authors found strong support for this hypothesis, concluding that "racial typification of crime is a significant predictor of punitive attitudes toward crime,"[22] controlling for other factors. And certainly there is no reason to believe this finding is any less true among white policy makers than among the white population overall.

MARC MAUER

In broad terms, we can see these dynamics most clearly in the contrast between our collective approach to white-collar crime as opposed to "street" crime. Consider the following instance of corporate crime. In July 2001, the Sara Lee Corporation pled guilty to two misdemeanor charges related to an outbreak of listeria from one of their "Ball Park Franks" hot dog factories.[23] The Bil-Mar factory, owned by Sara Lee, had stopped conducting bacteria tests for the listeria monocytogenes in November 1998. One month later, Sara Lee was forced to recall their hot dogs from store shelves due to an outbreak of listeria that resulted in fifteen deaths and six miscarriages. Federal prosecutors stated that they declined to pursue felony charges because there was not enough evidence to establish that Sara Lee was cognizant of the presence of listeria in the factory. This was despite the fact that it was known that during the replacement of a refrigeration unit in the factory, bacteria were dislodged and came in contact with the area where the hot dogs were processed. A Bil-Mar employee as well as a federal meat inspector stated in a Department of Agriculture investigation that managers had knowledge, up to eight months prior to the outbreak, that there were high levels of listeria in the factory.[24] This led the Agriculture Department to conclude that Bil-Mar "either knew or should have known" about the contaminated meats.[25] For this negligence, and the resulting deaths, Sara Lee was fined $200,000.

These acts are not limited to corporate misbehavior on a grand level, but are relatively pervasive among "average" Americans as well. A recent survey found that one-quarter of Americans believe that cheating at least a little on one's taxes is acceptable, and that figure has grown in recent years.[26] And for those so inclined, this is probably a rational act. While it is possible to receive a five-year prison term for possession of a small quantity of drugs, offenders who cheat on their taxes are generally not even brought into court. Instead, the matter is usually handled administratively by the IRS. The taxpayer is brought to account by the agency, given a reprimand, and made to pay the back taxes and perhaps a stiff penalty. Only in instances where there is clear evidence of fraudulent intent or the amount of the underpayment is substantial is criminal prosecution even considered.

This approach is not necessarily inappropriate. After all, large-scale prosecutions would only contribute to crowded court dockets, and any prison time imposed would affect working taxpayers and their families. So there are reasonable societal calculations, implicit or otherwise, in treating tax cheating as noncriminal.

But just as we take into account these personal and societal implications in regard to punishment of certain behaviors, our failure to do so for others calls into question whether this is a result of reasonable societal objectives or a two-tiered approach that is dependent on the public perception of the offender.

A study that a colleague and I conducted on societal approaches to different forms of substance abuse illustrates this as well.[27] The study examined the harm to society of two forms of substance abuse—drunk driving and drug possession. Both result in substantial numbers of arrests as well as societal harm, as measured by deaths caused by drunk driving or through drug overdoses or the violence of the drug trade. Yet despite high-profile advocacy on the issue of drunk driving, stiffer sentencing laws in many states are usually measured in mandatory days in jail compared to the years of imprisonment required in many drug cases. The societal response to drunk-driving arrests—78 percent of which are of white males—emphasizes keeping the person functional in the community while attempting to respond to the dangerous behavior through treatment. For drug offenders, far more likely to be persons of color, a heavy-handed criminal justice response has become the norm.

Whether or not sentencing policy is viewed as rational, it also represents just an end-stage in a court process where a variety of decisions have already been made. Most significant among these are law-enforcement decision making regarding deployment of resources and arrest strategies, and prosecutorial charging decisions. Each of these plays a critical role in determining who comes into the system and how severely they are treated, with potentially significant consequences for racial disparity. Until recent activity in regard to the practice of racial profiling, there has been relatively little oversight or evaluation of these actors to try to assess their public safety strategies and results.

Translating Racial Perceptions into Public Policy

To suggest that racial perceptions or bias influence the societal approach to crime or deviant behaviors still leaves open the question of the means by which this becomes translated into public policy. Absent a stated intent to punish based on an offender's race or class status, we still need to account for the means by which these biases play themselves out. Several institutions and processes are most relevant to this analysis.

The process is set in motion by a set of fiscal and other priorities that determine the type and quality of defense afforded indigent defendants. Among felony defendants in state courts nationally, 57 percent are African American.[28] These defendants overwhelmingly are represented by public defenders or assigned counsel. While common misperceptions about the quality of public defense are legion—defendants not infrequently are heard to comment, "I don't have a lawyer, I have a public defender"—in fact, many public defender offices provide high-quality representation.

The more significant concern is that compensation rates for public defense and assigned counsel are abysmally low in many jurisdictions: hourly rates of twenty to forty dollars for appointed counsel are common, often accompanied by statutorily limited maximum payments. In Virginia, court-appointed lawyers representing indigent defendants facing up to life in prison can be paid no more than a total of $1,096. Fulton County, Georgia, pays a flat fee of fifty dollars for each misdemeanor.

How a defendant has his "day in court" is also subject to fiscal and other priorities. An increasing tendency in many courts is to conduct bail hearings to determine pretrial release by video from a jail. Ostensibly designed to save on jail and court personnel costs, the process in many ways serves to dehumanize the defendant. Consider this exchange reported from a Baltimore courtroom regarding whether the bail review judge would use new video technology to improve the visual quality of the defendants to the courtroom observers:

> *Snapshot:* At a bail review last April, the public defender representing the detainees politely points out that now it is possible for the video camera to focus on each detainee's face.
>
> "Your honor, this new system zooms in . . .
>
> "It suits me," [Judge] Shuger says, interrupting the attorney.
>
> "Well, I'm not comfortable . . .
>
> "*It suits me*," Shuger repeats, cutting off the attorney again—and the camera continued showing an entire row of five orange jumpsuit clad detainees, instead of close-ups, for the rest of the afternoon.[29]

Changes in sentencing policy represent the most significant alteration in courtroom dynamics over the past twenty years, as seen most prominently in the spate of legislative initiatives that have given us mandatory sentencing, "three-strikes" policies, "truth in sentencing," and other new mechanisms generally premised on restricting the discretion of sentencing judges and increasing both the likelihood and length of a prison sentence. These policies have been critiqued from a variety of perspectives. There is little evidence that they provide any significant public safety benefits, but they impose substantial costs on society, as a result of both the fiscal cost of corrections and the social costs to offenders and their families.

But these policies have a significant racial component as well, one that is rarely addressed prior to adoption of such legislation and only occasionally after implementation. This results from two separate dynamics. First, it is a virtual certainty that any policy such as "three-strikes" or "habitual-offender" laws premised on increasing sanctions for repeat offenders will have a disproportionate racial impact. The reason is simple—African Americans and other minority groups on average are more likely to have a prior criminal history. Whether this is a result of actual greater involvement in criminal activity or the result of a racist criminal justice system, blacks, Latinos, and others will be disproportionately affected by such policies. Thus, for example, 44 percent of the offenders sentenced to twenty-five years to life under California's "three-strikes" law are African American, compared to their 31 percent share of the overall inmate population and 7.5 percent of the general state population.

The second factor that contributes to a greater impact on minority defendants is the result of a more subtle dynamic. Consider what it means to be a sentencing judge having to make the weighty decision of whether to imprison an offender or impose a less punitive sanction. Imprisonment, once we get away from the terminology of "corrections" and the like, essentially involves putting a human being in a cage for a number of years. To anyone with the least bit of compassion, this cannot be a very pleasant experience or decision to make. This would be even more true if the judge knew something about the offender and his or her family, and had to consider the pain that such an action would bring. In this regard, mandatory and similar determinate sentencing policies can represent almost a relief of sorts, essentially relieving the judge of that difficult responsibility. And the further removed the judge is from the offender by virtue of distinctions of race and class, the easier it becomes to impose the "caging" decision.

The above is not meant to suggest that most judges are unthinking or uncaring people, or to ignore the reality that many judges have been outspoken and eloquent in their challenges to mandatory-sentencing policies.

But as incarceration has become more commonplace and its imposition less unique, it becomes increasingly challenging for persons of conscience to remind themselves, and ourselves, of the gravity of the punishment that is being imposed.

But what are the social forces that have contributed to shaping this new climate of punitiveness? These are complex issues and result not only in harsher criminal justice sanctions but also in a host of altered perspectives in regard to welfare policy, immigration, educational access, and other areas. Without attempting to dissect these dynamics in full detail, let me just cover some of the more direct contributors.

Media imagery certainly has been a contributor to the representation of the problem as one defined by racial imagery. Numerous studies have documented that media outlets devote undue attention to crime stories, distort the level of violence within those crime stories, and display persons of color as criminal offenders to a greater degree than is actually the case.[30]

Some of these outcomes are influenced by the fiscal realities of mass media. To the producer of the nightly news on local television, crime coverage is a virtual godsend. Crime takes place every day, police scanners provide ongoing information and access to those crime scenes, and there is always a story to be told at the scene. All one needs to tell the story is a reporter, a camera, and the police lights and sirens. By contrast, covering developments at city hall or in a neighborhood is more difficult to capture visually and generally involves considerably more background preparation.

When the reporters do go out to cover crime, the visuals that accompany their stories often depict violence and racial minorities. Violence is featured because a murder scene is much more compelling than a stolen-car story, even though the latter are more common than the former by a factor of about seventy-five. As media outlets are usually located in urban areas, minorities are more likely to be represented among the defendant population there than in more suburban or rural areas. But the imagery that is transmitted about crime crosses those geographical boundaries and conveys a far less nuanced view of the problem than is generally the case.

Political dynamics represent the other significant focal point for the introduction of racial perceptions and disparities into crime policy. As the recent Enron scandal has shown us in excruciating detail, the development of public policy is very much influenced by access to decision makers, and access is obtained through financial clout and influence.

Needless to say, prisoners and their families are about the least influential group in society in these terms, and their voices are rarely sought or heard in policy debates about sentencing or incarceration policy.

But those directly affected by these policies are not the only "experts" with whom policy makers fail to consult. In the development of approaches to criminal justice, all too often policy is guided by polling and the demands of political campaigns, rather than consultation with knowledgeable people in the field. Few members of the American Society of Criminology, for example, have ever received a request from a congressional committee to lend their expertise to a consideration of proposed legislation. Instead, the imagery and direction of crime policy are more likely to be shaped by such instances as the "Willie Horton" campaign of George Bush Sr. in 1988 or Bill Clinton's dramatic trip back to Arkansas in the midst of the critical New Hampshire primary in 1992, in order to oversee the execution of Ricky Ray Rector, a mentally impaired black man who had blown out half his brain in the course of being apprehended for killing a police officer.

Conclusion

Changing these dynamics will not be simple, of course, but there are reasons for optimism today. First, with crime rates having declined for much of the past decade, sounding "tough" offers policy-makers less political gain. Debate continues regarding the impact of increased incarceration in contributing to that reduction in crime (most scholarship suggests that it was but one of a host of factors), but these developments open up the possibility of a more reasoned dialogue on the issues.

Second, the successful introduction of a host of sentencing and diversion options into court systems offers concrete evidence of viable alternatives for a range of offenders. These include such developments as drug courts, California's Proposition 36 drug-offender diversion initiative, and the more than three hundred sentencing advocacy programs nationally that present sentencing options to judges in serious felony cases. Not all of these programs have been thoroughly evaluated, but we do know that judges and communities have generally embraced the notion of having a broader array of options from which to choose than just the traditional choices of prison and probation.

MARC MAUER

Finally, what is needed in the public dialogue is greater understanding of more broad-based approaches to crime and public safety. This should incorporate a comprehensive examination of strategies framed around a simple proposition: How would we respond to the problems of a family member or someone we care about? While there are no easy answers to substance abuse, mental illness, or a host of other contributing factors to crime, we do know that our initial instinct in coping with the problems of a loved one is not to call the police, but rather to address the issue in as comprehensive a manner as time and resources permit. We should do no less for those in our society who may be less fortunate.

Notes

Thanks to Ryan King for research assistance for this article.

1. Many of the dynamics described in this essay may apply to racial and ethnic groups other than African Americans, but the focus here will be primarily on black-white distinctions due to the greater availability of data. Nor are these racial dynamics necessarily unique to the United States. See, for example, a review of these issues in Michael Tonry, "Ethnicity, Crime, and Immigration," in Tonry, *Ethnicity, Crime, and Immigration.*

2. *Racial Disparities in the Death Penalty* (Washington, D.C.: General Accounting Office, 1992).

3. Stephen Klein, Joan Petersilia, and Susan Turner, "Race and Imprisonment Decisions in California," *Science,* February 16, 1990.

4. Cassia Spohn, "Thirty Years of Sentencing Reform: The Quest for a Racially Neutral Sentencing Process," *Criminal Justice 2000: Policies, Processes and Decisions of the Criminal Justice System* 3 (2000): 460–61.

5. Reiman, *The Rich Get Richer and the Poor Get Prison,* 67–68.

6. Ibid., 68.

7. Beckett, *Making Crime Pay,* 86.

8. David Greenberg and Valerie West, "The Persistent Significance of Race: Growth in State Prison Populations, 1971–1991," paper presented to Law and Society Association, Aspen, Colo., June 1998.

9. Jacobs and Carmichael, "The Political Sociology of the Death Penalty: A Pooled Time Series Analysis."

10. Ibid., 125.

11. Musto, *The American Disease,* 4.

12. Ibid., 7.

13. Wright, as cited by Musto, 43–44.

14. Ibid., 219–20.

15. C. M. Goethe, as cited by Musto, 220.

16. Craig Reinarman and Harry Levine, "The Crack Attack: Politics and Media in the Crack Scare," in Reinarman and Levine, *Crack in America,* 18–51.

17. Marc Mauer and Steven Drizin, "Transfer Laws Victimize Fairness," *Chicago Sun-Times,* December 27, 2000.

18. Patrick Langan and David Farrington, *Crime and Justice in the United States and in England and Wales, 1981–1996* (Washington, D.C.: Bureau of Justice Statistics, 1998), 31.

19. Ibid.

20. Ibid., 33.

21. ImpacTeen Illicit Drug Team, *Illicit Drug Policies: Selected Laws from the 50 States* (Berrien Springs, Mich.: Andrews University, 2002), 96, 110.

22. Ted Chiricos, Kelly Welch, and Marc Gertz, "Racial Typification of Crime and Support for Punitive Measures," *Criminology,* 42, no. 2 (2004): 378.

23. Russell Mokhiber and Robert Weissman, "Corporations Behaving Badly: The Ten Worst Corporations of 2001," *Multinational Monitor* (2001): 22, 12.

24. "Allegations Made about Tainted Meat," *New York Times,* August 31, 2001.

25. Patricia Callahan, "US Agency Report Says Sara Lee 'Knew or Should Have Known' of Tainted Meat," *Wall Street Journal,* August 31, 2001.

26. Curt Anderson, "Cheating IRS More Accepted," *Washington Post,* January 20, 2002.

27. Cathy Shine and Marc Mauer, "Does the Punishment Fit the Crime: Drug Users and Drunk Drivers: Questions of Race and Class" (The Sentencing Project, 1993).

28. Brian Reaves, "Felony Defendants in Large Urban Counties, 1998" (Washington, D.C.: Bureau of Justice Statistics, 2001).

29. Joe Surkiewicz, "Bail Review: The Luck of the Draw," *Daily Record,* September 8, 2001.

30. See my discussion of these issues in Mauer, *Race to Incarcerate,* 171–77.

Complicity or Justice and Mercy?

Sexual Violence Challenges,
the Criminal Justice System,
and the Churches

LOIS GEHR LIVEZEY

As I was initially contemplating this chapter from my sabbatical vantage point in Cambridge, Massachusetts, Cardinal Law of Boston first refused, then very reluctantly agreed, to authorize the reporting of the sexual abuse of children and youth by priests to legal authorities. Speaking out on this "crisis of the church," he echoes the sensibilities of many church leaders who view the problem, the "wound" to the church, as a problem of too much publicity rather than as a profound, pervasive, destructive, and faithless habit of violation of the person—and the Gospel.[1] Like so many others, his primary loyalties are to the "institution" and its claim to protection from—as he sees it—outside agitators. We hear the same public complaint from many leaders in and out of the church who, in the name of "family values," are more concerned to protect the sanctity of marriage, the privacy of the home, and the institution of the family than to protect vulnerable family members from assault. These headlines are an appropriate starting point because issues of sexual and domestic violence confront us with the inextricable links between the criminal justice system and the religious pieties and practices that shape moral communities. For this presentation, however, I will first deal with sexual and domestic violence as an issue for the criminal justice system, and then turn to the role of the churches in doing justice to mercy—and to justice.

The Criminal Justice System

Issues of sexual and domestic violence bear a complex relationship to the criminal justice system. I will address two faces of this relationship: impunity and captivity.

THE CULTURE OF IMPUNITY: A CONSPIRACY OF SILENCE

The reality is that most cases of sexual and domestic violence are either unreported or they are reported to "authorities" that silence, further violate, blame, trivialize, and provide neither care nor justice. These cases do not even get into the sphere of the criminal justice system. That's the problem! Sexual and domestic violence is serious and pandemic, yet the criminal justice system has been largely unengaged—or co-opted. The conspiracy of silence and the culture of impunity reinforce each other. Genevieve Jacques of the World Council of Churches defines a culture of impunity as systemic: "the system as a whole, with its rules and with its codes of behaviour" normalizes violence and lack of accountability; impunity becomes the norm.[2] In this country, religious traditions, folk culture, powerful (patriarchal) interests collude to make violence against women seem "natural," inevitable, even God-ordained. Jacques argues that such a culture of impunity threatens the rule of law and, more basically, a society shaped by ethical principles. Jacques, influenced by the Truth and Reconciliation Commission (TRC) in South Africa, proposes "restorative justice," which seeks to restore dignity, justice, and healing to victims and perpetrators alike as well as to the community or communities involved. In a culture of impunity, the social fabric of silencing and lies requires breaking the silence through truth-telling. In the words of a TRC poster: "The Truth Hurts but Silence Kills." Jacques argues that truth-telling restores the human dignity of the victims by "granting them an opportunity to relate their own accounts of the violations of which they are the victims, and by recommending reparation measures in respect of them."[3] Truth-telling restores the human dignity of the perpetrators by granting them an opportunity to affirm their human capacity for responsibility and by holding them accountable. Holding perpetrators accountable requires a public and legal process of acknowledging wrongdoing and adjudicating punishment. For Jacques, the "visible justice" of a trial by a court of law, a properly functioning criminal justice system, is

LOIS GEHR LIVEZEY

a prerequisite to restorative justice and reconciliation, within a culture of impunity.[4] There can be "no reconciliation without transformation."[5]

Perhaps some definitions and statistics will help clarify the seriousness of this issue. Domestic violence is "a pattern of assaultive and coercive behavior." It may include physical, sexual, psychological-emotional, and/or spiritual abuse, economic coercion, neglect. This violence, whether perpetrated against children or adults, spouses or siblings, elderly persons or persons with disabilities, violates elemental dimensions of our common humanity. It inflicts harm and suffering on body and spirit alike. It coerces for the sake of control, a violation of consent and choice. It is a betrayal of trust that destroys relationships and isolates. It terrorizes. Indeed, the experiences of sexual and domestic violence bear many of the marks of the six dimensions of the "theatric of terror" described in this volume and elsewhere by Mark Taylor.[6]

The haunting words of Ntozake Shange's famous poem "with no immediate cause" lodge in our memories as statistics never will: "Every three minutes a woman is beaten / every five minutes a woman is raped / every ten minutes a little girl is molested." Yet numbers matter. In the United States alone:

- at least 4 million cases of domestic violence against women are reported every year;

- more than 4 million women are raped by an intimate partner every year;

- 15–25 percent of pregnant women are battered by their intimate partner;

- over 3 million cases of child abuse were reported in 1998;

- over 1 million cases of elder abuse were estimated (National Center of Elder Abuse 1996); and

- an average of 28 percent of high school and college students experience dating violence; 40–60 percent of known sexual assaults within families are committed against girls fifteen years old or younger.[7]

THE EMERGENCE OF A LEGAL FRAMEWORK

A legal framework for addressing sexual and domestic violence is relatively new and still very much in process. The dramatic emergence of the child welfare and women's movements of the 1960s and 1970s testifies

---

to the power of breaking the silence and to the perseverance and courage of the many associations of women ("the feminist revolution") and other concerned groups. It was these advocacy organizations that persuaded hospitals and social service agencies, legislatures and attorneys general to acknowledge the rights of children and women to protection from violence, including the violence inflicted by family members. Our current sexual and domestic violence legislation has been developed since this period. In the 1960s, following the 1962 publication of Henry Kempe et al., "The Battered Child Syndrome," in the *Journal of the American Medical Association,* all fifty states passed legislation that required designated professionals to report suspected cases of child abuse, and in 1974 the federal government passed the Child Abuse Prevention Act, which led to the establishment of the National Center on Child Abuse and Neglect. The criminalization of wife battering and other forms of violence against women came more slowly. During the 1970s and 1980s, a series of class-action suits challenged the criminal justice system's refusal to take wife battering seriously and gave impetus to legislative and procedural reforms.[8] Laws already on the books have undergone radical changes of definition, scope, and procedures. Rape laws, for example, were revised to encompass male as well as female victims, marital rape, acts of sexual coercion that do not involve sexual intercourse, and assaults in which there is no evidence of resistance or physical harm. In June 1986, the Supreme Court declared that the sexual harassment of women in the workforce constitutes discrimination on the basis of sex and is therefore illegal under Title VII of the Civil Rights Act. Every year, additional patterns of violence within families become matters of public concern: child sexual abuse, sibling abuse, elder abuse by adult children, corporal punishment.

This emergent federal and state legislation represents a paradigm shift, not only as a matter of law but of culture. What was taken for granted, justified (if justification was thought necessary) with recourse to the Bible or the laws of nature, is now illegal. It will take some time for us to get beyond the jokes, the defensiveness and denial, and the outright lawbreaking, and learn to live a new way of life. All of us need basic training and communities of encouragement to change.

In the meantime, the implementation of "justice" proceeds slowly and unevenly. The legal process requires not only good law but also fair and effective implementation. It requires training police, lawyers, judges, teachers, doctors and pastors. In a culture of impunity, this training must acknowledge the challenges and initiate transformation-oriented processes of consciousness-raising and reeducation.[9] It requires dealing with the impact of race, gender, and class on judicial procedures. It requires timely and inclusive mechanisms for evaluating effective and ineffective policies and procedures. Sometimes, state irresponsibility in matters of sexual and domestic violence is subtle. For example, current policies regarding the homeless and welfare recipients ignore the flight of many of these people from situations of domestic violence. Residency requirements in some states deny subsistence-level benefits to the many women and their children who move across state lines to escape domestic violence. We have to recognize that, in dealing with the response of the criminal justice system to sexual and domestic violence, sometimes there are no easy answers—but the struggle must continue.

Sexual and domestic violence does not stop at the water's edge. In the 1990s, the international human rights regime began to respond to the cries of anguish, the increasingly publicized horror stories, the mind-numbing statistics on the prevalence of sexual and domestic abuse in all countries of the world, and to the organized efforts of women across the globe. In December 1993, The United Nations General Assembly adopted the *Declaration on the Elimination of Violence against Women.* The document firmly and clearly defines violence against women as a violation of human rights within the responsibility of the states, and this is reinforced and extended by the work of NGOs:

> recognizing the urgent need for the universal application to women of the rights and principles with regard to equality, security, liberty, integrity of all human beings . . . [which] are enshrined in international instruments, including the *Universal Declaration of Human Rights,* the *International Covenant on Civil and Political Rights,* the *International Covenant on Economic, Social and Cultural Rights,* the *Convention on the Elimination of All Forms of Discrimination against Women,* and the *Convention against Torture and other Cruel, Inhuman or Degrading Treatment or Punishment.*[10]

Amnesty International (AI) investigates, publicizes, and develops policy recommendations related to the ratification and implementation of the various international human rights covenants and conventions. In 2001, as part of AI's campaign against torture, the organization published three reports: *Broken Bodies, Shattered Minds: Torture and Ill-treatment of Women; Hidden Scandal, Secret Shame: Torture and Ill-treatment of*

Children; and *Crimes of Hate, Conspiracy of Silence: Torture and Ill-treatment Based on Sexual Identity.* In the first report, AI states: "AI considers that acts of violence against women in the home or the community constitute torture for which the state is accountable when they are of the nature and severity envisaged by the concept of torture in international standards and the state has failed to fulfill its obligation to provide effective protection."[11]

In addition, there is a growing body of literature that argues for the connections between sexual and domestic violence, on the one hand, and the experience of political prisoners, holocaust survivors, and other groups who have been deprived of "rights" recognized in the Universal Declaration of Human Rights, on the other.[12]

> We have struggled for and witnessed enormous changes in the law in
> the past ten to twenty-five years. We have also experienced obstruction
> of justice, backlash, and erosion of support for efforts to end sexual and
> domestic violence through recourse to the criminal justice system. Every
> day we celebrate the shifted weight of the law from silence to condemna-
> tion; and every day we face the reality: the rule of law is precarious in a
> continuing culture of impunity.

THE DYNAMICS OF CAPTIVITY

I confess to a certain hermeneutics of suspicion. Just as the criminal justice system begins to embrace, at least in principle, the right to protection and the duty of accountability in these everyday situations of terror and torture that we call sexual and domestic violence, we find ourselves appealing to a system under indictment.

Yet, I concur with the indictment of the criminal justice system voiced in these essays. The experience of battered and sexually abused women confirms it. Inadequate police intervention, ineffective orders of protection, intimidating court appearance processes, delays and more delays, and low conviction rates leave women and children whose abuse is reported at risk of greater danger. For example, while the conviction rate for child sexual abuse may be improving, available evidence puts it at about 1 percent of reported cases, and most such abuse goes unreported.[13] The likelihood of unjust resolutions of such cases is exacerbated by racism and immigrant status. Nor is it likely that prison is rehabilitative, given the conditions and intentions of the current prison system.

LOIS GEHR LIVEZEY

Second, we need to pay attention to the escalating rate of incarceration of women, many of whom are incarcerated for nonviolent crimes; specifically for their participation in the sex industry, substance abuse, or shoplifting. The "collateral damage" of their arrest and conviction for these offenses is a criminal record that in turn blocks their opportunities to find alternative work. A few are serving time for homicide or attempted homicide—often of an abusive husband or other intimate. Various studies of these women demonstrate they have a common experience of prolonged abuse, battery, and sexual abuse as adults—often reaching back to their childhood. The National Coalition against Domestic Violence estimates that 65–95 percent of incarcerated women are victims of prior abuse.[14] The life-threatening character of their abusive situations is designed to cause terror; it contributes to their isolation and disconnection from wider circles of relationships; and, ultimately, it creates a sense of entrapment in relationships that not only establish a reign of terror but often include forced sex work or drug abuse or other illegal activities. Judith Herman calls this "captivity" a hostage situation.[15] The criminal justice system fails when it refuses to pay attention to the coercive environment of these women's lives.

Instead, the constraints this violence imposes on women's choices must be analyzed carefully. For example, in virtually every case of female homicide of a male intimate, there is a substantial record of calls to the police in previous situations of the man's battery of the woman. Often, too, there is a pattern of her previous attempts at suicide. Angela Browne's analysis of the comparison between battered women who kill their husbands and battered women who do not reveals no pattern of differences among the women studied. Rather, the differences are found in *the behavior of the men involved.* Prior to the homicide or attempted homicide, these men were more violent or caused more severe injuries, raped their partners, abused the children, engaged in substance abuse.[16] When these issues are not addressed in the legal proceeding, the process often mimics the trivialization of the clear and present danger to which these battered women are subject. For minority women or women whose status or work is illegal, experience with the criminal justice system breeds well-founded mistrust and, again, justice-seeking options narrow.

The criminal justice system does not address these women's concerns for their connection with and the well-being of their children—nor their more general need for community. In these situations of isolation, in the absence of access to relationships, incarcerated women are especially vulnerable to control, continuing abuse, and violation of their basic needs, including the right to dignity of the person. Theirs is a world of systemic injustice in which these women find themselves both victim and agent, ever trying strategies of survival amidst narrowing options.

Moreover, these women find prison to be an arena of ongoing sexual violation and a quite intentional system of dehumanization. In prison, rape continues to be used as a weapon of terror, captivity, control, and disrespect. We need to take seriously the needs of all victims of prison-based sexual violence, but especially those for whom the experience of sexual violence in prison further traumatizes.

As Marc Mauer and Jonathan Rothchild discuss more generally in this volume, mandatory sentencing and "three-strikes" legislation exacerbate the situations of incarcerated women. Richard Snyder notes that

> one of the most devastating consequences [of mandatory sentencing] has been on the many poor women from Third World countries who have been either forced (at threat of their lives or their children's lives) or duped into becoming couriers of drugs. Often referred to as "drug mules," these women have been the targets of inordinate and insensitive punishment automatically meted out to them. Even when it is clear that they were forced into such actions, the judge has no alternative but to enforce the sentence.[17]

Similarly, "three-strikes" legislation (which the Supreme Court has agreed to review) is especially egregious for such women, when the third strike may be not a third felony, but a misdemeanor property crime (in one case, the theft of a bottle of vitamins from a supermarket, according to an April 2, 2002, *New York Times* report).

A related and very serious issue is the incarceration of children and the relegation of youth offenders to adult status for trial procedures, sentencing, and assignment to prison. Ironically, the court-mandated institutionalization and incarceration of children and youth are in part the bitter fruit of good works: compulsory education; homes for homeless, neglected, and abused children; treatment centers for the mentally retarded, chronically ill, or otherwise disabled; a "juvenile justice" system to discipline and rehabilitate children declared "ungovernable" (by their parents or schools) as well as youth who have committed crimes. What has developed is a massive, ungovernable, and costly institutional complex maintained by political and economic interests that are either incapable of or uninterested in the safety and well-being of the children in their care.

The moral imperative of respect for the dignity of the person gives way to an ethos of control, humiliation, and abuse. Many of these institutions do not provide care, including medical treatment and psychological counseling, nor education, nor even the pretense of moral formation and rehabilitation. Living conditions are often deplorable, and physical and sexual abuse is systemic. A four-year-old child disappears from the child welfare system, and her disappearance is not noticed for fifteen months.[18] Stories of abuse and death become routine. So does suicide and attempted suicide. Status offenders, many of whom are runaways from abusive homes or truants from schools where they are humiliated, begin a long pattern of institutionalization that, far from making them productive citizens, makes them criminals instead. Institutions that were founded to provide care, education, and opportunity for transformation have become, instead, prisons whose organizing principles are control, domination, and punishment. In addition, we are witnessing escalating pressure to treat crime-committing youth as adults and incarcerate them with adults, which leaves them subject to regular, humiliating, and harsh physical and sexual abuse.

Thus, children and youth as well as battered and sexually abused women who encounter the criminal justice system provide ample evidence for its indictment: patterns of law enforcement that either neglect or target the vulnerable rather than the powerful; prison conditions that establish control by systematic abuse as well as by denying basic life needs and the dignity of the person; political and economic stakeholders that effectively maintain the status quo, which has become a very lucrative enterprise.

Faith Communities: From Complicity to Justice and Mercy

> "You shall love your neighbor as yourself, I am the Lord. . . ." "You shall love the Lord, your God, with all your heart, with all your soul, and with all your might." (Lev. 19:18 with Deut. 6:5, cited in Mark 12:28–31)
>
> Rabbi David says: "How do you love your neighbor as yourself? By allowing yourself to be silenced by your neighbor's pain, a silence of awe and of openness. And by *not* allowing yourself to be silenced by your

neighbor's pain, by speech which is powerful and comforting. And how do you love the Lord, your God, with all your heart? By allowing yourself to be silenced in the presence of God, a silence of amazement and of receptivity. And by *not* allowing yourself to be silenced by God, by speech which is strong and just." [19]

As we turn to the obligation of the churches to do justice, love mercy, and walk humbly, we ought to begin with a prayer of confession. With respect to issues of sexual and domestic violence, the churches, like the criminal justice system, have silenced the neighbor's pain and offered no word of comfort. Churches have fallen silent rather than confront the neighbor's violence and offered no word of justice. Historically, too, churches have been a theological as well as an ecclesial sanctuary for abuse. Nevertheless, I believe churches and other religious organizations have resources to draw on, if we appropriate them critically and constructively. Second, I believe we best access those resources by attending to the ordinary practices of communities of faith.

ENDING THE CULTURE OF IMPUNITY:
THE STRUGGLE FOR JUSTICE

Faith-based institutions and communities ought to be engaged in the public realm. "God so loved the world" that the congregations that have grown up in the shadow of God's grace can do no less. How congregations do so is highly contested territory. One fundamental ground rule of a democratic and heterogeneous public is that participants do not speak *ex cathedra* but are willing to listen as well as speak and to persuade by appealing to principles of justice for all.[20] Let me offer a few brief observations about churches' justice-making responsibilities.

First, from the earliest practices of baptism to contemporary formulations of confessions of faith, Christians are called upon to *renounce evil,* denounce idolatry.[21] Communities of faith are expected to "speak truth to power." In this context, churches are called to recognize the dynamics of captivity of women and men in the criminal justice system. They are called to support, protest, advocate for a system that does not demean but rather insists on respect; a system that protects from further violation, encourages connections with children and other nonabusive family members as well as the larger community, refocuses the system on the accountability of the violent rather than simply targeting the most vul-

LOIS GEHR LIVEZEY

nerable. Persons who are victimized by violative homes and streets and again by the criminal justice system are doubly jeopardized; they are the poorest of the poor, the most marginalized. Moreover, such women and children are often ignored or condemned by churches and other "respectable" advocacy organizations. Jesus did not tell the story of the women caught in adultery for nothing; we are the religious leaders who picked up the stones. We are the ones who crossed to the other side of the road, ever attentive to our very important religious business while the "other" recognized what God requires of us all.

Second, churches are explicitly value-bearing institutions, constituted to consider issues of criminal justice within the larger normative framework of a community's life. Churches ought to articulate a vision of the good ordering of society that is deeply rooted in an understanding of our common humanity. Such a faith-based vision carries with it the obligation to seek justice for all and the fulfillment of *the common good*. It requires that public institutions of lawmaking and law enforcing strengthen rather than diminish the dignity of every person. It requires support for a thickly textured web of relationships, responsibilities, and creative possibilities that reach beyond the letter of the law to a spirit of care and justice that some might call shalom/salaam. Shalom, Nicholas Wolterstorff reminds us, is characterized by nonviolence, well-being, community, and delight.[22]

Third, religious organizations ought to "practice what we preach," which requires *critical and constructive institutional engagement in the public realm*. We know that laws are not enough. At every stage of the way we need social movements and social support systems, associations that create social space for imagination and "voice," strategies that sustain political participation that makes a difference. We have already seen that such legal framework as exists to deal with sexual and domestic violence emerged from the child welfare and women's movements of the 1960s and 1970s respectively, and laws of protection and access continue to develop as groups organize around an issue of injustice (for example, abuse of the elderly, discrimination against people with disabilities). Public engagement might take the form of cooperation with community agencies of caregiving. These groups include a diversity of providers of the wide-ranging "services" that are essential to sustain efforts to care for the abused, the abuser, the families and the communities impacted by sexual and domestic violence. Or it might lead to participation in community organizing, legislative advocacy, legal watchdogging. As churches negotiate the complex territory of their involvement with public and private "secular" institutions, critical discernment will be necessary.[23] Discernment—and risk. At heart, I am a "Niebuhrian," who emphasizes the need for critical discernment but who embraces the ineluctably "dirty-hands" quality of political action in the confidence that the struggle for justice is inseparable from the promise that "salvation" is a matter of grace, not grit.[24]

Fourth, and finally, some specifics: in a time such as this, when the abolition of domestic violence through law is so precarious, religious organizations and their leaders have a specific and important role. First, *know the law*—that means state law in the state in which you practice pastoral or other professional leadership: How does the law define rape, domestic violence, rights of victims? What are the procedures for reporting, orders of protection, law enforcement? What supporting services are available? Second, *communicate* this information so that the whole congregation is prepared to act effectively. *Use it* in situations of abuse. *Join coalitions that advocate* for laws where there are none or changes in the laws where they are ineffective or "dehumanizing." *Create (or support) networks of shelter and support for victim-survivors* as they encounter health care, criminal justice, and other "systems" in situations of pain, isolation, poverty, and terror (risk). Become educated about and advocates for *effective treatment programs* for abusers (whether incarcerated or not) and also effective treatment and support services for incarcerated women and children who are victim-survivors of violence.

BREAKING THE SILENCE: THE QUALITY OF MERCY

Breaking the silence requires *the practice of hospitality* (for further theological analysis, see Matthew Myer Boulton's essay in this volume). Historically, hospitality is connected with welcoming the stranger into the household (opening the door), discerning their needs, and responding with respect. Meeting basic human needs, as we all know, is not simply a matter of offering safety, food, and shelter but also of welcoming the voice of another. The practice of hospitality is the practice of inviting the unspeakable to be spoken. Being the church means welcoming the presence of an abused person and welcoming her or his voice as a blessing. Churches have durable traditions of hospitality on which to draw.[25] Churches have the physical and spiritual resources to offer safe space or, perhaps more accurately, "respite space" [26] required for remembering, truth-telling, reconnecting, healing. Churches practice hospitality—and so mercy—in the caregiving that listens to the cry of suffering and hears the victim-survivor's own capacities for survival and faith. Churches practice hospitality—and so mercy—in the justice making that supports the cry of mourning as it comes to be expressed in protest and challenge. Christine Pohl emphasizes another element of hospitality: the practice of shared meals as boundary-crossing events. "So then you are no longer strangers and sojourners, but you are fellow citizens with the saints and members of the household of God" (Eph. 2:19 RSV). Citizens and house-holders: in their practices of eating together, churches witness the gift of God's gracious act of inclusion in the community of life.

Second, the *recovery of the Psalms of lament* is a crucial resource for showing mercy to victim-survivors of sexual and domestic violence; biblical expressions of lament are a much-neglected resource in contemporary church life.

> Give ear to my prayer, O God; do not hide from my supplication. . . . My heart is in anguish within me, the terrors of death have fallen upon me. Fear and trembling come upon me, and horror overwhelms me. And I say, "O that I had wings like a dove! I would fly away and be at rest. . . . It is not my enemies who taunt me—I could bear that; it is not adversaries who deal insolently with me—I could hide from them. But it is you, my equal, my companion, my familiar friend. . . . But I call upon God, and the Lord will save me." (Psalm 55: 1, 4–6, 12–13, 16)

The Psalm of lament is an eloquent account of suffering; it invites the practice of mourning. The Psalm of lament is an act of protest and a call for change; it inspires resistance to evil. It is significant that most lament Psalms are not confessions of sin but the cry of the "sinned against." [27] In my experience, lament Psalms give encouragement to people of faith who experience abuse or who stand with those who experience abuse. Lament Psalms portray a community of people who claim their voices before God in their pain, anger, and confusion; they reveal an "assertive" rather than a submissive people. They give voice to the anguish of human life— but also to hope. Lament Psalms portray a God who hears—and does not turn away from—those who cry out and speak up from the depths of abuse, a God who expects us to speak up, and who promises to be faithful. The requirement—and the risk—for the church is to become a faith-based communal context in which lament, protest, and healing can be safely voiced, truly heard, and patiently supported.

"THINKING WHAT WE ARE DOING": THINKING THEOLOGICALLY

In this volume, we have engaged one another in rich interdisciplinary conversation. Perhaps we have caught the spirit of Hannah Arendt and, specifically, her insistence in this challenging time that we "think what we are doing." We have a lot of thinking to do. As participants in religious and political communities, we need to examine our practices. We need to listen to the stories of those most directly affected and "hear them to speech," in Nelle Morton's marvelous phrase.[28] We need serious inquiry—and it must include a serious critical and constructive theological inquiry.

Thinking theologically about sexual and domestic violence begins with the reality of unequal power relations and requires us to think theologically about power and our images of power. The *UN Declaration on the Elimination of Violence against Women* argues that violence against women is fundamental to the social structuring of women's subordination and vulnerability: "violence against women is a manifestation of historically unequal power relations between men and women, which have led to domination over and discrimination against women by men and to the prevention of the full achievement of women, and . . . violence against women is one of the crucial social mechanisms by which women are forced into a subordinate position compared with men."[29]

In order to better understand the complex meanings of power, I am led to ask the question of what it means to be human in the presence of God and how these theological understandings inform an interpretation of power. Elsewhere I have argued that four elements of our common humanity, grounded biblically and theologically in Christian tradition, offer significant resources of the faith for standing with a survivor and for standing against sexual and domestic violence: (1) integrity of body and spirit; (2) freedom, the idea that human beings are created centers of conscience, consent, and choice; (3) covenant, the idea that human beings are created through and for relationships; (4) joy.[30] Fully developed, this argument requires a critical and constructive reappropriation of these traditions in light of their historic complicity in Christian rationalizations of sexual and domestic violence. Reconstructed, this argument in theological anthropology provides a thick description of sexual and domestic violence as an abuse of power. In this perspective, the various forms of abuse violate our very humanity as essentially body-spirits, characterized by moral agency, embedded in and ever forming and transforming relationships, created to rejoice.

Power is often abused. But power is also essential to healing, caregiving, and justice making. There is positive, indeed essential, life-giving and world-transforming power. Sexual and domestic violence seek to leave the victim powerless—and the victim often feels powerless. So healing requires taking back the home, the night, the streets, one's life and connection to community and world. How do we understand theologically the "right use" of power? How do we recognize "empowerment"? How do churches become resources for these capacities of being human to emerge, take root, and grow? How do churches become the place in which our neighbors can sing with the psalmist: "You have turned my mourning into dancing!" (Psalm 30). These are crucial questions for the intellectual and practical future of the churches.

This theological inquiry is directly related to the capacity of religious organizations to be effective resources on sexual and domestic violence in the public realm. Congregations can be a significant locus for confronting these issues; they can be potent resources of caregiving and justice making; they can be strategic in the struggle to end violence within families. But churches will become such a resource only when they reframe the issues of sexual and domestic violence as issues of power and investigate the spiritual, biblical, and theological roots of these meanings and uses of power.

Notes

1. *New York Times,* April 1, 2002.
2. Jacques, *Beyond Impunity,* 3.
3. Ibid., 24; see also 36.
4. Ibid., 34–35.
5. Ibid., 55.
6. Taylor, "The Executed God: The Way of the Cross in Lockdown America," *Princeton Seminary Bulletin* 21, no.3 (2000): 301–23.

7. Presbyterian Church USA, *Turn Mourning into Dancing!* (2001), 9–10.

8. Gelles and Cornell, *Intimate Violence in Families,* 29–30, 129–32; Finkelhor, *Stopping Family Violence,* 17ff.

9. This is especially important for police officers, among whom the rate of domestic violence is disproportionately high.

10. *Declaration on the Elimination of Violence against Women,* General Assembly resolution 48/104, December 20, 1993. Office of the United Nations High Commission for Human Rights, Geneva, Switzerland. Likewise, The Fourth UN World Conference on Women held in Beijing in 1995 emphasized the importance of issues of violence against women. It should be noted, however, that the 1979 *Convention on the Elimination of All Forms of Discrimination against Women* did not mention violence against women or sexual and domestic violence—although the document specifically addresses issues of marriage and family life, women's health, and sex-role stereotyping and prejudice.

11. Amnesty International, *Broken Bodies, Shattered Minds,* 5.

12. See, for example, Blumenthal, *Facing the Abusing God;* Herman, *Trauma and Recovery;* and Nussbaum, *Sex and Social Justice.*

13. Poling, *The Abuse of Power,* 51.

14. 1993 IL Attorney General report on Domestic Violence. I am told that these estimates hold true for incarcerated men as well.

15. Herman, *Trauma and Recovery,* 74ff.

16. Browne, *When Battered Women Kill,* 127.

17. Snyder, *The Protestant Ethic and the Spirit of Punishment,* 6.

18. *New York Times,* July 1, 2002.

19. Blumenthal, *Facing the Abusing God,* dedication page.

20. Young, *Justice and the Politics of Difference,* chap. 6.

21. Reference to the sacrament of baptism in the *Book of Common Worship* and to the "Brief Statement of Faith—Presbyterian Church (U.S.A.)," *Book of Confessions,* Presbyterian Church, USA.

22. Wolterstorff, *Until Justice and Peace Embrace,* 69ff.

23. On this point, see Bane et al., *Who Will Provide?*

24. Niebuhr, *The Nature and Destiny of Man,* vol. 2, chap. 9.

25. Pohl, *Making Room.* Pohl's narrative account of the church's practices of hospitality illumines its historic importance to the well-being of ancient cultures, including the early church. She analyzes the changing definition and role of hospitality in changing institutional contexts, and argues for the critical reappropriation of practices of hospitality today.

26. West, *Wounds of the Spirit,* 178. West offers the term "respite space" to note that "safety" is not available under the social and cultural conditions in which black women live.

27. Park and Nelson, *The Other Side of Sin.*

28. Morton, *The Journey Is Home,* 29.

29. *Declaration on the Elimination of Violence against Women,* General Assem-

bly resolution 48/104, December 20, 1993. Office of the United Nations High Commission for Human Rights, Geneva, Switzerland.

30. Livezey, "Sex and Power Politics: A Theological Reflection," *Working Together* 19, no. 2 (Spring 1999), a publication of the Center for the Prevention of Sexual and Domestic Violence, Seattle. See also PCUSA, *Turn Mourning into Dancing*, 15–19.

Echoes of Grace
From the Prison to the State House

ERNIE LEWIS

I approach this essay on doing justice and mercy from two perspectives, that of a Christian who received an M.Div. degree from Vanderbilt some twenty-nine years ago, and that of a twenty-five-year state public defender. I am presently serving as the Kentucky Public Advocate, the chief administrator of a statewide public defender system, a role that finds me approaching public policy questions often utilizing both perspectives.

Jesus said in Matthew 5:38–39 and 43–44 the following: "You have heard that they were told, 'An eye for an eye, a tooth for a tooth.' But what I tell you is this: Do not resist those who wrong you. If anyone slaps you on the right cheek, turn and offer him the other also. . . . You have heard that they were told, 'Love your neighbor and hate your enemy.' But what I tell you is this: Love your enemies and pray for your persecutors, only so can you be children of your heavenly Father, who causes the sun to rise on good and bad alike, and sends the rain on the innocent and the wicked."

Jesus offers a challenge to the criminal justice system of today. The American criminal justice system is one where wrongs are taken very seriously, and where cheek turning is rare. Hating the enemy, whether he be the criminal, the police, the judge, or the defense lawyer, is all too often the norm. It is in this context that Jesus asks us: "You have heard it said that an eye and a tooth will be taken in the criminal justice system for wrongs committed. Where then is the place in such a system for mercy? When, if ever, do forgiveness or reconciliation or grace break through?"

The Problems of the Criminal Justice System Are Familiar

The criminal justice system is a tough place to look if you are trying to find mercy, much less grace. Neither characterizes the present American criminal justice system. But if you look, and if you listen, you will hear echoes and see signs of both. The system itself is one of America's flash points. It is highly sensitive to the events of the day, to politics, to anecdotal lawmaking, and even to demagoguery. Ours is a system of mostly retributive justice. The norm is that of the system frustrating victims, grinding up offenders and their families, and burning out participants from prosecutors to defenders, from probation and parole officers to police. I am not going to sugarcoat the system in an effort to locate the echoes of mercy, because that is all they are, echoes, barely heard, unreal and from another place. But they are detectable nonetheless.

I want to look at a handful of issues in my search for these echoes. The issues are the death penalty, race, and sentencing. I could choose others. However, these are the issues where the picture is often at its most grim, and where echoes of mercy and grace are least detectable. These issues go to the heart of our system; I believe the present way the death penalty is used, the manner is which race plays out in criminal justice, and how sentencing policies have been implemented harm the community and reduce the moral authority of the state to punish.

Communities Have a Place in the Discussion

I applaud the focus of this volume on communities as they are the right place to start. It is no accident that criminal cases in my state are entitled the "Commonwealth vs. Joe Defendant." It is communities in addition to individual victims who are harmed by crime and many criminal justice policies. The fabric of community life is torn by the commission of many crimes. Trust is broken. Memories of violence are seared into young children, who revisit their memories as they become adults. Family life is scarred by domestic violence. Commerce, which relies upon the easy flow of goods and services in return for currency, is slowed by shoplifting and white-collar crime. Individual lives are wasted by drug addiction, with potential for a life well-lived lost. Entire generations of young men are wasted by policies resulting in the incarceration of large numbers of minority males.

Many observers have missed the damage that crime has inflicted on community life. Liberals have too often been insensitive to the harm inflicted by crime on the community, by the brokenness of the community's peace and harmony. Conservatives too have been insensitive to the manner in which communities are offended by the breaking up of families by overincarceration, overcharging, "three-strikes" laws, racial discrimination, the death penalty, the searching of probationers and parolees, and other similar practices.

We must probe the question of whether incarceration, which at its core is an exile from the community, is or should be the default crime policy in our nation. We must seriously examine how we can keep individuals accountable for the harm they have inflicted while at the same time building communities that include victim and offender alike. We must craft a criminal justice system that satisfies communities. We must understand that communities hold the key if offenders are to be restored to the community and victims to wholeness. If over a half million felons are coming back into our communities each year, we must have a strategy of restoration if communities are to be able to tolerate this infusion of broken persons. Individual accountability must be balanced with communal responsibility.

Holding individuals accountable in our existing criminal justice system is not the problem. Our laws are based upon holding individuals accountable for the wrongs that they have done. Indeed, we sometimes hold persons responsible for their unintended actions, affirming the maxim that ignorance of the law is no excuse. While many of my clients avoid personal responsibility, our criminal justice system is quite good at holding them ultimately accountable.

The irony, however, is that there seems to be a lack of community or corporate accountability. The mocking of the "abuse excuse" is prevalent. We as a community do not want to accept our own responsibility for the problem of crime. We look the other way when the subject of our responsibility for poverty, neglect, abuse of children, the gulf between rich and poor in education, health care, and housing arise.

The answer is to achieve a proper balance between corporate and individual responsibility. Of course we want to hold individuals responsible for the harm that they do to the victim and to communal peace. We want to require restitution for the victim, making the victim whole. At the same time, we must listen to the stories of communal responsibility, of mentally ill persons being ignored, of families torn apart by social policy, of children taken from poor families too early or left in violence-laden families too long. We must be open to the fact that criminals are our children, and that we helped create them.

The Death Penalty Is Broken

I am an unapologetic abolitionist. I have been an abolitionist since divinity school, borne of a belief in the Creator God who made all things good, and who reserves judgment for the ultimate time. I also am a public defender who has spent much of my career defending persons accused or convicted of capital crimes. I have defended fifteen capital cases, fourteen at the trial level. I have death qualified six juries, and one case I defended resulted in a judgment that landed my client where he is today, on Kentucky's death row. I once put a Christian ethicist from the Louisville Southern Baptist Seminary on the witness stand during the penalty phase to testify to the ethical concerns prevalent in the case I was trying. I remain convinced that the church has a fundamental role to play in the discussion on the death penalty.

The death penalty is the criminal justice system at its worst. I have seen normally good judges make horrendous result-oriented decisions in capital cases. I have seen otherwise decent prosecutors hide evidence or engage in other outrageous misconduct in order to achieve a death verdict. I have seen defense lawyers lose their moral bearings in the face of this horrendous penalty. I have seen police officers plant physical evidence, coerce confessions, and lie on the witness stand. We have all witnessed policy makers hold to this dreadful penalty despite evidence that the death penalty does not deter, that it is racist, that it results in innocent persons being convicted, that it features only the poor and mentally ill or retarded being sentenced to death. These policy makers have turned our system on its head, a system that traditionally affirms through the reasonable doubt standard that it is better for one hundred guilty people to go free than one innocent to be incarcerated. That has been replaced by the belief that we must risk innocent deaths in order to maintain capital punishment.

I agree with the Columbia University study whose primary contention is that the death penalty system in America is broken. That study showed that there is a 68 percent reversal rate across this county in capital cases. In my own state, we feature a 62 percent reversal rate. In no other enterprise would we tolerate such faulty quality control. One can only imagine the fate of an airline industry where 68 percent of its planes went down.

The causes identified in the study and elsewhere (such as the Ryan Commission Report and the Constitution Project's 18 Reforms) are many.

Primary among them are the flawed reliance upon eyewitness identification testimony, the use of informants, prosecutorial misconduct, junk science, and incompetent defense lawyers, many of them appointed counsel. This reversal rate exists despite efforts by Congress through the Antiterrorism and Effective Death Penalty Act of 1996 (AEDPA) to avoid reversals in federal court by insulating constitutional violations from federal review.

Indigent defense is one of the primary reasons why the death penalty is broken in this country. We simply are not willing to place sufficient resources into indigent defense, particularly across the South, in order to rely upon that system to defend individuals accused of capital crimes. In Kentucky, the first and only involuntary execution since 1976 involved an alcoholic attorney appointed by an exceptionally pro–death penalty judge. Many places in the South still have little or no system for providing indigent defense, places that refuse to organize a system, that provide little money for the defense of capital cases either at the trial or post-trial level. Federal Resource Centers, once beacons of justice in the death belt, were abolished by a result-oriented Congress displeased by the success of these sturdy but poorly funded capital lawyers. Sleeping defense lawyers involved in multiple capital cases in Texas are defended by the Texas Attorney General's Office as being "effective." Effective counsel apparently does not mean counsel who has even awakened from slumber in Texas. And former Governor George Bush vetoed an indigent defense system in Texas in deference to the opinions of trial judges and private criminal defense lawyers. Fourteen of Illinois' 159 inmates on death row were represented at trial by attorneys who have been disbarred or suspended. We've had a similar although less dramatic experience in Kentucky.

Innocence and the Death Penalty

One of the shocking parts of the death penalty system is how we are tolerating evidence of actual innocence. Over one hundred persons have now been freed from death row, having been found innocent—some were within hours of being executed, freed after DNA proved their innocence. Governor George Ryan of Illinois said in a January 2003 speech at DePaul University College of Law: "We had exonerated not one, not two, but 13 men from death row. They were found innocent. Innocent of the charges for which they were sentenced to die. Can you imagine? The state nearly killed innocent people, nearly injected them with a cocktail of deadly poisons so that they could die in front of witnesses on a gurney in the state's death chamber."

Death Penalty Echoes of Mercy

Where can you find mercy on this issue? Where are the echoes of grace and mercy among the death rows of this nation? You can find mercy among those who work on improving conditions on death row. You can hear echoes of mercy among those who work on changing indigent defense systems. You can find mercy among those who study existing problems with the death penalty and call for changes to eliminate racism, bad lawyering, junk science. You can find mercy among those who seek to depoliticize the death penalty.

If you listen, you will hear very specific echoes. You will hear it in the Constitution Project's 18 Reforms, a project that moved past the tired debate of deterrence versus abolition and sought to reform this area pending a resolution. You can hear it among the work of Steve Bright and Bryan Stephenson, Professor Marshall and Helen Prejean. You can hear grace working in the death row ministry of Paul Stevens of Kentucky, and the Murder Victims for Reconciliation. You can hear it among the leaders in the United States Congress working today on the Innocence Protection Act.

You can clearly find echoes of mercy when people work to discover those innocent men now on our death rows. With the use of DNA, 110 innocents have now been exonerated, many of them on death row. The Innocence Project, leading the way, locates one man at a time and pulls him back from death's door.

Most recently you can hear echoes in the U.S. Supreme Court decision of *Atkins v. Virginia* and *Ring v. Arizona*. In a landmark decision, the nation's highest court held that the execution of the mentally retarded violated the Eighth Amendment's cruel and unusual punishment clause. The Court said that a national consensus had developed over the previous eighteen years since *Penry v. Texas* had said that the execution of the mentally retarded was not unconstitutional. Thereafter, in a second landmark case within a week of the other, the Court affirmed that juries alone can sentence a person to death, invalidating hundreds of death penalty verdicts across the nation.

Something extraordinary is going on; poll numbers favoring the death penalty are dropping. Justices O'Connor and Ginsburg have expressed serious doubts about the manner in which the death penalty is being implemented. The Constitution Project, the American Bar Association, the Ryan Commission, the Innocence Project are casting serious, fundamental doubts about whether this penalty can survive. Echoes are joining together, not quite a chorus, but voices nevertheless, and they are being heard.

A Faint Echo: The Kentucky Racial Justice Act

The death penalty nationwide has had a troubling racist past, particularly in the South. Of the 455 persons executed for rape between 1890 and 1950, 90 percent were black men. No white men were executed during the same period of time for raping a white woman. Two-thirds of the 288 children executed in this country have been black. All forty children executed for the crime of rape have been black. Death row populations today include 42 percent African Americans, compared to 13 percent of the population.

Studies have abounded connecting the race of the defendant and the race of the victim to the incidence of the death penalty. One of the most recent was Professor David Baldus, who published a 1998 study in the Cornell Law Review revealing that race of victim and defendant continue to be significant factors in New Jersey and Philadelphia, a finding similar to his previous studies from Georgia in the 1970s and 1980s.

This past was implicitly affirmed in the Supreme Court case of *McCleskey v. Kemp*. There the Court ignored clear evidence of a pattern of race discrimination in the implementation of the death penalty in Georgia. A study showed that the defendant's odds of getting the death penalty were 4.3 times higher if the victim were white. The majority opinion stated that allowing such statistical proof would throw "into serious question the principles that underlie our entire criminal justice system."[1] Justice Brennan in dissent wrote that the majority "seems to suggest a fear of too much justice."[2]

It was out of this past, and specifically the *McCleskey* case, that the Kentucky Racial Justice Act was born. In 1992, a group of people in Kentucky began to advocate for a state version of the national Racial Justice Act. A study was ordered by the General Assembly. The study, conducted by Professors Thomas J. Keil and Gennaro F. Vito of the University of Louisville, found that "blacks accused of killing whites had a higher average probability of being charged with capital crimes by the prosecutor and sentenced to die by the jury than other homicide offenders."[3]

Despite the study, the Racial Justice Act failed to pass the Kentucky General Assembly in either 1994 or 1996 sessions of the Kentucky General Assembly. However, Senator Gerald Neal of Louisville, Father Pat Delahanty of Louisville, and attorney Ed Monahan of the Department of Public Advocacy and others persisted and finally obtained passage of this bill, the one and still the only such act in existence in the country.

The bill is simple. It prohibits a sentence of death sought on the basis of race, demonstrated by showing that race was a significant factor in decisions to seek the sentence of death at the time the death sentence was sought. It further allows for the use of statistical data to show that death was being sought more frequently upon persons of color than upon white persons.

The passage of this bill is an echo of grace heard across the cacophony that is the death penalty. It is a sign that if we are going to continue to implement the policy of having a death penalty, then we must deal with race.

Race Permeates the American Criminal Justice System

Any discussion of race and the criminal justice system must begin with slavery. In 1862, Frederick Douglass said that "justice is often painted with bandaged eyes, she is described in forensic eloquence as utterly blind to wealth and poverty, high or low, white or black, but a mask of iron however thick could never blind American justice when a black man happens to be on trial. . . . It is not so much the business of his enemies to prove him guilty, as it is the business of himself to prove his innocence. The reasonable doubt which is usually interposed to save the life and liberty of a white man charged with crime seldom has any force or effect when a colored man is accused of crime."[4] How little things have changed in the last 140 years.

Of the practice of racial profiling, Tracey Maclin points out that racial profiling has an ancient pedigree. Philadelphia in 1693 gave city officials power to stop and detain any black, free or slave, who was "gadding abroad" without a pass. South Carolina in 1696 required slave patrols to search slaves' homes weekly for concealed weapons. By 1738, Virginia authorized mandatory searches of the homes of all blacks.[5]

Judge A. Leon Higginbothom Jr., former chief judge of the U.S. Court of Appeals for the Third Circuit, has said that: "the impact of our heritage of slave laws will continue to make itself felt into the future. For there is a nexus between the brutal centuries of colonial slavery and the racial polarization and anxieties of today. The poisonous legacy of legalized oppression based upon the matter of color can never be adequately purged from our society if we act as if slave laws never existed."[6] Many commentators have held that racial bias influences every aspect of the criminal justice system. African Americans, Latinos, and members of other racial minorities and marginalized groups are more likely than similarly situated white people to be stopped by police, to be arrested after being stopped, put in choke holds by arresting officers, denied bail, denied probation, and given harsher sentences, including the death penalty.

The Police/Citizen Encounter and Race

One of those places where race is most problematic is during the police/citizen encounter. It is also one of the places where communities may become most broken. The killing of Haitain immigrant Amadou Diallo, the killing of Haitian immigrant and security guard Patrick Dousmaid, the brutalization of Abner Louima with a broom handle in the New York police station bathroom, the Ramparts scandal in Los Angeles, all demonstrate the dramatic end result of racism during the police/citizen encounter.

Much of the relationship between police and citizens is controlled, at least theoretically, by U.S. Supreme Court case law. A Supreme Court opinion from 1968, *Terry v. Ohio,* has continued to poison the police/citizen encounter over the last thirty years. Tracey Maclin states that *Terry* ultimately vitiates the Fourth Amendment's values. *Terry*'s holding was mistaken because the Court neglected the larger historical and social picture: widespread police practices were causing perilous friction between police and minority communities and making a mockery of the Fourth Amendment rights of minority citizens.[7]

A more recent opinion, *Whren v. United States,* has given the green light to pretextual searches, that is, the practice of stopping a car or person who has committed a minor traffic or other violation for reasons of crime control. In *Whren,* the police stopped a car being driven by minority youth for speeding and having been at the stop sign too long. The inference was that they were stopped for reasons of racial profiling. The

Court stated that the pretext for the stop did not matter as long as there was probable cause to believe a crime had been committed. *Whren* featured a similar blind eye to racism shown previously in *McCleskey.*

Wardlow v. Illinois also held recently that presence in a high-crime neighborhood combined with flight from the police offer sufficient reason to stop the person fleeing, so-called "running while black." Like *Whren,* the opportunity to utilize racist motives in the police/citizen encounter is apparent.

Echoes: The Kentucky Racial Profiling Act and Restoration of Civil Rights Act

The battle for civil rights in this country has been long and effective for two centuries. There have been giants among us who have brought justice to minorities in many areas, education, housing, employment, voting.

The criminal justice system has seen fewer of these efforts, however. There have been successful efforts to stop racial profiling in New Jersey and Florida. Two recent bills in the Kentucky General Assembly are echoes of grace and mercy. In 2001, the Racial Profiling Act was passed by the Kentucky General Assembly. This bill simply outlaws the practice, and puts financial teeth (the officers' salaries) behind its prohibition. That same year, the Restoration of Civil Rights Act was passed in Kentucky, this time streamlining the procedure for obtaining voting and other rights for convicted felons. Both bills indicate that a history of racism can be broken, even in the criminal justice system, even in the South.

Sentencing Practices

Nothing indicates the direction of our present criminal justice system like sentencing patterns and practices (see also Jonathan Rothchild's essay in this volume). A couple of patterns stand out: we are incarcerating at a dramatically high level; we are incarcerating in a racially discriminatory manner; and we are incarcerating in a way that ignores individual differences.

In 1972, 196,000 persons were incarcerated in America. There were 130,000 persons in jail. One in 625 was incarcerated. By 1997, those figures exploded. The number in prison had risen from 196,000 to 1,159,000. The number in jail had risen from 130,000 to 567,000. One of every 155 citizens was incarcerated, up from 1 in 625. Today that figure has increased further to 1 in 145, with a total of 1,965,495 in our jails and prisons. American prisons hold more of our citizens than those of any other nation in the world except Russia. Exile at this level makes communities hemorrhage.

This dramatic increase has had a disparate impact on minorities. In 1926, during the worst days of separate but equal, African Americans comprised 21 percent of prison populations, compared to 60 percent of prison admissions today. Today, blacks account for fewer than half of arrests for violent crimes, over half of the convictions, and 60 percent of prison admissions. In 1998, 36 percent of the 3.9 million persons who were disenfranchised temporarily or permanently as a result of their being convicted of a crime were African American. According to the Sentencing Project, one black man in seven is kept from voting as a result of his convictions. One young black male in three in 1995 was under the control of the criminal justice system. One adult black male in fourteen is locked up on any given day.

Our sentencing practices have turned away from individualized consideration. "Three-strikes" laws are locking up more and more people, often for nonviolent offenses. Mandatory sentencing guidelines are as a policy matter requiring judges to ignore individual situations. What does it mean when we incarcerate so many of our citizens? Why do we provide billions for prison construction but become parsimonious with treatment dollars? Where is an echo of grace here?

The Sentencing Project of Washington, D.C., certainly has brought the truth to power on this issue. Persistently, the Sentencing Project has published the statistics and told the stories of what we are doing in the sentencing arena. As illustrated by Mauer's own essay in this volume, Marc Mauer's book *The Race to Incarcerate* has done this as effectively as any other. There are also echoes of grace and mercy in the restorative justice movement, that movement that tries to bring victim and offender together in order not only to restore both of them but also to bring healing to the community. There are also echoes of grace in the growth of problem-solving courts, including drug, family, homeless, and mental health courts, all of which are attempting to focus on the offender and the victim and are using solutions other than exile.

Another Echo: The National Mood

I am hesitant to try to gauge public opinion, particularly with the exigencies post-9/11. The criminal justice system is being pushed at the national level to deal with an unprecedented situation. Traditional rights, including the right to counsel, the right to be held only upon probable cause, are being threatened by the War on Terrorism.

However, a recent poll conducted by the Peter D. Hart Research Associates entitled "Changing Public Attitudes toward the Criminal Justice System" points to a readiness among the public to seek new answers to the crime problem. The results of that poll, announced February 13, 2002, indicated that the public believes by 65 percent to 32 percent that public policy should deal with the roots of crime over strict sentencing. Americans now favor dealing with drug abuse as a medical problem that should be handled through counseling and treatment rather than prisons, by 65 percent to 31 percent. Fifty-six percent of Americans favor elimination of "three-strikes" and other mandatory-sentencing laws. Fifty-four percent believes the nation's approach toward crime is wrong. Seventy percent believes the War on Drugs is a failure. Nearly two-thirds of Americans believe that rehabilitation through education and job training is the best way to reduce crime.

One Last Echo

The problems in the criminal justice system are long-standing and appear intractable. Problems of injustice have been with us for centuries. Yet if you look, and if you listen, even in this arena you can hear echoes of grace and mercy.

In Kathleen Norris's *Cloister Walk,* she states of the psalms that they "remind us that the way we judge each other, with harsh words and acts of vengeance, constitutes injustice, and they remind us that it is the powerless in society who are overwhelmed when justice becomes institutionalized."[8]

Notes

1. For the *McCleskey* decision, please see http://www.law.umkc.edu/faculty/projects/ftrials/conlaw/mccleskey.html.

2. Ibid.

3. See Keil and Vito, "Race and the Death Penalty in Kentucky Murder Trials."

4. Douglass, "The United States Cannot Remain Half-Slave and Half-Free," in *The Life and Writings of Frederick Douglass, Reconstruction and After,* 4: 357.

5. Maclin, "Race and the Fourth Amendment."

6. Cited by Steven Bright, director, Southern Center for Human Rights, in "Keep the Dream of Equal Justice Alive," Yale Law School commencement address, May 24, 1999.

7. See Maclin, "*Terry v. Ohio*'s Fourth Amendment Legacy: Black Men and Police Discretion."

8. Kathleen Norris, *Cloister Walk* (New York: Riverhead Trade, 1997).

Recapturing the Good, Not Merely Measuring Harms

Rehabilitation, Restoration, and the Federal Sentencing Guidelines

JONATHAN ROTHCHILD

As the essays in this book demonstrate, the current criminal justice system faces significant challenges: overcrowding, racial disparities, financial shortfalls, increases in juvenile inmates, and the collapse of families and communities of those incarcerated. These challenges impel critical reflections on the basic purposes of criminal punishment on both a theoretical and practical level. According to the *United States Commission Guidelines Manual* (November 2000), the four basic purposes of criminal punishment are deterrence, incapacitation, just punishment, and rehabilitation.[1] Each of these purposes has garnered extensive support, and debates among the different proponents have been polemical at times. Within the last decade, the general consensus has acknowledged incapacitation as "the principal justification for imprisonment in American criminal justice."[2] While incapacitation does function to remove immediate threats to the wider public, the notion of "warehousing" criminals lacks a capacious vision of individual and social flourishing and appears condemned to a self-perpetuating system of revolving doors.

The purpose of this essay is to begin to explore the features that may constitute such a capacious vision. Specifically, I focus on rehabilitation and the extent to which it has declined and, in many circles of criminal justice discourse, disappeared altogether. Understanding reasons for the disfavor shown toward rehabilitation requires historical and theoretical analyses that lay bare the problems with and prospects of retrieving rehabilitation within our current system. Rehabilitative ideals manifest themselves in diverse scopes and distinct contents, but, broadly construed, rehabilitation designates any method (or constellations of methods that may or may not be religious in character) established for purposes of transforming individuals so as to redress harms; restore social relationships and reintegrate offenders into society; repudiate cycles of vengeance; and replenish moral, social, and individual goods.[3] I argue that rehabilitation—underpinned by expansive conceptions of self and society illuminated by theological resources and restorative models of justice— more fully accommodates the procedures of justice and the claims of mercy than other modes of punishment. While portions of the current system can be preserved with minor modifications, I contend that the current trend of incapacitation must be reconceived in order to avoid settling for reductive solutions.

There are two principal sections of the essay: the first as a longer, more descriptive and analytical exercise and the second as a more constructive project. The first section undertakes a historical excursus that traces the implementation of rehabilitative objectives in the United States from the 1800s to the 1970s. The trajectory reveals the formation of different rehabilitative techniques that, at least in their earliest forms, have religious origins. The charting of significant developments helps one to conceptualize the ramifications of rehabilitative models. In the 1970s, the paradigm shifted from rehabilitation to incapacitation and just punishment; the determinate, minimal mandatory sentencing introduced by the 1987 Federal Sentencing Guidelines encapsulated the diminishing reliance upon rehabilitative programs. Extended exegesis of the Federal Sentencing Guidelines, in conversation with its critics, will enable us to consider determinate sentencing vis-à-vis justice and mercy.

The second section considers rehabilitation in the current criminal justice system. Three thematic questions orient my discussion: (1) who is involved in crime and punishment? (2) what methods of punishment are suitable to justice and mercy? and (3) what theological resources can illuminate matters of justice and mercy? To offer modest responses to these questions, I will explore alternative solutions to imprisonment, including programs that strive to engender rehabilitation through restorative justice. Restorative justice attends to various matrices of the criminal justice dynamic between victim, offender, and community, and not merely offender and state as in retributivist models. Restorative justice does not seek leniency for offenders, but rather it situates them within frameworks of reciprocity and accountability. I answer the third inquiry by highlighting the unique contributions of theology to social problems such as criminal justice. These contributions include marshaling critiques of finite systems as well as fostering profound images of self and society. I consider the import of theological symbols from the Protestant and Catholic traditions, including Richard Snyder's *The Protestant Ethic and the Spirit of Punishment* and United States Conference of Catholic Bishops' *Responsibility, Rehabilitation, and Restoration: A Catholic Perspective on Crime and Criminal Justice.*

Strategies of Incarceration: A Historical Analysis

REHABILITATIVE IDEALS IN AMERICA: 1800S–1970S

Resonating with Clark Gilpin's analysis in this volume of penology in the colonial period, our historical narrative begins in the late 1700s with Philadelphia's Walnut Street Jail. This invention of the Pennsylvania Quakers is often considered to be the origin of modern imprisonment. Norval Morris explains that rehabilitative ideals undergirded the Quakers' humanitarian mission, where prison practices included "removal from corrupting peers, time for reflection and self-examination, [and] the guidance of biblical precepts."[4] The elimination of capital punishment further testified to these practices as spiritual exercises intended to induce disciplined transformation and to save individual souls. Consonant with coeval, international trends in reform, characterized by Michel Foucault as trends toward humanization focused on the soul rather than the body, prison officials methodically organized and closely supervised inmate life, where each moment was seized to expatiate on morals and to instruct the soul. The resonance with monasticism is rather pronounced: disciplined obedience and divine guidance were the levers of the rehabilitative machine.

Similar to the discipline and hard work encouraged by Bentham's panopticon (although distinct in that Bentham championed deterrence as the chief purpose of punishment), the Quaker system of solitude and interiority conforms to Foucault's study of the historical shift from public execution to punishment as "the most hidden part of the penal process."[5] This concealed quality of punitiveness intensified the dynamic between prisoner and supervisor; knowledge of the individual, according to Foucault, became paramount and determinative for the treatment of prisoners. The stress on knowledge of the individual—knowledge of behavior before and after incarceration that provided a criterion for transformation—"made it possible to divide [prisoners] not so much according to their crimes as according to the dispositions that they revealed. The prison became a sort of permanent observatory that made it possible to distribute the varieties of vice or weakness."[6] For Foucault, this permanent observatory amounted to a "mechanism of coercion";[7] such criticisms would fetter models of rehabilitation throughout the next two centuries.

These rehabilitative objectives continued in the early 1800s, when two rival systems of penitential organization—the Auburn system of New York and the Pennsylvania plan—became the dominant options within American penology. Both plans emphasized isolation, obedience, and rigorous labor, for reformers envisioned these techniques as critical for reforming corrupt human lives. As Foucault observes,[8] both systems advocated complete silence as foundational; however, whereas Philadelphia practiced absolute isolation and cultivated rehabilitation of the conscience, Auburn brought inmates together in silent interaction and cultivated rehabilitation of the social individual. Debates soon emerged regarding the ostensibly religious connotations of conversion in reference to rehabilitation. Was the goal of transformation the experience of a Pauline *metanoia* or heartfelt contrition or the recovery of proper moral sensibilities to return to normal civic life?

To appreciate the significance of the Auburn and Pennsylvania systems, it is important to attend to both their political and religious contexts. Though these contexts were significantly intertwined, let us begin with the political context. In studying the historical development of the American asylum (and its different modalities such as the almshouse, the workhouse, the home for the insane, various child-care institutions, and the rise of the penitentiary), David Rothman observes that distinct shifts—informed by political and religious sensibilities—helped account for the initial success and gradual decline of these institutions. Colonial legal codes were harsh (e.g., whippings, stocks, and pillory) and, at times, inhumane (e.g., public cage or disfigurement), and they frequently lacked an institutional basis because criminal offenses were conceived in terms of sin. In an effort attributable to tremendous increases in general population and population

JONATHAN ROTHCHILD

density as well as the widespread dissemination of Enlightenment conceptions of sovereignty and reason, the new republican government sought to reform the legal system and forms of punishments through institutionalized structures. Rothman explains that asylums arose during the Jacksonian period as envisioned panaceas for rising social instability.[9]

Rothman asserts that Americans generally no longer conflated criminality and individual sinfulness and divine judgment; he argues that political exigencies superseded religious beliefs and thus rendered them ancillary or superfluous to the criminal justice process. While below I will problematize Rothman's thesis about the disenfranchisement of religion from criminal justice, Rothman does provide insight into the rehabilitative character of the asylum. The optimistic spirit of the Jacksonian era witnessed mass construction of uniformly designed asylums;[10] these institutions placed emphasis on obedience and respect for authority as integral for rehabilitation. Rothman writes that this institutionalized rehabilitation soon lost momentum, however, when "the decline from rehabilitation to custodianship"[11] became pronounced in the period between 1850 and 1880. The ideals of Jacksonian reform were trumped by rising recidivism, overcrowding (attributable partially to inundations of lower-class immigrants), and new theories of science. The Auburn and Pennsylvania prisons could not escape these phenomena; by 1866 the Philadelphia penitentiary discontinued its exclusive use of solitary confinement, and the two prisons' rehabilitative plans succumbed to concerns for peace and security.[12]

Despite his illuminating work on the sociopolitical contexts that influenced perspectives on criminal justice and the development of penal institutions, Rothman, in my judgment, fails to appreciate the theological contributions that elevated the prominence of rehabilitative programs as well as the Auburn and Pennsylvania systems.[13] It is inaccurate to assert that the Quakers were the only religious group who influenced the development of criminal justice in the United States. Christopher Adamson describes the "interdenominational"[14] character of societies supporting prison reform in the early 1800s (e.g., the Philadelphia Society for Alleviating the Miseries of Public Prisons and the Boston Prison Discipline Society), which included the perspectives of Calvinists, Unitarians, Methodists, Quakers, and Universalists. These religious groups became steadfast critics of various criminal justice practices, and they successfully persuaded several states to discontinue public executions in the 1830s.[15] These religious groups did not share monolithic views, including their views of the religious dimensions of rehabilitation. Disparate understandings of religious doctrine brought disagreements about the proper method of criminal punishment and rehabilitation. The Calvinists and Unitarians, for example, held divergent conceptions of redemption: whereas the Calvinists viewed the will as corrupt and bound where salvation existed only for the elect, the Unitarians adopted a more egalitarian model that emphasized the individual decision for transformation. These religious views, in turn, accounted for their divergent perspectives vis-à-vis the Auburn and Philadelphia models. Christopher Adamson explains this difference: "Calvinist values are discernible in the organization of Auburn prison discipline—in the uniformity of treatment, in the strict rules governing communication"; by contrast, the Pennsylvania plan

> made each felon responsible for his own reformation, [and] was consistent with [Unitarian William Ellery] Channing's doctrine of personal reformation according to which God's grace would be bestowed only on those who chose to reform. Someone who did not in heart want to change could never be forced to do so. The objective of Unitarian philanthropy should therefore be to aid human beings in their personal search for moral perfection, not frighten them into obedience by reminding them of their innate depravity.[16]

To be sure, as Rothman argued, theological influences became increasingly marginalized with respect to rising administrative and social concerns and promising scientific theories; however, in ways undervalued by Rothman, these theological influences, sustained by changing doctrines and practices, were significantly operative during the incubation and development of rehabilitative practices in the United States.[17]

Though the Auburn system gained popularity among state prisons attributable to its cost effectiveness vis-à-vis the Pennsylvania system,[18] the middle of the nineteenth century presented considerable obstacles for rehabilitative efforts. The Civil War and its aftermath disrupted social and political life in all its matrices (e.g., lack of communal cohesiveness, social problems such as poverty, and the emotional trauma of those returning from war). Perhaps the most conspicuous impact on prisons was the modern phenomenon of overcrowding. Overcrowding presented new challenges—challenges that complicated strategies of isolation and rehabilitation of the individual. Despite these challenges, there were mid- to late nineteenth-century American penal institutions that dedicated themselves to reform of the prisoner. One such institution was New York's Elmira Reformatory, established in 1870. Reflecting the influence of penologists from around the world,[19] the Elmira Reformatory advocated rehabilitation and reconstruction of the self over against punishment and deterrence. Hard work constituted the central task of the prisoners, but also Elmira introduced comprehensive educational programs to complement this industriousness. These educational programs not only taught basic competency, but they cultivated virtue through a program of moral education. The foundation for Elmira's moral education program was Kant's ethical rationalism: "Kant's philosophy was given credence in the rational and humanitarian vision being inculcated at the reformatory. D. R. Ford, a school director at Elmira, outlined the ideas underlying the curriculum that verified the harmonious union of Kantian and liberal Protestant philosophies."[20] The Kantian-based curriculum of moral education appeared to reduce successfully the likelihood of repeat offenders. According to Robert Waite, the recidivism rate among those released from Elmira remained low; consequently, "Elmira provided the model for prison construction and programs in the United States in the First World War."[21] Rehabilitation remained consistent with the objectives of incarceration, and the Elmira Reformatory provided a good model of the effectiveness of rehabilitation despite growing discomfort with such models.

By the turn of the twentieth century, the emergence of behavioral sciences transformed notions of rehabilitation into curing the offender (see Peter Paris's essay in this volume). The construal of criminality as illness impacted the criminal justice system: "The opening of penology to psychiatrists and behavioral scientists spurred on the design and appeal of indeterminate sentencing statutes. Release from prison became the equivalent of release from a hospital."[22] The conflation of prisoner and patient diminished the importance of the actual crime committed but intensified the necessity of psychological classifications, where evaluative designations differentiated prisoners' "symptoms." These evaluative designations dictated the conditions of sentencing, and, hence, sentences were indeterminate. The rehabilitative ideal was now less analogous to a monastic lifestyle, but knowledge of individual dispositions remained prominent. Rehabilitation was measured according to psychologically informed predictions about the potential for recidivism. Congress's establishment of a federal parole system in 1910 further confirmed the newly conceived emphasis on "expert" determination of rehabilitation. In the wake of wider social optimism after World War II, there was renewed confidence in rehabilitation as a primary purpose of incarceration.

In the turbulence of the 1960s, amidst the evolution of the modern prison system punctuated by prison riots and the recognition of prisoners' rights, debates raged concerning punishment versus therapy that foreshadowed the decline of rehabilitation. On the one hand, thinkers such as psychiatrist Karl Menninger defended therapy and indeterminate sentencing as invaluable tools for restoring individual health and social order; Menninger envisaged that scientific diagnostic centers would afford prisoners dignified ways to reassimilate into civilized society. On the other hand, legal theorists such as Francis Allen offered the rejoinder that therapy offered ambiguous proposals that encouraged "procedural laxness and irregularity."[23] Allen adumbrated reasons for the decline of the rehabilitative ideal (e.g., it threatened democratic sensibilities, and it lacked scientific evidence that demonstrated its effectiveness), and his work functioned as a catalyst for wider movements against rehabilitation. The deterioration of prison conditions precipitated concerns about the feasibility of rehabilitating the individual. While the law continued to embrace the rehabilitative ideal (e.g., the Model Penal Code of 1962), critics argued that the system of psychological classifications and indeterminate sentencing was coercive and subject to enormous abuse.

Among these critics were retributivists who maintained that rehabilitation precluded just punishment. A paramount retributivist precept derives from the criminal's merited or deserved punishment. Kant declared that a community, were it to resolve to disband, must first execute all murderers as that was their deserved punishment and social debt.[24] Hegel insisted that the execution of a murderer reconciles the rights of society, law, and offender by canceling out the offender's violation of rights and dignity in a rationally determined way. Hegel therefore concludes that "[p]unishment is inevitably deserved; that is inescapable."[25] Contemporary retributivist Jeffrie Murphy appropriates a Kantian theory of criminal punishment.[26] This theory adheres to the moral law and to the social contract: citizens enjoy privileges and obligations in virtue of social membership, such that criminal offenders deserve punishment lest they gain an unjust advantage over other citizens and vitiate the formal structure and categorical nature of the moral law. Based on these principles, Murphy castigates therapy as paternalistic and coercive. He contends that therapy does not reflect desert but rather a perceived need that necessarily involves the "involun-

JONATHAN ROTHCHILD

tary deprivation of liberty."[27] He submits that he does not oppose rehabilitation as such, but he claims it is disingenuous, attenuates prisoners' volition, eschews accountability, and cannot restore social order. While I cannot here fully engage retributivism on a critical level, it is important to note that the position of Murphy and other retributivists attained momentum in the 1970s.

THE ROAD TO DETERMINATE SENTENCING: THE FEDERAL SENTENCING GUIDELINES

In the 1970s, the system of sentencing was indeterminate, predicated on the evaluations of judges, parole officers, psychiatrists, and other officials. Criticisms continued to proliferate outside (e.g., law-enforcement groups) and within the prorehabilitation community (e.g., psychiatrists who became less sanguine on prediction).[28] Judge Marvin Frankel, through his influential work *Criminal Sentences: Law without Order,* became a leading advocate for determinate sentencing that relinquished the objectives of restoring personalities and the methods of psychological predictions and relied less heavily upon judicial discretion. Frankel is often credited as forging a catalytic point of departure for the framework of the Federal Sentencing Guidelines. While federal judges did strive for consensus building through the voluntary exchange of information about cases and sentences, there were no mechanisms that could ensure uniformity in sentencing at the federal level.

Consequently, there were increasing concerns about the seemingly limitless nature of judicial discretion and the inconsistency of measures such as parole. On a legislative level, Maine established precedence on a state level by abolishing parole in 1975, and the California Determinate Sentencing Legislation dismissed focus on rehabilitation in 1976. On a broader political level, neither conservatives (who argued that indeterminate sentencing amounted to a soft position on crime) nor liberals (who argued that indeterminate sentencing invited racial bias and unjust disparities) were content with criminal justice sentencing structures. Pursuit of sentencing uniformity compelled members of Congress—spearheaded by Senator Edward Kennedy but supported by staunch Republicans such as Strom Thurmond—to pass the Sentencing Reform Act of 1984, which created the United States Sentencing Commission and laid the groundwork for the Federal Sentencing Guidelines (effective November 1, 1987).

The putative aims of the legislation were to establish "honesty in sentencing," "uniformity in sentencing," and "proportionality in sentencing."[29]

The sentencing guidelines were designed to be presumptive, that is, sentences were presumed to be appropriate for all generic cases. The commission therefore developed the sentencing guidelines through an empirical approach drawn from ten thousand presentence investigations and forty thousand summary reports of convictions. It extrapolated a sentencing table that is constituted by a 258–cell grid and two axes: a horizontal scale of criminal history and a vertical scale of offense tabulation. The scale of criminal history reflects the extent of past criminal offenses (which range from category 0 in the case of a first offender to category VI in the case of a "career offender" or third felony offender);[30] and the offense tabulation scale provides forty-three different levels that account for the specific details (e.g., the addition or subtraction of levels based on factors such as the aggregate financial damage or physical harm caused; the amount of drugs and violence involved; the violation of a position of trust; evidence of contrition and acceptance of responsibility) of the presently charged offenses. Upon clarifying the two axes via legal argumentation between defendants and prosecutors, federal judges must consult the table by reading the convergence of the two axes: this "score" provides the monthly parameters for sentencing, wherein the statutory regulation mandates that the maximum of any range cannot exceed the minimum by more than the greater of 25 percent of six months (according to 28 U.S.C. 994 (b) (2)). The sentences established for felonies and misdemeanors are to be served in full, less reductions through good behavior. In 1987 the system of parole was abolished on the federal level, where only supervised release existed after the duration of the sentence. The cumulative effect has extended prison sentences, particularly, as Marc Mauer points out above, for young African American male offenders. While, as stated above, the United States Sentencing Commission continues to uphold four purposes for punishment, the sentencing guidelines appear to render rehabilitation less and less a tenable option.[31]

CRITICAL ASSESSMENTS OF THE GUIDELINES:
GUIDING WHOM, BY WHAT STANDARDS?

Critics, particularly federal judges,[32] have maintained that the sentencing guidelines, while well intended and ameliorative of earlier abuses within

JONATHAN ROTHCHILD

judicial discretion, perforce divest judges of their legitimate capacities for judging. There is a constellation of reasons for the purported failure of the guidelines. Some refer to the fact that only three of the original seven persons on the federal Sentencing Commission had ever been a judge. Others point to the specific political context and criminal justice conditions out of which the legislation for the sentencing guidelines originated that appear to lack suitability for today's milieu.

Given the purposes of this essay, I want to isolate three reasons for the general dissatisfaction with the guidelines. First, the emphasis on determinate sentencing gives new prominence to prosecutors; prosecutors can intentionally alter sentencing procedures by charging criminals with different types of crimes that warrant disparate sentences according to the guidelines. Thus, plea bargaining,[33] wherein prosecutors agree to reduce sentences in exchange for offender cooperation with investigators, has become increasingly common in federal cases. The utility of plea-bargained information complicates sentencing uniformity, for it appears to exchange one type of disparity for another.[34] Equally important, it works to eviscerate the difficult deliberation entailed in evaluating the claims of offender, victim, and community and negates the necessity of decision (see William Schweiker's essay in this volume and his discussion of Augustine and the necessity of judgment). Plea bargaining obviates these claims, as well as the three purported aims of the guidelines themselves, because its largely unregulated role in criminal justice invites, according to Albert Alschuler, "a prosecutor's paradise" whereby "the guidelines are bargaining weapons—armaments that enable prosecutors, not the sentencing commission, to determine sentences in most cases. In operation, the guidelines do not set the sentences; they simply augment the power of the prosecutors to do so."[35]

This augmentation of prosecutorial power truncates the contribution of judges to the federal sentencing system and raises further questions about justice and mercy. Stated baldly: if the system merely "warehouses" its prisoners, are federal judges relegated merely to stocking the warehouses? Kate Stith and José Cabranes summarize the precarious position of judges and the guidelines' impact on questions of justice and mercy: "Without moral authority, neither mercy nor moral condemnation are possible. Under the Guidelines, mercy, by which the full application of the law is relaxed in furtherance of the law's ends, has been rendered largely obsolete. Without the possibility of mercy, rigid adherence to the law cannot express severity of judgment. No moral judgment can be expressed at all."[36]

Indeed, federal judges are bound to uphold federal statutes in accordance with constitutional principles, but the structure of the sentencing guidelines reduces their judgments in many cases to the mere application of limited, quantified variables. I contend that nuancing these variables in a prudent, sensitive, and critical manner in conjunction with a holistic vision of offender, victim, and community allows for notions of transformation that do not preclude the pursuit of rational judgment or honesty in sentencing.

The second and third reasons pertain to departures. The second reason that judges experience frustration stems from the limited adjudicating factors; as explained above, the sentencing table accounts only for previous criminal history and the specific details of the current offense. According to the *United States Commission Guidelines Manual,* "age (including youth)," "mental and emotional conditions," "family ties and responsibilities," and other factors such as educational or vocational skills, public service, abuses suffered, or charitable service "are not ordinarily relevant in determining whether a sentence should be outside the applicable guideline range."[37] This public policy decision, designed to thwart special privileges for middle-class, white Americans, reduces the uniqueness of individuals to banal numbers and fails to take into account the complexity of human life: it merely calculates the quantitative total of harms caused without recognizing additional factors such as individual and public goods (e.g., unique contributions of individuals to society, critical roles played by individuals within structures of family). Albert Alschuler describes the extent to which aggregation has become the dominant paradigm in contemporary legal and social thought— a paradigm he characterizes as "the bottom-line collectivist-empirical mentality"—wherein "[w]e seem increasingly indifferent to individual cases and small numbers."[38]

Despite its claims to objectivity, the mechanical calculus of the sentencing table does not circumvent political concerns. As noted by Marc Mauer in this volume and elsewhere,[39] the mandatory minimum penalty for crack cocaine (more common among African American users) is disproportionate to the same penalty for an equal amount of powdered cocaine. Such discrepancies are exacerbated by the fact that over 40 percent of federal cases involve some type of drug offense. On a wider plane within criminal justice, the quantitative apparatus of determinate sentencing in general cannot achieve perfectly just sentencing. For example, determinate sentences such as "three-strikes" laws in California are predicated on sequence: "When these three defendants are sentenced in their third conviction, they have identical criminal records in every respect but sequence. It is the defendant with the least serious current offence who receives the most severe prison sentence."[40] The internal logic of the determinate sentencing system itself can be self-defeating in that it imposes unequal sentences on seemingly equivalent crimes.

Furthermore, equally troubling for many students of the guidelines, the United States Sentencing Commission has adopted measures that seem to disenfranchise poor and minority offenders. Michael Tonry provides two examples that demonstrate the commission's resistance to considering extenuating circumstances that may mitigate presumptive sentencing. In *United States v. Big Crow,* 898 F. 2d 1326 (1990), an appellate court approved a lower departure for a Native American victimized by abuse but recognized for his outstanding work. The commission responded by reconceiving its departure standards and disavowing the relevancy of good works. In *United States v. Lopez,* 945 F. 2d 1096 (1991), another appellate court upheld deviation from the suggested sentencing to a lower one predicated upon a defendant's disadvantaged upbringing. The commission, in turn, determined that such variables were not germane to matters of sentencing.[41]

The third reason, interrelated to the second, underlying the disillusionment with the guidelines concerns the inability of judges to depart from the parameters framed by consulting the sentencing table. Judges do possess liberty to depart from the table, but the commission forecasts that "they will not do so very often"[42] and asserts that federal appellate courts will frequently overturn such departures through an abuse of discretion standard. The commission cites a Supreme Court decision, *Koon v. United States* 116 S. Ct. 2035 (1996), which holds that departures can be justified based on unusual circumstances that fall outside the "heartland" of cases. In writing the majority opinion in *Koon,* Justice Kennedy affirms that "[the Sentencing Reform Act of 1984] did not eliminate all the district court's discretion" because judges have authority "to depart in cases that feature aggravating or mitigating circumstances of a kind or degree not adequately taken into consideration by the Commission."[43] The difficulty arises because the commission fails to articulate the explicit nature of the aggravating or mitigating circumstances that warrant departure; it merely demands conformity to the prescribed sentencing parameters.[44]

Recent legislation, hastily passed as the Feeney Amendment in April 2003, has raised additional concern related to departures. Subsumed under the Protect Act as a rider to the Amber Alert Bill, the amendment seeks to eliminate unwarranted downward departures. In Section 401, entitled "Sentencing Reform," the amendment develops a strategy "to ensure that Department of Justice attorneys oppose sentencing adjustments, including downward departures, that are not supported by the facts and the law."[45] A substantial portion of this strategy entails monitoring judicial decisions: United States attorneys report to the Department of Justice names of judges departing downwardly and the stated reasons for these departures. Attorney General John Ashcroft then compiles a report for the Committees on the Judiciary of the House of Representatives and the Senate. Ashcroft, in a July 2003 memorandum to United States attorneys, submits that the Feeney Amendment "enacts several key reforms designed to ensure that the Sentencing Guidelines would be more faithfully and consistently enforced, thereby achieving the consistency and predictability that Congress sought in the Sentencing Reform Act."[46] The desire for predictability and a Holmesian law as power inform Ashcroft's memorandum.

Does the amendment promote this "consistency and predictability"? Opponents ranging from the Judicial Conference of the United States, the NAACP, and the late Supreme Court Justice William Rehnquist[47] maintain that this monitoring is effectively tantamount to intimidating judges as it not so subtly dissuades downward departures. The Feeney Amendment is also controversial because there is debate about the number of departures. Immigration lies at the heart of the debate, given that the three districts leading the nation in downward departure rate are the District of Arizona and the Southern District of California (two districts bordering Mexico) and the Eastern District of Washington (bordering Canada). In an April 2003 letter to Senators Hatch and Leahy, the United States sentencing commissioners argue that prescinding from these immigration departures reveals a minimal number of downward departures: "If those districts with departure policies crafted to address these high volume immigration caseloads are filtered out, the non-substantial assistance departure rate is reduced to 10.2%."[48] Moreover, to what extent does the Feeney Amendment violate judicial authority to depart as provided by the Sentencing Commission and upheld by the Supreme Court in *Koon v. United States?* In the same letter mentioned above, the United States Sentencing Commission itself raises concerns that "[t]he amendments being proposed in this legislation change not only departure guideline policy, but also alter the traditional way in which guideline revisions are implemented."[49] The Feeney Amendment thus blurs the separation of powers.

In light of these reasons, one can raise questions about the character of determinate sentencing: can it account for the whole person? Michael Tonry sheds light on the difference between the narrow construal of determinate sentencing and the more expansive perspective of indeterminate sentencing:

> The two-axis grid reifies thinking about punishments into a calculus that takes account only of criminality. Under indeterminate sentencing, the goal of individuation of punishment to achieve rehabilitative ends, combined with an absence of sentencing rules, forced judges to adopt a holistic approach. That approach led to unwarranted disparities and unacceptable risks of invidious bias and consciousness, but at its best allowed judges to take account of the crime, all of the relevant circumstances, and the likely consequences of alternate possible sentences.[50]

There are shortcomings entailed in indeterminate sentences, as we have seen above with respect to previous judicial bias. Yet indeterminate sentences can provide judges with flexibility to consider past actions in relation to present responsibilities and future possibilities. Judicial flexibility does not lapse into relativism: rather, it enables judges to attend to individual circumstances, legal practices, and moral imperatives as well as a holistic vision of the offender that appreciates transformation as an ongoing process. Judges can consequently interpret the criminal act within the narrative of a criminal's life. By contrast, determinate sentencing concerned with retribution and incapacitation concentrates too exclusively on past offenses and not on individuals. To be sure, the goals of the Federal Sentencing Guidelines—honesty, uniformity, and proportionality in sentencing—must remain, but there must be a recognition of inexorable tensions, particularly between uniformity and proportionality. The Feeney Amendment, in my judgment, glosses these tensions in an unsophisticated manner. Stith and Cabranes similarly recommend a strategy for overcoming these tensions: "This should be our foremost goal—the avoidance of sentences that are arbitrary, unreasonable, or inexplicable *in context,* not the achievement of national uniformities devised by persons deliberately alien to the case at hand." [51]

Justice, Mercy, and Alternative Models of Criminal Justice

Having now traced the historical decline of rehabilitation and critically assessed the present system exemplified in the Federal Sentencing Guidelines, I now turn to alternatives that may reintegrate rehabilitation into the accepted purposes of punishment. Let me reiterate that it would be nearly impossible to eliminate the guidelines altogether and that problems with determinate sentencing do not necessarily translate into the efficacy of indeterminate sentencing solutions. Rather, I seek to appropriate criminal justice and theological models to help recommend ways the guidelines might be reconceptualized to engender possibilities for rehabilitation with regard to justice and mercy. There are three thematic questions that I will consider: (1) who is involved in crime and punishment? (2) what methods of punishment are suitable to justice and mercy? and (3) what theological resources can illuminate justice and mercy?

OFFENDERS, VICTIMS, AND THE COMMUNITY

An obstacle to rehabilitation immediately arises when one conceives of crime and punishment solely in terms of offender and state. Indeed, the state does possess a central role: thinkers from Paul (Rom. 13:1–7) to Thomas Aquinas to Martin Luther to Hegel have asserted the priority of the state to punish offenders to secure the common good and to restore civil order. How can rehabilitation become integrated into this process? Earlier we observed the critiques advanced by Foucault and Jeffrie Murphy, who censured rehabilitation as coercive and paternalistic. Edgardo Rotman distinguishes between two types of rehabilitation, authoritarian and humanistic, or liberty-centered. While thinkers such as Foucault and Murphy endorse the possibility of the former, Rotman argues that the latter "offers inmates a sound and trustworthy opportunity to remake their lives. Thus this model seeks to awaken in inmates a deep awareness of their relationship with the rest of society, resulting in a genuine sense of social responsibility." [52] This awareness of social responsibility, rather than mere submission to state power or guilt for deserved punishment, conveys a sense of transformation that transcends mere restoration

JONATHAN ROTHCHILD

of the individual. By expanding the scope of criminality to interpenetrate offender (as an individual), victim, society, and state, one can more fully demonstrate the potential outcomes of rehabilitative strategies. Decline in recidivism rates should marshal support for rehabilitative programs, but recidivism rates do not exhaust the meaning of rehabilitation. The inclusion of victims and society within the criminal justice process facilitates broader conceptions of rehabilitation.

This expanded scope of rehabilitation is frequently referred to as restorative justice. Restorative justice perceives crimes as offenses against the community, not merely the state, and thus it can disengage itself from merely retributive modes of thought. Restorative justice models recently have garnered international attention through the work of the Truth and Reconciliation Commission (TRC) in South Africa. Rather than seeking vengeance against those responsible for apartheid, the TRC has sought to recover the truth and restore social relations. The TRC relies upon dialogue between victims and offenders with the criterion of truth as the determining factor. Restorative justice applies to crimes that directly violate an individual or individuals but also that deeply affect community consciousness in more implicit ways. The explosion of hate crimes, or at least crimes now officially counted as hate crimes, instantiates the importance of restorative solutions. Those offenders who commit crimes that "manifest evidence of prejudice based on race, religion, sexual orientation, or ethnicity"[53] provoke visceral reactions and deserve amplified punishment. Intensification of punitive measures, however, will not work to heal the wounds of hate and violence. Communities must perform extraordinary measures—such as the risk of embracing both offender and victim—before restoration and rehabilitation can achieve fruition. There are few examples of programs dedicated to restorative justice in the United States, although the numbers are increasing.[54] Let us now turn to some proposals for alternative methods.

ALTERNATIVE METHODS OF PUNISHMENT

A rehabilitative model must adopt variegated methods that attend not only to offender, community, and victim but also to justice and mercy. One innovative method deemphasizes imprisonment and retrieves a traditional form of punishment: shame. While shame as stigmatization remains embedded in the criminal experience, shame also functions as a strategy of deterrence and of rehabilitation. Shaming can deter corporate corruption by jeopardizing one's professional reputation, particularly among the white-collar criminals that comprise 8 percent of federal inmates. Dan Kahan and Eric Posner argue that shaming deters by engendering "strong economic and psychological disincentives against crime."[55] These deterrent aspects may well help obviate further corporate scandals, but the rehabilitative dimensions of shaming, in my judgment, hold more promise for reforming the current system. Shaming does not seek to evacuate the sociality of offenders as lengthy prison sentences can;[56] rather, shaming reinforces the responsibilities of such sociality.

While perceiving a rehabilitative dimension in shaming, John Braithwaite contends that shame cannot be disengaged from punishment. He points to cultures such as Japan where shame as punishment functions collectively: the shame from individual offenses are borne by the collective entity of which the individual is a member. Individual accountability remains crucial because the individual experiences consternation at subjecting the community to public scrutiny and dishonor. Yet, the ultimate telos of the shame is the moral restoration of individual and community, which Braithwaite denominates as reintregrative shaming. He writes: "*Reintegrative shaming* is shaming which is followed by efforts to reintegrate the offender back into the community of law-abiding or respectable citizens through words or gestures of forgiveness or ceremonies to decertify the offender as deviant."[57] Transformation therefore is experienced at the individual and communal level as it is definitively shaped through reciprocal interactions—that is, a dialectic consisting of rebuke, contrition, and forgiveness—between offender, victim, and the community.

Braithwaite's inclusion of "forgiveness" introduces a dimension of mercy that appears to create tensions with the procedural requirements of justice. Does not rehabilitation imply leniency, a free ride for offenders, at the expense of the rights, the properties, and even the lives of victims? This tension can be rendered productive through careful distinctions about the types of mercy involved. Paul Ricoeur offers a clarifying distinction that allows one to appeal to mercy without severing completely the claims of justice. Ricoeur submits that pardon, not amnesty, provides the means to absolve offenders from debt without denying the reality of the offense: "All the detrimental effects of forgetting are contained in this incredible claim to wipe away the traces of public discord. It is in this sense that amnesty is the contrary of pardon, which, as I shall insist, requires memory."[58] Rehabilitative models, such as the aforementioned re-integrative shaming and restorative justice, do not therefore dispense with punishment, the claims of victims and communities, and the memory of pain and suffering; rather, they can preserve the tragedy and brokenness of the past, the complexity of interactions in the present, and the prospects of resolution and hope in the future. As with theological models that do not uncouple judgment and forgiveness, these models uphold profound opportunities for genuine transformation.

These opportunities can be found in less obvious forms. Restitution constitutes another alternative to imprisonment that can incorporate rehabilitative ideals. In addition to community service and electronic monitoring, Sweden has instituted a day-fine system—wherein offenders pay fines correlative to their annual income—that has reduced incarceration numbers. Offenders therefore pay restitution (through fines or community service that can function as job-skills training), but they can more readily resume the normal activities of their lives without the disruption of familial or vocational responsibilities. Restitution comports well within a system of restorative justice, where offenders provide compensation to the state, the community, and victims as reparations for prior offences. Importantly, this restitution should be accompanied by dialogue, for it is transparent that mere monetary compensation does not restore moral, cultural, and political integrity. Hence, attempts by economists to construct sophisticated formulae that capture the "costs" of crime are too reductive and dismissive of nonquantifiable goods and values.[59]

Restitution alone cannot alleviate the problems of the system.[60] It should be employed, therefore, in concert with other methods, including what Morris and Tonry designate as intermediate punishments that are "more severe than probation and less severe than protracted imprisonment."[61] Intermediate punishments, increasingly appropriated by states, provide flexibility to judges and other criminal justice officials; whereas the current guidelines system imposes a binary between prison and non-prison, intermediate punishments can provide regularity and allow for judicial discretion on a case-by-case basis. Morris and Tonry envision that one could subsume intermediate punishments within the current guidelines system: "If intermediate punishments are to take their proper place in a comprehensive system of structured sentencing discretion, there must be some interchangeability between incarcerative and non-incarcerative punishments *within* some of the boxes of the guideline grid."[62] Intermediate punishments better enable judges to consider the individual as an individual, to adjudicate the concerns of justice with the claims of mercy, and to maintain proportionality within sentencing. In fulfilling these objectives, the sentencing guidelines are not abandoned but modified to consider all the variables involved. Theological resources can help facilitate this goal.

THEOLOGICAL SYMBOLS

To this point, I have discussed issues pertaining to the political, social, and economic spheres of criminal justice. Yet, it will be soon evident that theological resources have informed my approach.[63] Theological perspectives generally prefer restorative justice to retributive justice. Anthropological notions of the deeply flawed, but redeemable character of human beings resonate with rehabilitative objectives in criminal justice. Whether cast in terms of justification, sanctification, atonement, conversion, or regeneration, the notion of transformation has played a central role within the Christian tradition. To be sure, theologians can neither presume hegemonic dependence on tradition-specific narratives nor over-determine policy recommendations through insulated discussions among themselves. Theological methods must engage in conversations with psychology, criminology, economics, and other disciplines germane to these recommendations; theologians must listen to the complex interactions of cultural and economic developments, political movements, and scientific discoveries, that is, to the "situation" (Paul Tillich) or the "signs of the times" (Vatican II). Nevertheless, theology possesses an important autonomy that enables it to critique finite structures of social existence. Kathryn Tanner, for example, describes this critical function by analyzing notions of divine transcendence: "If divinity is the locus of what is ultimately true or good, and the human cannot be identified with the divine, appeals to a transcendent God are a possible focus for criticizing rather than reinforcing what passes for right belief and action in a particular society."[64] Theological language about divine transcendence or prophetic judgment or radical agape remains crucial for adjudicating social problems because it helps navigate solutions between the extremes of relativism and absolutism.

In *The Protestant Ethic and the Spirit of Punishment*, T. Richard Snyder demonstrates the capacities of theology to censure the current criminal justice system, but he also applies them as self-reflexive critiques of theology. Snyder notes the contentious but enriching relationships among culture, morality, and religion. On the one hand, Snyder draws upon Christian symbols as the groundwork for a restorative model that contrasts with the current retributive models of violence; on the other hand, he marshals arguments against theological, that is, primarily Protestant, notions of punishment that exacerbate the punitive spirit pervasive in the United States. Snyder contends that Protestantism's distorting tendencies (in the form of its limited notions of the grace of creation and its individualistic conception of redemptive grace) intensify the spirit of punishment that envelops American society.[65] In light of this pervading spirit, Snyder appeals to counterproposals vouchsafed in restorative models, including the Truth and Reconciliation Commission, Sweden, youth courts in New Zealand, Native American sentencing circles, and Victim Offender Reconciliation. These models integrate victim, offender, and society through balanced procedures of justice that seek transformation of individuals and communities. They do not neglect harms (e.g., abuses of human rights in the case of the Truth and Reconciliation Commission), but they promote the goods of the community (e.g., solidarity through tribal consensus in Native American sentencing circles) and alternatives to incarceration (e.g., electronic monitoring in Sweden that preserves familial and professional obligations). Though he remains vigilant against the hypocritical character of religious beliefs that can reinforce systems that contradict these beliefs, Snyder contends that Judeo-Christian symbols offer individuals essential models for reconceiving criminal justice. He identifies covenant (that signifies mutual accountability), incarnation (that engenders respect for the other), and trinity (that discloses reality as essentially relational and loving) as fundamental symbolic resources for an alternative vision of criminal justice.[66] These symbols robustly portray self, other, and world in ways that motivate hospitality and transformation, not violence and retaliation.

Catholic theologians also utilize theological symbols as substantive norms for reconsidering notions of rehabilitation. The Committee on Domestic Policy of the United States Conference on Catholic Bishops explores restorative justice and the constructive and rehabilitative purposes of criminal justice in *Responsibility, Rehabilitation, and Restoration.* Theological symbols have direct relevance to current criminal justice; for example, the Bishops hold that contrition, confession, satisfaction, and absolution are "the four traditional elements of the sacrament of Penance [that] have much to teach us about taking responsibility, making amends, and reintegrating into community."[67] The Bishops do uphold incapacitation and deterrence as legitimate purposes of punishment (and, as indicated above, these strategies of incarceration are not antithetical to rehabilitative ideals), but they contend that these strategies in themselves are not sufficient to overcome the present culture of violence. The Bishops resist attributing criminality to social pressures, for they seek to preserve individual accountability. Yet, in consonance with earlier critiques of the Federal Sentencing Guidelines, the Bishops condemn simple and reductive solutions ("One-size-fits-all solutions are often inadequate")[68] and seek restorative practices. The Bishops advocate for funds to be redirected from prison building to programs that assist community healing, educational programs and vocational training, substance-abuse treatment, and other projects that apply to individuals but ultimately enrich personal safety, social order and solidarity, and the common good. These objectives, according to the Bishops, cannot be met without the demands of mercy, forgiveness, and healing, values intrinsic to the Christian tradition.[69]

Concluding Reflections

While they envisage a shift from collective incapacitation to selective incapacitation in the coming decades, Franklin Zimring and Gordon Hawkins attribute incapacitation's perduring popularity to its "capacity to control rather than influence."[70] Control of criminals has consistently remained prominent, and future technological advancements, signaled by the emergence of "supermax" prisons, will no doubt continue this trend. Yet, as this essay has attempted to demonstrate, recent strategies of rehabilitation to "influence" criminals have not only promoted individual transformation but also repaired social relationships, rectified harms against victims, and recovered moral and public goods. Rehabilitation programs in nineteenth- and twentieth-century America had certain advantages and disadvantages, but their intention to reshape personalities was fettered by sentencing disparities and judicial abuses. The 1987 Federal Sentencing Guidelines ushered in an era of determinate sentencing that rectified many abuses, but it also disqualified judges from their roles as critical adjudicators and reduced criminals to quantifiable data. Retributivism and incapacitation soon dominated theories of punishment.

Through criticisms of the guidelines and examination of alternative rehabilitative models such as restorative justice, I have argued that the system can be conceived in ways that value harms and goods, offenders and victims, and justice and mercy. I am cognizant that my proposals are quite inchoate and must be developed in more detail on a policy level. Whatever form future criminal justice proposals take, theological symbols and resources should challenge critically what we are and portray models of what we might become.

Notes

My knowledge of the Federal Sentencing Guidelines has been enhanced by conversations with United States District Judge Joan Gottschall. I take full responsible for any errors, and my analysis should not be construed as representing her position.

1. *United States Commission Guidelines Manual,* chap. 1, pt. A, "The Statutory Mission," 1.

2. Zimring and Hawkins, *Incapacitation,* 3. Zimring and Hawkins contend that incapacitation achieved this status by default by virtue of the collapse of confidence in rehabilitation and deterrence (cf. Morris and Tonry, *Between Prison and Probation,* 13).

3. Space limitations preclude a more detailed nuancing of the types of goods—e.g., moral, "premoral" or "nonmoral," common, and public—and of their inevitable conflicts. For further discussion on the articulation of and conflict between these goods, see Charles Taylor, *Sources of the Self,* and Schweiker, *Responsibility and Christian Ethics.* My point is that the current system privileges harms over goods in its assessment of the purposes of punishment.

4. Morris, *The Future of Imprisonment,* 4.

5. See Foucault, *Discipline and Punish,* 9. For a discussion of the Quakers and the rival Auburn and Pennsylvania plans mentioned later in this essay, see David Rothman, "Perfecting the Prison: United States 1789–1865," in Morris and Rothman, *The Oxford History of the Prison.*

6. Foucault, *Discipline and Punish,* 126. Foucault notes that the structure of this discipline served as the blueprint for other, newly developed institutions, such as armies, hospitals, and schools.

7. Ibid., 231.

8. Ibid., 238.

9. Rothman, *The Discovery of the Asylum,* xxxiv.

10. These included insane asylums (ibid., 130) and the rapid spread of childcare institutions by 1830 (ibid., 207).

11. Ibid., 239.

12. See ibid., 242, 237.

13. Andrew Skotnicki observes the religious bases for the proliferation of the Auburn system in the 1830s. He notes the contributions of religious leaders such as the Reverend Louis Dwight of Massachusetts. See Skotnicki, *Religion and the Development,* 44.

14. Adamson, "Wrath and Redemption," 75.

15. In 1833, Rhode Island abolished public executions, followed by Pennsylvania in 1834, and Massachusetts, New Jersey, and New York in 1835.

16. Adamson, "Wrath and Redemption," 87, 98. Skotnicki, in *Religion and the Development,* further describes the affinities between Calvinism and the Auburn system: "the specific attributes of orthodox Calvinism—obedience and discipline—as well as the identification of moral worth with pragmatic concerns, were critical factors that often came to govern the content of penal legislation and institutional practice in the Auburn model" (50–51). Skotnicki additionally identifies features of Calvinism within the Pennsylvania system that complement the dominant Quaker views (59).

17. Adamson, in "Wrath and Redemption," nicely summarizes the relationship between religious doctrines and penal practices: "The transformation that occurred in penal attitudes and practices during the early decades of the nineteenth century was made possible by an ongoing theological shift according to which the doctrine of inherited sin gave way to a more subtle theory that specified that sin, although it was inevitable as a universal feature of human action, was the product of sinning, and not a quality inherent in the individual prior to action" (100).

18. Rothman, "Perfecting the Prison: United States 1789–1865," in Morris and Rothman, *The Oxford History of the Prison,* 119.

19. These penologists were reformers who included John Howard (Britain), Captain Alexander Maconochie (New South Wales), and Walter Crofton (Ireland). For further discussion of their significance, particularly with respect to Elmira, see Waite, "From Penitentiary to Reformatory."

20. Skotnicki, *Religion and the Development,* 126.

21. Waite, "From Penitentiary to Reformatory," 100.

22. Rotman, "The Failure of Reform: United States 1865–1965," in Morris and Rothman, *The Oxford History of Prison,* 178.

23. Francis Allen, "Criminal Justice, Legal Values, and the Rehabilitative Ideal," in Murphy, *Punishment and Rehabilitation,* 187. For an extended critique of the predictive elements of therapy, see Morris's *The Future of Imprisonment.*

24. For further description, please see Kant's *The Metaphysical Elements of Justice,* 99–106 (reprinted in "The Right to Punish" in Murphy, *Punishment and Rehabilitation,* 20–23). Kant remarks that those who fail to exercise this punishment "may be regarded as accomplices in this public violation of legal justice" (22).

25. Hegel, *Early Theological Writings,* 226. Hegel's more extended formulation is as follows: "The law cannot forgo the punishment, cannot be merciful, or it would cancel itself. The law has been broken by the trespasser; its content

no longer exists for him; he has canceled it. But the form of the law, universality, pursues him and clings to his trespass; his deed becomes universal, and the right which he has canceled is also canceled for him. Thus the law remains, and a punishment, his desert, remains."

26. To be sure, while Murphy summarily concurs with Kant's position, he does acknowledge that "it tends perhaps to encourage blindness to the way things are and to give rise to smugness and self-righteousness." Murphy, "Kant's Theory of Punishment," in his *Retribution, Justice and Therapy*, 90.

27. Murphy, "Preventive Detention and Psychiatry," in his *Retribution, Justice and Therapy*, 161 (original emphasis).

28. For a comprehensive discussion of the decline of rehabilitation, including discussion of Francis Allen's work and political and legislative developments, see Zimring and Hawkins, *Incapacitation*, esp. 5–12.

29. *United States Commission Guidelines Manual*, chap. 1, pt. A, "The Basic Approach (Policy Statement)," 2.

30. For the Sentencing Commission's definition of a career offender, see ibid., chap. 4, "Criminal History and Criminal Livelihood," pt. B, "Career Offenders and Criminal Livelihood," 319.

31. Indeed, it would be fallacious to deny the existence of rehabilitative programs within the federal system. The guidelines manual describes programs administering "community confinement" (e.g., community treatment center, halfway house, mental health facility). See chap. 5, "Determining the Sentence," pt. F, "Sentencing Options."

32. Hundreds of written judgments by federal judges have expressed opposition to the guidelines on constitutional grounds. The Supreme Court, in *Mistretta v. United States*, 488 U.S. 361 (1989), 109 S. Ct. 647 (1989), upheld in an eight-to-one decision the constitutionality of the guidelines and the Sentencing Commission. Nonetheless, judicial discontent remains. Michael Tonry cites a 1994 Federal Judicial Center survey that revealed that 58.9 percent of appellate judges and 68.5 percent of trial judges were "strongly" or "moderately" opposed to retention of "the current system of mandatory guidelines." See Tonry's *Sentencing Matters*, 11.

33. There are different types of plea negotiation, including charge bargaining (reduced or substituted charges), fact bargaining (mitigation of the severity of original offenses), and sentence bargaining (influence on the type and duration of sentencing).

34. James M. Anderson, Jeffrey R. Kling, and Kate Stith, in "Measuring Interjudge Sentencing Disparity," *Journal of Law and Economics* 42 (1999): 303, describe this phenomenon: "Unfortunately, the very success of the Guidelines in reducing interjudge disparity by constraining judicial discretion may have exacerbated the impact and the degree of disparity at earlier stages of the criminal justice process through the elimination of parole and the severe reduction in the judiciary's ability to compensate for interactor disparity earlier in the criminal justice process."

35. Alschuler, "The Failure of Sentencing Guidelines," 926.

36. Stith and Cabranes, *Fear of Judging*, 84.

37. See chap. 5, "Determining the Sentence," pt. H, "Specific Offender Characteristics," particularly 367–69.

38. Alschuler, "The Failure of Sentencing Guidelines," 904, 905. He explains that aggregation, despite its envisioned aims to the contrary, promotes inequality in and through its neglect of the individual: "Equality does not mean sameness; the term more commonly refers to the consistent application of a comprehensive principle or mix of principles to different cases. Excessive aggregation—treating unlike cases alike—can violate rather than promote the principle of equality" (916).

39. For Mauer's insightful studies on drug offenses, African American offenders, and the effects of incarceration, see *The Race to Incarcerate*.

40. Zimring, Hawkins, and Kamin, *Punishment and Democracy*, 19. The authors further criticize the nonproportional impact of "three-strikes" penalties, exemplified in the stealing of a slice of pizza as equivalent to a third strike. This confounding situation is explained by the fact that "any petty theft is a felony in California if committed by a person with a prior felony theft conviction, and any felony generates the mandatory third-strike minimum" (190). The authors censure other aspects of California's three-strikes law, notably "its deliberately confrontational and destabilizing intention" (23) and its excessive application, for California sentenced 40,000 three-strike offenders "when none of the other [states'] jurisdictions had yet accumulated 1,000" (20). In the March 5, 2003, *Ewing v. California* decision, the Supreme Court upheld California's three-strikes law as constitutional based on a determination that it does not constitute cruel and unusual punishment (and thereby does not violate the Eighth Amendment).

41. For more details on these cases and the commission's response, see Tonry, *Sentencing Matters*, 77.

42. *United States Commissions Guidelines Manual*, chap, 1, pt. A, "The Guidelines' Resolution of Major Issues (Policy Statement): (b. Departures)," 6. The fact that sentences on the federal level are nearly mandatory differs from the departure rate of several states that have constructed state sentencing guidelines. Minnesota, which established its own sentencing guidelines prior to the federal ones, has a departure rate of over 30 percent. Moreover, in terms of international comparisons, the Swedish criminal code, *Brottsbalken*—codified in 1962 and implemented in 1965—offers special cases of mitigation: e.g., BrB 29:3(3) renders young offenders less culpable, and BrB 28:9, 34:6, and 38:2a assert deductions in connection with revocation of probation. For more on sentencing in Minnesota and Sweden, see Andrew von Hirsch, "Proportionality and Parsimony in American Sentencing Guidelines: The Minnesota and Oregon Standards," in Clarkson and Morgan, *The Politics of Sentencing Reform*, 149–67; Nils Jareborg, "The Swedish Sentencing Reform," in ibid., 95–123; and Nils Jareborg, "Sentencing, Law, Policy, and Patterns in Sweden," in Tonry, *Penal Reform in Overcrowded Times*, 118–24.

JONATHAN ROTHCHILD

43. *Koon v. United States,* in Weinreb, *Leading Constitutional Cases on Criminal Justice,* 1153, 1154. Kennedy adds: "We do not understand it to have been the congressional purpose to withdraw all sentencing discretion from the United States District Judge" (1166).

44. Alschuler states an alternative procedure vis-à-vis judicial discretion and individual case factors: "Guidelines should be binding rather than voluntary or advisory, but they should bind trial judges only in the way that the rulings of higher courts bind them. When a judge could reasonably distinguish the case before him or her from a 'normal case' treated in the guidelines, he or she should be permitted to choose a different sentence" ("The Failure of Sentencing Guidelines", 945).

45. "Provisions of Feeney Amendment as Enacted into Law as Part of Protect Act," *Federal Sentencing Reporter* 15, no. 5 (2003): 362.

46. "Memorandum from Attorney General John Ashcroft Setting Forth Justice Department's Sentencing Policies," *Federal Sentencing Reporter* 15, no. 5 (2003): 375.

47. In his 2003 year-end report on the federal judiciary, Chief Justice Rehnquist, a Nixon appointee, criticizes the passage of the Feeney Amendment. Submitting that the Protect Act (the act under which the Feeney Amendment was subsumed) "was enacted without any consideration of the views of the Judiciary," Rehnquist contends the act usurps the unique place of judges to exercise discretion in sentencing decisions: "Judges have, again by Constitutional design, an institutional commitment to the independent administration of justice and are able to see the consequences of judicial reform proposals that legislative sponsors may not be in a position to see" (statement released January 1, 2004, on www.supremecourt.gov).

48. "Letter to Congress from Sentencing Commission," *Federal Sentencing Reporter,* 15, no. 5 (2003): 341.

49. Ibid., 342.

50. Tonry, *Sentencing Matters,* 20.

51. *Fear of Judging,* 172 (original emphasis).

52. Rotman, *Beyond Punishment,* 77. Put differently, Rotman insists that "[o]nly true rehabilitation offers the option of a nonmechanical reaction that might overcome the contradiction between the offender and society" (113).

53. Hate Crimes Statistics Act, Public Law 101–275 (1990), as cited in Stephson, *Gender Bias Crimes,* 5. For analogous cases on an international level, see David Scheffer's essay in this volume discussing atrocity crimes.

54. For a description of these programs, see Michael Tonry's "Penal Developments in America" in his *Penal Reform in Overcrowded Times,* 17–30. Currently, Minnesota has the only state-funded office of restorative justice planning in the United States.

55. Dan Kahan and Eric Posner, "Shaming White-Collar Criminals: A Proposal for Reform of the Federal Sentencing Guidelines." *Journal of Law and Economics* 42 (1999): 368.

56. Ricoeur notes the debilitating social consequences of extended sentences: "We can assume that beyond a certain time span the execution of a sentence is equivalent to an accelerated process of desocialization." Ricoeur, "Sanction, Rehabilitation, Pardon," in his *The Just*, 142.

57. Braithwaite, *Crime, Shame, and Reintegration,* 100–101 (original emphasis). There is a resonance between Braithwaite and Foucault in that both maintain that the public aspect of punishment has profound impact on offenders and communities.

58. Ricoeur, "Sanction, Rehabilitation, Pardon," in his *The Just*, 143–44.

59. See, among other things, Gary Becker's "Crime and Punishment: An Economic Approach," in *The Economic Approach to Human Behavior.* Becker measures harms and gains to ascertain net cost: "For example, the cost of murder is measured by the loss of earnings of victims and excludes, among other things, the value placed by society on life itself" (44). He contends that criteria for punishment should be based on "the damages from offenses, the costs of apprehending and convicting offenders, and the social costs of punishments" (51). For a critique of cost-benefit analysis approaches to crime and punishment, see Zimring and Hawkins, *Incapacitation.*

60. Even in systems that fine proportionally to income, one confronts problems on either end of the poverty-wealth spectrum. On the one hand, the impoverished may lack sufficient funds for restitution; on the other hand, the opulent will gladly pay fines that, while prohibitively expensive for the majority of the public, have little effect on their overall wealth.

61. Morris and Tonry, *Between Prison and Probation,* 3.

62. Ibid., 56.

63. Theology here refers to no one specific religious tradition; I will, however, restrict my comments to the Christian tradition in this essay.

64. Tanner, *The Politics of God,* 57. While she notes the ambiguities of divine transcendence, Tanner affirms that "[t]he transcendence of God functions as a protest against all absolute and unconditional claims" (69). Tanner identifies further import of theological claims for social problems, e.g., the "respect for oneself as God's creature [that] inclines one toward cooperative ventures" (234).

65. For Snyder's argument, please see his *The Protestant Ethics and the Spirit of Punishment,* particularly 1–73.

66. Ibid., 116, 120, 122.

67. *Responsibility, Rehabilitation, and Restoration,* www.usccb.org/sdwp/criminal.htm. According to the text, contrition expresses genuine sorrow and regret; confession signals true acceptance of responsibility for one's harmful actions; satisfaction is an external sign of one's desire to amend one's life; and absolution represents the forgiveness of sin and the welcoming back into the community.

68. Ibid. Hence, the Bishops gainsay "three-strikes" sentencing and rigid mandatory sentencing.

69. According to the Bishops, restorative justice resonates with this pursuit of forgiveness and healing: "Restorative justice also reflects our values and traditions. Our faith calls us to hold people accountable, to forgive, and to heal. Focusing primarily on the legal infraction without a recognition of the human damage does not advance our values."

70. Zimring and Hawkins, *Incapacitation,* 157; for their comments on the future of incapacitation, see 171–72.

A Place for Mercy

ALBERT W. ALSCHULER

In some situations, justice requires mitigating a wrongdoer's punishment. Mitigation is a moral duty. In other situations, justice forbids mitigation. Any mitigation is improper. If these situations exhaust the field, mercy is an impossible virtue.[1] Mercy must be an act of grace, not duty. It is the paradigmatic example of supererogation.[2]

To make room for mercy as a supererogatory act is to make room for inequality. If individuals and governments are morally obliged to treat like cases alike, supererogatory acts have no place. This essay considers whether the concept of justice is so expansive that it leaves no room for mercy. Focusing primarily on criminal justice officials rather than private individuals, it offers the fuzzy answer "not quite."

Justice as the Starting Point

While criminal justice serves many purposes, its core is retributive. A retributivist believes that the imposition of deserved punishment is an intrinsic good. This proposition defines her as a retributivist, and it is the only proposition to which she must be committed. This proposition departs sharply from the view that punishment is an intrinsic evil, the view endorsed by Jeremy Bentham when he wrote: "All punishment in itself is evil. If it ought at all to be admitted, it ought only to be admitted in as far as it promises to exclude some greater evil."[3] A retributivist need not believe that imposing deserved punishment is a categorical imperative or that it is the *only* good. Although the retributivist position is deontological, a retributivist who emphasizes the beneficial consequences of her position is not cheating.

Retributivism rests on a core truth about human beings. An implicit "giving-receiving" ratio informs our sense of justice. A few people called saints may give regardless of whether they receive anything in return. Other people may take and never give. Most people, however, fall into neither of these categories. Some of them give two, three, or ten times what they receive, yet even these people are likely to cease giving when they sense that the "return-for-giving" ratio has grown too far out of line. Criminal punishment is one of the social institutions that help to keep the "return-for-giving" ratio in rough balance.[4]

I have previously used a parable of parking violation to illustrate this thesis.[5] Several years ago, Adam moved to a neighborhood in Chicago in which parking regulations were seldom enforced. He frequently found his way and his vision blocked by unlawfully parked, unticketed cars. As Adam grew accustomed to the realities of life in this neighborhood, his own parking behavior changed.

Adam still does not park in spaces reserved for the handicapped, but when the only available parking space is too close to an intersection, he takes it. Adam was a nicer person and a better citizen when he lived in Colorado. He also was happier. Like most people, Adam preferred cooperating with his neighbors to struggling with them. When he could improve other people's lives (or, more modestly, facilitate their driving and parking) with confidence that most of them would do the same for him, he felt better about himself and his community.

The lack of parking-law enforcement in Adam's neighborhood has affected his behavior. The principal reason for Adam's law violation, however, is not that he knows he can get away with it. It is not that he fears punishment less than he did in his former neighborhood. It is not that he is less concerned about incurring social disapproval. It is not that he has a lesser understanding of the risk, harm, and inconvenience caused by illegal parking.

Adam would desist from his lawlessness (he really would) if his neighbors would desist from theirs. When Adam must endure the burdens of life among incorrigible parking violators, however, he thinks himself a fool not to capture a portion of the benefits. Adam is unwilling to do much more than his share. He would prefer a regime of mutual cooperation to one of every person for himself, but he prefers a regime of every person for himself to one of "cooperation for suckers." In Adam's neighborhood in Chicago, the bonds of the social compact have weakened. Sanctions matter to Adam less because his own principal reason for law observance is the fear of punishment than because sanctions applied to others reinforce his sense of reciprocity and mutual obligation.

Is Justice the Finishing Point Too?

Adam's case helps to bring mercy into focus. Withholding punishment is inappropriate when doing so would encourage people to conclude, "Everyone else is looking out for themselves, and I'll be a fool unless I become a little bit like them." When withholding criminal punishment leaves the giving-receiving ratio out of balance, the failure to punish makes selfish action more likely. When mercy significantly weakens our sense of justice and our sense of social obligation, it is improper.

Sometimes, however, withholding punishment does not undercut the sense of justice or the sense of reciprocity and obligation. The wrongdoer may not seem to be a free rider; he may appear to be more sinned against than sinning; he may have had no real choice; he may have been subjected to extraordinary temptations; he may have suffered enough; we may accept his apology and expression of remorse as sincere. When we withhold punishment for one of these reasons or for any other good reason, how should we characterize our act? Are we doing justice or granting mercy?

The more sophisticated the concept of justice becomes, the less room justice leaves for mercy. The word "retributivism" often makes people uncomfortable because it seems to tie punishment to harm. Using "retribution" as a prompt in a game of free association probably would evoke one response more frequently than any other: "an eye for an eye." If one envisions justice simply as an eye for an eye, mercy has a great deal of work to do.

Hagit Benbaji and David Heyd lean strongly toward this position. They describe mercy as the product of a gestalt switch or change of perspective. They compare it to the switch from seeing a line drawing as a duck to seeing it as a rabbit. In this gestalt switch, a person's focus moves from an act and its consequences to the actor. A vindictive person who alters her perspective in this way may become less vindictive, and Benbaji and Heyd declare that the two perspectives—justice and mercy—are equally valid.[6]

Benbaji and Heyd's "justice" perspective, however, makes me shudder. As I see it, this perspective is not a valid alternative to their "mercy" perspective at all. Contrary to Benbaji and Heyd's depiction, desert de-

ALBERT W. ALSCHULER

pends as much or more on circumstances and personal characteristics as upon physical actions and harm. The Benbaji-Heyd view of mercy rests on a primitive vision of justice. Disregarding circumstances and personal characteristics altogether is unjust.

One virtue of moving circumstances and personal characteristics from the mercy side of the ledger to the justice side is that this move encourages reflection about when considerations other than the wrongful act and its consequences warrant mitigation and when they do not. This move encourages equal treatment. Mitigation of punishment does not depend simply upon whether one looks at an ambiguous drawing as a rabbit or a duck or on whether full or partial forgiveness seems like a good idea at the time.

Our ability to articulate principles of justice is limited, but even when we afford discretion to criminal justice officials, we can charge them, not to grant mercy as a matter of grace, but to judge as best they can what punishment offenders deserve.

Two Places for Forgiveness in the Criminal Justice System

Should our goal be to refine the concept of justice to the point that the concept of mercy vanishes altogether? I suggest hesitantly that mercy remains appropriate for criminal justice officials in two situations (and there may be others). In the first, officialdom seeks to exempt an offender from punishment without creating a precedent for the future and without making a commitment (at least an explicit commitment) to treat like cases alike. I believe that low-visibility, one-time exemptions can be appropriate and, with some reservations, that these exemptions can fairly be described as acts of mercy. In the second, the criminal justice system adopts the well-being of crime victims as one of its goals. When the purposes of punishment include advancing the interests of individual victims, the justice system must make room for their mercy.

TICKETS GOOD FOR THIS DAY AND TRAIN ONLY

Saul Touster describes cases in the first category.[7] He examines the minor theft, bribery of officials, and black marketeering that survivors of the Holocaust committed in post–World War II Europe. Survival in the concentration camps had depended on "organizing" by theft and barter, and these activities continued during the *Bricha,* a movement that "in the two years between 1946 and 1948 brought 250,000 Jewish survivors from eastern Europe to the American zone in the west, in clandestine, mostly illegal, underground operations."[8] In Touster's words, "an evil system ha[d] fallen but its nefarious works and effects had not yet been extirpated."[9] Widespread hunger threatened. In this setting:

> One stole a pound of butter and another exchanged an army shirt for cigarettes. Each of these received a three-month sentence—which meant a criminal record that might further lead to being barred from immigration to the United States. Even the American officer in command of the Landsberg Jewish DP camp called these prosecutions "insane" and the sentences "outrageous." In an UNRRA report we can find a list of comparable offenses: "a mother of two who the Army said had excess soap and chocolate; a mother of six who had excess soap, chocolate, and cigarettes; a father who had a flashlight; a camp leader who had four tins of cookies; a teacher who had cigarettes, food and chocolate." In these cases, UNRRA was able to report that "three days later all food was returned to camp and all charges dropped."[10]

Touster comments:

> I tried to think of comparable times in history when an evil regime had fallen and left a class of victims, disabled by circumstances and prior socialization, to be brought into a new and presumably benign society. What came first to my mind was the period following the American Civil War. The slaves were "free" but the conditions of a collapsed Confederacy left them without power, impoverished, and in terrible danger. . . . Like the later Jews, they searched for family members who had been sold off and separated. . . . And the legal situation was comparably chaotic. The same questions arose: How to treat the former slaves who "stole"—or, one might say, "organized"—food for their sustenance from the plantation fields or stores; or "organized" horses and wagons to go searching for kin.[11]

A former slave who took a wagon to search for members of his family might assert a defense of necessity. Recognizing this "legal" defense, however, would affirm that he had chosen the lesser evil and would encourage others to engage in similar conduct.[12] Approving this defense would effectively license the former slave to continue to appropriate wagons until he achieved his goal. Rather than present this issue to the courts, a humane

ALBERT W. ALSCHULER

prosecutor might have declined to file charges. He also might have taken up a collection to buy the former slave a wagon.

Would a prosecutor who took this course be doing justice or granting mercy? Neither characterization would strain the English language. One might reasonably declare that prosecuting and punishing the former slave would be unjust. Indeed, one might sensibly declare that failing to provide affirmative assistance would violate the moral duty of someone who could help without difficulty. Affirmative assistance like the gift of a wagon, however, also could be regarded as supererogatory. Perhaps the refusal to prosecute could be regarded as supererogatory as well.

Just how far the prosecutor's moral and legal duty extends is debatable, but however this issue is resolved, a prosecutor who declined to prosecute would have made the right choice. What Meir Dan-Cohen calls acoustic separation—promulgating "conduct rules" that differ from a system's "decision rules"[13]—is often problematic, but the circumstances described by Touster make a case for it. Some cases are better resolved through low-visibility, discretionary mechanisms (refusal to prosecute, jury nullification, and executive clemency) than through the rule of law. If the rule of law is regarded (artificially) as the measure of justice, Touster's examples are cases in which mercy is appropriate. In situations like those of Touster's Holocaust survivors and emancipated slaves, the criminal justice system should bark harder than it wants to bite.

PRIVATE MERCY AND PUBLIC JUSTICE

I hesitate to characterize Touster's cases as appropriate cases for mercy only because, in the end, the rule of law obviously is not the measure of justice. Acts presented as merciful dispensations from law-ordained justice may themselves be obligatory. These acts may be required even when the law is sufficiently just that one wishes to keep it, allowing it to threaten punishment even if not to impose it. If a second slave stole a wagon in the same circumstances as the first, an honorable prosecutor could not treat him less favorably without a reason. I am less hesitant, however, about the second situation. When the criminal justice system seeks to advance the welfare of crime victims, it must make a place for them to be merciful.

It is doubtful that, apart from extending ordinary courtesies like information and respect, the criminal justice system should advance the welfare of individual victims in ways that do not simultaneously advance the welfare of the community as a whole. Not long ago, the victim was described as the forgotten person in the criminal process.[14] Today she sometimes is remembered too well. The separation of criminal law from tort law—of public justice from private redress—was a milestone of civilization. The awareness that crime wrongs all of us fades when the decision to punish is redelegated in significant part to victims. With this delegation, the criminal justice system affords authority over offenders' lives to people whose personal interests would disqualify them from serving as judges or jurors. Moreover, giving influence or authority to victims ensures inequality. An offender's punishment depends in part on whether he has harmed a vindictive or a charitable person.

Today's partial delegation of criminal punishment to victims is most evident in our treatment of the death penalty inside and outside the courtroom. Franklin Zimring notes that closure for survivors has now become the principal justification offered for capital punishment. Execution is seen as a governmental service for private parties—a form of state-sponsored psychotherapy. Noting that the word "closure" did not appear in a news story concerning the death penalty until 1989, Zimring charts the increase in the use of this word since then. More than five hundred death-penalty stories spoke of it in 2001.[15] One implication of viewing "closure" as the principal justification for capital punishment is that a survivor should be allowed to say, "My path to closure is one of mercy, not killing."

Prominent news stories in 1998 described the murder of Matthew Shepard. Aaron McKinney and Russell Henderson lured him from a bar and beat his skull repeatedly with a .357 Magnum. Then they burned him and left him strung to a fence to die. They killed Shepard because he was gay. After McKinney's conviction, Shepard's parents convinced a reluctant prosecutor not to seek the death penalty. Here are some excerpts from Dennis Shepard's extraordinary courtroom remarks on the subject of mercy:

> My son was taught to look at all sides of an issue before making a decision or taking a stand. . . . When he did take a stand, it was based on his best judgment. Such a stand cost him his life when he quietly let it be known that he was gay. He didn't advertise it, but he didn't back away from the issue either. For that I'll always be proud of him. He showed me that he was a lot more courageous than most people, including myself. . . . Matt's beating, hospitalization and funeral focused worldwide attention on hate.

ALBERT W. ALSCHULER

Good is coming out of evil. . . . [Mr. McKinney, y]ou made this world realize that a person's lifestyle is not a reason for discrimination, intolerance, persecution, and violence. . . . [M]y son has become a symbol, a symbol against hate and people like you. . . . I would like nothing better than to see you die, Mr. McKinney. However, this is the time to begin the healing process. To show mercy to someone who refused to show any mercy. To use this as the first step in my own closure about losing Matt. . . . I'm going to grant you life . . . because of Matthew. . . . I give you life in memory of one who no longer lives. May you live a long life, and may you thank Matthew every day for it.[16]

Like their son Matthew, Dennis and Judy Shepard favored the death penalty for some crimes. They regarded their decision as supererogatory, and we can too.

The power of survivors to forgive must be limited. If Aaron McKinney had killed a second young man whose parents wanted the other sort of closure, the prosecutor might not have allowed the Shepards to save his life. Moreover, if the Shepards had been merciful enough to propose a sentence of community service and therapy, someone would have had to say no. When society delegates the decision to forego capital punishment to survivors like the Shepards, there is no blinking the fact that one murderer may live and another die simply because the first murderer selected a victim whose parents were more magnanimous. If this inequality seems tolerable—if sparing one McKinney can be a legitimate act of charity while executing a second McKinney is a legitimate act of justice—we have found a place for mercy.

Notes

1. See Bernard Williams, "Toleration: An Impossible Virtue," in Heyd, *Toleration: An Elusive Virtue,* 18.

2. *The Random House College Dictionary* (rev. ed., 1975) defines *supererogatory* as "going beyond the requirements of duty."

3. Bentham, *An Introduction to the Principles of Morals and Legislation,* in Bentham and Mill, *The Utilitarians* 162, 166.

4. The golden rule—"do unto others as you would have them do unto you"—prescribes nonreciprocal altruism, the saintly kind. Reciprocal altruism is the more natural kind. See Goldsmith and Zimmerman, *Biology, Evolution, and Human Nature,* 136–37 (describing the evolution of reciprocal altruism in nonhuman species).

5. See Alschuler, *Law without Values,* 149–50.

6. Benbaji and Heyd, "Forgiveness and Toleration as Supererogatory," *Canadian Journal of Philosophy* 31 (2001): 567, 585.

7. A note on the subheading: Dissenting in *Smith v. Allwright,* 321 U.S. 649, 669 (1944), Justice Owen Roberts (the first Justice Roberts) protested that the majority's decision to overrule a recent precedent "tends to bring adjudications of this tribunal into the same class as a restricted railroad ticket, good for this day and train only." For Touster's description of the cases in the first category, see *The Treatment of Jewish Survivors of the Holocaust.*

8. Ibid., 8.

9. Ibid., 9.

10. Ibid., 10.

11. Ibid., 12–13.

12. See American Law Institute, Model Penal Code § 3.02 (official draft 1962) ("Conduct which the actor believes to be necessary to avoid a harm or evil to himself or another is justifiable, provided . . . the harm or evil sought to be avoided by such conduct is greater than that sought to be prevented by the law defining the offense charged").

13. Dan-Cohen, "Decision Rules and Conduct Rules: On Acoustic Separation in Criminal Law," *Harvard Law Review* 97 (1984): 625.

14. See S. Re No. 532, 97th Cong., 2nd sess., 10, reprinted in 1982 *US Code Cong & Adm News* 2515, 2516 (concerning the Victim and Witness Protection Act of 1982) ("Too often the victim has been 'the forgotten person' of the criminal justice system").

15. Zimring, *The Contradictions of American Capital Punishment,* 60.

16. Dennis Shepard's statement appears at http://www.matthewsplace.com/dennis2.htm.

Why International Law
Matters in God's World

DAVID SCHEFFER

One of Isaiah's prophecies against Judah intones, "Mankind will be brought low, everyone will be humbled" (Isa. 2:9). That prophecy bore truth in our lifetimes, on our watch. If you have difficulty imagining the reality of the Devil, or if you do not believe in the Devil, or of evil forces that undeniably exist, then take a walk with me.

- Imagine walking through a still-burning camp in the eastern Congo, near Goma, in August 2000, where scores of internally displaced persons have been burned alive in their tents or gunned down trying to escape— not an uncommon event in the worst humanitarian crisis on the face of the earth.

- Imagine standing in a small hospital in Freetown, Sierra Leone, in February 1999. Scattered before you are scores of mutilated children. One young girl, no more than ten, is burned only on the front side of her body, from her face to her toes, because rebels had thrown her into the fire of her burning home. Another teenage girl lies still, her eyes having been incinerated with acid following her gang rape by rebels.

- Imagine witnessing thousands of Kosovo-Albanians flee across the Macedonian border in early April 1999 with tales of sheer horror at the hands of Serb paramilitary and police units sweeping across Kosovo, and in the rain-drenched night visiting families whose babies had died from exposure only moments before.

- Imagine visiting a near-abandoned town deep in the interior of southern Sudan in June 1999 and learning of the years of torture, death, and destruction visited upon its Christian population by the Sudanese army and paramilitary and listening to the few remaining children describe how they saw their neighbors being shot by soldiers and stuffed down the town's major water well, where their bodies continued to decay.

- Imagine investigating a still-smoldering massacre site in northwest Rwanda in 1997, a crime scene larger than any ever encountered by the FBI prior to the terrorist attack on the World Trade Center in 2001. Those Tutsis lucky enough to survive are huddled in a nearby hospital with horrific wounds from grenade blasts, gunfire, hatchets, and machetes. A young girl's brain has just been stuffed back into her head by the sole doctor on the site, who is entering his fifty-sixth hour of surgery and care of the wounded.

- Imagine touring the missing-persons identification morgue in Tuzla, Bosnia, right after the delivery of almost three hundred well-preserved Muslim bodies in Yugoslav army body bags dug up from a mass grave found near the border with Serbia, and learning that a mother just hours earlier had identified her husband and all four sons among the carcasses, each one screaming at her with waxy skin stretched by the collapse of the victim's jaw.

But you do not have to imagine any of this. It all happened before my eyes. In America, the terrorist attacks of September 11, 2001, brought home the kind of horror experienced by millions in foreign lands in this age of atrocities. So we need no longer plead with Americans to imagine such assaults on humankind. Genocide, war crimes, and crimes against humanity are very grim reapers of death and sorrow in the lives of so many innocent human beings, and none of us holds any exclusive rights to the spectacle.

What happened in the Congo, in Kosovo, in the Sudan, in Rwanda, in Bosnia, and in so many other atrocity zones, and which continues today across the globe, has a lot to do with law and with religion. There are millions of citizens of the world who every day need the protection of what I call "atrocity law" and who, as believers in God, still trust in Him to keep them alive despite the ravages of evil forces that none of us would ever want to confront.

In these essays we are examining the most fundamental proposition about how we respond to atrocities: whether justice or mercy, punishment or forgiveness, military might or religious pacifism can coexist in a violent world or whether we should chose one over the other in the conduct of human affairs. I can bring some practical perspective to the discipline and some rather blunt assessments of how I believe society should address the relationship between justice and religion. Let me begin by stating three conclusions:

1. A useful terminology for identifying the relevant crimes and relevant law for an examination of justice and religion should be the identification of "atrocity crimes" and "atrocity law." Once we understand what these terms mean, the religious equation becomes clearer.

2. The popular notion that a pagan ethos, dismissive of international law, is required to effectively confront international terrorism, aggression, and other forces of evil is a seriously flawed argument.

3. Accountability and forgiveness are not incompatible and in fact reinforce each other. But in the realm of atrocity crimes, accountability under a credible system of justice must be the primary means of responding to the perpetrators of such heinous crimes even though military force may be required to stop or deter the criminal conduct. The arrival of the permanent International Criminal Court will create a dynamic process of accountability for atrocity crimes that may clarify the limitations of mercy.

Atrocity Crimes and Atrocity Law

During the last decade of the twentieth century, a remarkable number of international criminal tribunals were negotiated and, in some cases, actually established.[1] The landmark tribunals at Nuremberg and Tokyo after World War II were finally eclipsed with a new generation of international criminal jurisprudence. Today we no longer have to begin and end our discussion about enforcing the laws of armed conflict, of punishing leaders for actions constituting the crime of genocide, or examining witness testimony about crimes against humanity with historical nuggets from the prosecution of Nazi or Japanese warlords. A large body of scholarly research and courtroom trials for massive crimes committed in our own time has appeared. Since 1993 much law, institution building, practice, and scholarship have occurred.

That institution building includes the International Criminal Tribunal for the former Yugoslavia, the International Criminal Tribunal for Rwanda, the Independent Special Court for Sierra Leone, the still emerging Extraordinary Chambers for Cambodia, and the International Criminal Court. We need a reality check about the character of the crimes and of the law that are the raison d'être for these courts.

No single category of crimes or body of international law accurately and thoroughly describes the foundation for any of these courts. The crimes include war crimes, genocide, terrorism, and crimes against humanity, and within the latter term can be found crimes of torture or slavery or apartheid. The evolving crime of ethnic cleansing crosscuts each of these major categories of crimes. The crime of aggression may surface relatively soon in one of the courts. In some of the criminal tribunals, domestic criminal law figures prominently. The international law that is or will be applied by each court varies in description: we speak of the laws of war, customs of war, the laws of armed conflict, military law, international humanitarian law, international criminal law, and human rights law. This cacophony of crimes and laws is a lawyer's feast and explains, I believe, the proliferation of scholarly treatises and articles seeking to understand afresh the origins and meaning of each category of law and to define as precisely as possible the crimes that are on deck for prosecution.

I am going to plead for a new category of crimes that would be called "atrocity crimes" and a new category of international law to facilitate the prosecution of those who commit such crimes. That body of law I would describe as "atrocity law." It is essentially the law of the criminal tribunals. This may seem like heresy to serious scholars and practitioners who have developed great expertise in distinguishing between crimes and laws and who may advocate broader and broader application of a particular category of established law, such as international humanitarian law. But the statute of each criminal tribunal uniquely embraces atrocity crimes and atrocity law. It is also extremely important for lawyers to appreciate the need to communicate to the general public in terms that they can easily identify with and begin to grasp what the phenomenon of mass crime and international prosecutions is all about. You walk up to anyone on Main Street USA and say, "international humanitarian law," and he or she will look bemused and ask if you really work on overseas child abuse cases. Or if you challenge the guy walking his dog with, "international criminal law," he is likely to start mumbling about Colombian drug traffickers.

The word "atrocity," or "atrocities," derives from Roman military law. It described acts that were illegal even though performed pursuant to military orders, an issue that today we call "superior orders" and the defense of superior orders. Mark Osiel, in his book *Obeying Orders,* writes: "This word [atrocities] never became a legal term of art, however, with a settled meaning distinct from ordinary Latin. It no longer occupies any place within the formal language of international military law."[2] For that very reason I would argue that we have a fairly clean slate to work with now in using the term "atrocity" as a legal term and, indeed, as a descriptive term in religious discourse, particularly in light of what has occurred in the last decade and the manner in which the term "atrocity" has been used by governments, international organizations, and the media.

The crimes of greatest interest to the international community, those crimes that have triggered demands for international criminal tribunals and that are increasingly being excluded from domestic amnesty deals (the civil equivalent of forgiveness), are crimes that cumulatively fit the following profile:

- The crime must be of significant magnitude, meaning its commission is widespread or systematic or is a part of a large-scale commission of such crimes. The crime must involve a relatively large number of victims, such as a fairly significant number of deaths or casualties or impose other very severe injury upon noncombatant populations (such as massive destruction of private property), or must subject a large number of combatants or prisoners of war to violations of the laws and customs of war.

- The crime can occur in time of war, in time of peace, or in time of violent societal upheaval of some organized character, and it can be either international or internal in character.

- The crime must be identifiable in conventional international criminal law as the crime of genocide, a violation of the laws and customs of war, the crime of aggression (if and when it is defined for individual criminal culpability), the crime of international terrorism, a crime against humanity (the precise definition of which has evolved in the development of the criminal tribunals), or the emerging crime of ethnic cleansing.

- The crime must have been led in its execution by the ruling or otherwise powerful elite in society (including rebel and terrorist leaders) who planned the commission of the crime and can be identified as the leading perpetrators of the crime.

Why International Law Matters

- The law applicable to such crime, while it may impose state responsibility and even remedies against states, is also regarded under customary international law as holding individuals criminally liable for the commission of such crime, thus enabling the prosecution of such individuals before a duly constituted court for such purpose.

A crime that meets all of these five criteria would be, in my opinion, an atrocity crime. In nonlegal terms, I am clearly pointing toward high-impact crimes that are of an orchestrated character, shock the conscience of humankind, result in a significant number of victims, and on which you would expect the international media and the international community to focus as meriting an international response that at least would hold the leading perpetrators accountable before a court of law.

There is, of course, the dilemma posed by the threshold of criminal conduct associated with atrocity crimes. We might speak of "significant magnitude," "high threshold," "extreme gravity," and "significant numbers." In the Rome treaty on the International Criminal Court, the text refers to "unimaginable atrocities that deeply shock the conscience of humanity," asserting that "such grave crimes threaten the peace, security and well-being of the world," and that they are "the most serious crimes of concern to the international community as a whole." Examples of atrocity crimes—such as those that appear at the beginning of this essay—abound during the last thirty years.

Atrocity law applies the criteria of atrocity crimes to the many categories of conventional law that cover such crimes some of the time, but none do so all of the time. These categories include international humanitarian law, international criminal law, international human rights law, military or court-martial law, and the identification of serious crimes under international law. But in conventional legal terminology, no term describes precisely what the criminal tribunals seek to prosecute. The crimes are not only genocide, crimes against humanity, or war crimes; they need a unifying term. The law is not only international humanitarian law, not only international criminal law, not only international human rights law, not only military law, and not only serious crimes under international law.

The law of the criminal tribunals is uniquely crafted, the enforcement mechanism is uniquely conceived, and the political mandate of each of these courts is uniquely tailored. They need a truly relevant term to describe the reality of their jurisdiction and their role in framing legal responses to war crimes, genocide, crimes against humanity, mass terrorism, and other heinous crimes.

We have been at this juncture before in history. The crime of genocide was identified by an American, Raphael Lemkin, after he found that the Holocaust could not be properly defined or prosecuted as simply a crime against humanity. The constituent parts of the crime were unique, and conventional international law did not address those unique characteristics of intent, of target, and of context. With Lemkin's perseverance, the Genocide Convention defined the new crime of genocide.

In a similar vein, today we are confronted with an inadequate lexicon for the crimes and law that underpin the criminal tribunals. In a fundamental way, the relatively rapid establishment of the criminal tribunals has outstripped the capacity of the law to remold itself into an easily identifiable legal weapon for those courts. It is no idle matter, this quest for terminology. Getting the terminology right is part of the accuracy and integrity of the process, and it is part of the selling job to the public about the credibility and utility of these judicial institutions. If you lose public support for international prosecution of atrocity crimes because what you describe appears threatening or incomprehensible to the average guy, then you have lost the war as a lawyer and as a champion for international justice. Those of us who believe strongly in international justice know how difficult that struggle is within our own borders with the American public.

We should be mindful of the following characteristics of atrocity law drawn from the tribunals of accountability:

- No two criminal tribunals share exactly the same law. The law is selected and edited to conform to the circumstances of the crimes and the context within which they were committed. In both the Sierra Leone and Cambodia tribunals, domestic law also figures prominently. The principle of complementarity in the Rome treaty invites a significant and potentially exclusive role for national criminal law in achieving the objectives of the permanent court.

- Personal jurisdiction is limited either implicitly by virtue of the seriousness and threshold level required of the crime and, one might argue, the practical limitations of the tribunal (ICC, ICTY, ICTR) or explicitly by the terms of the statute itself (Sierra Leone, Cambodia).

- Some categories of atrocity law evolved and acquired greater precision with more recently established tribunals.

- We can look beyond the statutes of the tribunals to case law for a further understanding of atrocity crimes and atrocity law. So far, the judgments of the ICTY and ICTR have assisted in further defining the relevant crimes and the companion law. We can also look to the Elements of Crimes of the International Criminal Court for guidance on the scope of atrocity crimes, guidance that doubtless will bleed over into the other tribunals.

If atrocity crimes and atrocity law were to become our lexicon for the criminal tribunals, they would help us address these issues:

- The criminal tribunals are having the perhaps unintended effect of encouraging a shift away from state responsibility to individual criminal responsibility and from low-magnitude crimes to high-magnitude crimes as the focus of judicial enforcement. We are loath to allege collective criminal responsibility; we emphasize the responsibility of individual leaders and military commanders. States refuse to acknowledge their own commission of atrocities, and are far more willing to associate individuals with such crimes. The proposed terminology places greater emphasis on the high-magnitude crimes of concern to the criminal tribunals and leaves no doubt about the seriousness of the crimes for which individuals will be prosecuted.

- There remains a need to more dramatically identify and criminalize responsibility for atrocities in order to achieve the deterrence objective of international justice. The proposed terminology uses the term "atrocity" bluntly and in association with common words, "crimes" and "law," to emphasize the severity of the crimes and the precise character of the law being applied by the criminal tribunals.

- Use of the proposed terms enhances the unique character and accuracy of the conventional terminology, which otherwise risks becoming blurred with overlapping applications and incomplete descriptions of what the criminal tribunals actually enforce. In other words, we do not have to fudge the meaning of international humanitarian or criminal law, or the law of war, to describe the applicable law of the criminal tribunals.

DAVID SCHEFFER

• The presumption of the criminal tribunal is that the leading perpetrators of the atrocity crimes would be prosecuted before the criminal tribunal, whereas the mid- and low-level perpetrators either would be prosecuted before competent domestic courts or handled through a nonjudicial mechanism, such as a truth and reconciliation commission, determined at the national or local level. By focusing on atrocity crimes and atrocity law in describing the jurisdiction of the criminal tribunals, we more clearly delineate between the international and domestic mechanisms of justice that are in fact evolving. Theoretically, of course, a criminal tribunal should have the legal tools to prosecute the foot soldier for a grave breach of the Geneva Conventions, or a local policeman for participating in mass rape during a genocidal rampage. But the international community and national governments are drawing a different line, using scarce resources for criminal tribunals that prosecute the leading perpetrators of crimes meeting the criteria I have set forth and encouraging alternative mechanisms at the national level for the typically much larger number of mid- and low-level perpetrators. Atrocity crimes and atrocity law better distinguish between those two levels of justice and rehabilitation.

• Humanitarian intervention, a highly controversial area of international law, might be better understood and more supportable politically if the objective of the intervention were to end or prevent an atrocity crime, rather than have politicians, military commanders, and their government lawyers and spokespersons claim that such massive military measures are required to confront war crimes, or crimes against humanity, or violations of international humanitarian law. The crime of genocide can be left untethered as a powerful public rationale for humanitarian intervention. But short of literally calling the crime "genocide," which we know from experience is a struggle for governments, we need a powerful and accurate term that can be readily understood as justifying the extraordinary and legally controversial initiative of a humanitarian intervention. The technical terms may be accurate, but humanitarian interventions require the building of popular support, as well as international support, to sustain them in times of great crisis and to preserve the right and ability to intervene for humanitarian purposes again. It might be novel to link in this manner the criminal tribunals with the use of military force to confront the types of crimes being prosecuted by the tribunals, but if we actually call what the criminal tribunals prosecute "atrocity crimes" and the law at stake "atrocity law," then the rationale for humanitarian intervention would be strengthened and more politically acceptable. The public would gain a greater appreciation for the need for military intervention to confront the atrocity crimes with which criminal tribunals are increasingly identified, thus better educating the public about what is at stake. The legality of any particular humanitarian intervention is a separate debate. Here I am arguing for the utility of a more focused jurisdictional description for criminal tribunals in relation to atrocity prevention and termination.

The religious equation becomes, in my view, clearer once we have established the terminology of atrocity crimes and atrocity law. We are more easily positioned to consider punishment and forgiveness, and I will address that challenge shortly.

The Danger of the Pagan Ethos

First, however, I want briefly to examine a dangerous trend in contemporary political dialogue that, if adopted by our leaders, would essentially remove religious considerations from the conduct of America's foreign and military policies in much the same way as it would remove international law from the execution of those policies.

In his recent book *Warrior Politics: Why Leadership Demands a Pagan Ethos,* Robert Kaplan writes:

> While international law grows in significance through trade organizations and human rights tribunals, it will play less of a role in the conduct of war because war will increasingly be unconventional and undeclared, and fought within states rather than between them. The concept of "international law" promulgated by Hugo Grotius in seventeenth-century Holland, in which all sovereign states are treated as equal and war is justified only in defense of sovereignty, is fundamentally utopian. The boundaries between peace and war are often unclear, and international agreements are kept only if the power and self-interest are there to sustain them. In the future, do not expect wartime justice to depend on international law; as in ancient times, this justice will depend upon the moral fiber of military commanders themselves, whose roles will often be indistinguishable from those of civilian leaders.[3]

DAVID SCHEFFER

Kaplan also criticizes "classical liberal values" that evoke the demand that "something must be done!"[4] I see all of this quite differently; indeed, we must do something. That is my view of what America, as the dominant power in the world, is all about. Otherwise, our understanding of dominance becomes so insular and self-protective that it no longer is dominance, no longer leadership, and no longer the moral high ground. It is just plain lethargic power, intimidated by the challenges of the world. The issue, when confronted with atrocities, is what must be done, not whether something should be done.

International law is not incapacitated by the complexities of modern warfare; it is challenged just as is modern politics and religious doctrine. For a long time now, international law has been developing with respect to unconventional and undeclared wars.

We do not win at any cost or by any means. American national security does not rest on unfettered discretion, on unchecked power, or on the character of a single commander. We do not subscribe to creating chaos in order to defeat chaos. We are a democracy firmly established under the rule of law and with a significant commitment to morality guided by religion, and we must act democratically, legally, and morally.

There is a burden that attaches to dominance. There indeed may be a higher standard that attaches to the privilege of dominance. For every retreat in international law that Kaplan would endorse, there would emerge yet another risk that the abandonment of law would expose the United States to reciprocal treatment that we would fiercely oppose, at times with our own blood and treasure. The momentary glory of Mr. Kaplan's leadership ethos would create a future of perpetual risk in how international affairs would be managed within any kind of legal framework or broadly acceptable morality.

Doubtless, Kaplan's thesis has a very attractive, albeit misguided, appeal. What builds character in a leader? Is it the freedom to act recklessly in pursuit of victory? Or does law bring some value to a leader's choices? Is not a leader's and a commander's character shaped by how he or she understands and responds to the law? A leader who respects the law, and who leads in the enforcement of law, may well demonstrate the more worthy character that Kaplan is seeking. You can always skirt the sharper edges of international law, perhaps of God's law also, to protect the national interest and defend our democratic way of life, and you can seek

new rationales within the law to defend state policy, but the abandonment of international law as proposed by Kaplan is no strategy at all. It
merely removes the rudder from the leader's boat and trusts that the leader
will rediscover how to guide his own boat, our nation, toward shore.
The rather tempting view among intellectuals like Kaplan and Charles
Krauthammer and George Will that law inhibits, rather than liberates,
leaders and nations has its mass appeal, but I would argue it is a red her-
ring. In the long run, the work of the successful leader, the strategy that
will build a lasting victory in warfare, and the ability to sustain our dominance in world affairs will turn on how well we influence the development of international law and demonstrate our compliance with it rather
than on how dismissive we are of its importance in the shaping of our
policies, particularly military policy in times of conflict.

Accountability and Forgiveness

If we reject the pagan ethos, then we must confront the tension that can
exist and does exist between the strong movement for accountability of
recent years and the equally powerful voices of reconciliation and forgiveness that have swept through societies. Let's begin at the beginning.[5]

A good Christian forgives. The power of forgiveness is a pillar of Christianity, and I would submit that any evangelical Christian, in particular,
who ignores or belittles the act of forgiveness would be in serious conflict with the Scriptures. Did not Luke remind us of what Jesus said on
the cross: "Father, forgive them; they do not know what they are doing"
(Luke 23:34). Did not Mathew counsel us: "For if you forgive others the
wrongs they have done, your heavenly Father will also forgive you; but if
you do not forgive others, then your Father will not forgive the wrongs
that you have done" (Matt. 6:14–15). And did not Mark record the ad-
monition of Jesus: "[W]hen you stand praying, if you have a grievance
against anyone, forgive him, so that your Father in heaven may forgive
you the wrongs you have done" (Mark 11:25).

A recent book entitled *Burying the Past*, edited by Nigel Biggar, minimizes retributive justice and supports restorative justice emphasizing nonjudicial remedies and rehabilitation.[6] Biggar argues for forgiveness and
nonpunitive justice. He claims that punishment is not the primary aim
of criminal justice, and then weaves a theory that would lead to milder
punishments of perpetrators of genocide, crimes against humanity, war

crimes, and torture, with the real aim being other forms of vindicating the victim. For Biggar, the victim comes first; but he presumes—incorrectly, in my view—that the victim can tolerate something less than maximum punishment for the perpetrator. Biggar writes that "my main point has been that criminal justice is primarily about the vindication of the victim, and that there are ways of vindicating the victim that do not involve the punishment of the perpetrator: namely, by recognizing the injury, supporting the victim, and discovering the truth."[7] As for punishment, he argues:

> it is retributive, but not in the sense of aspiring to annul the crime by imposing suffering on the perpetrator "equal" to that criminally inflicted on the victim. Rather, punishment's retributive character lies in its being a response to someone who has actually broken the law . . . ; and insofar as the penalties that it imposes are designed, as far as possible, to annul the relative advantages unfairly seized in the criminal act and/or to express the community's opprobrium.[8]

Judges on international criminal tribunals and on domestic courts (not to mention the victims) may find it a bit difficult, after hearing the evidence of heinous crimes taking the lives of thousands with unbounded cruelty, to apply this antiseptic formula. Try out the "take-it-easy" theory on the mothers of Srebrenica, and see how they react.

Biggar's approach is supported by Donald Shriver, in his essay in *Burying the Past* entitled "Where and When in Political Life is Justice Served by Forgiveness?" Not surprisingly, Shriver relies heavily on theology, and finds in the Bible a stronger connection between justice and mercy than support for retributive justice. He advocates restorative justice with a heavy dose of forgiveness. Biggar concludes this book of very fine essays by cautioning against "righteous" justice, arguing that "compassion is one of the basic motives behind forgiveness; and it is one that recognizes in forgiveness, not only a means to a good end (reconciliation), but also something intrinsically fair and, in that sense, just."[9] In the final sentence, he opts for eschatological hope as the means to look far beyond "our deep and humane yearning for justice in time and space."[10]

In my view, however, forgiveness and accountability are not incompatible; instead, they reinforce each other. In practice, neither should overwhelm the other. The Ninety-ninth Psalm tells us: "O Lord our God, you answered them; / you were a God who forgave them, / yet you called them to account for their misdeeds." The pathway between forgiveness and accountability is repentance by the sinner. The perpetrators of the most serious crimes that can be committed against humans, namely, atrocity crimes, are rarely repentant and rarely surrender voluntarily, and when they do repent, it usually is in the face of criminal charges that will lock them away for life, or worse.

Among civilized societies guided by the rule of law, and particularly among democratic societies, it would be untenable to conduct world affairs largely on the basis of some idealistic theory of forgiveness. What accountability can offer—whether before a court of law or, for example, before a truth commission that requires confession to avoid judicial sanction, such as the one created in South Africa—is a means for society at large to forgive in a civilized and meaningful way those mortal human beings who have committed such heinous crimes. Accountability deters, or at least seeks to deter, further atrocity crimes. Forgiveness must not be manipulated to reward the perpetrators of atrocity crimes with freedom. Rather, we can all forgive and yet still hold an individual accountable under the law. Forgiveness is a personal decision that reflects an individual's relationship to whatever deity he or she believes in, if any. But forgiveness by some individuals does not absolve other individuals of taking responsibility for their actions. Accountability is society's collective judgment about how both to forgive and to punish, in this case for crimes that directly assault humankind as a whole and the very meaning of faith among the world's leading religions. For these crimes, the courtroom remains the great leveler, addressing both the perpetrators and the victims through the revelation of the truth and also through the knowledge that consequences flow from evil actions.

"No peace without justice" is a catchy slogan for rallying activists, but transitions are much more complicated. What kind of justice? Increasingly, there are those who would challenge this slogan with modifications such as "no peace without some form of restorative justice coupled with strong doses of forgiveness" or "no peace without transitional justice that may include almost no justice at all." With the arrival of the permanent International Criminal Court (ICC), the tug-of-war between judicial and nonjudicial remedies, and between international and domestic mechanisms, will intensify. I do believe that the existence of the ICC will significantly limit, if not eliminate, viable options to implement strategies of forgiveness or reconciliation for the leading perpetrators of atrocity crimes. Either they will have to be investigated and prosecuted at the national level or the ICC will seize the case. The international community and its support for the ICC simply will not tolerate forgiveness for the masterminds of atrocity crimes.

We may find that there will be more willingness and tolerance for non-judicial remedies at the national level for mid- and low-level perpetrators, as they almost certainly will not seize the attention or resources of the ICC. For these individuals, there may be local preference for some kind of forgiveness scheme. But I would not underestimate the growing power of accountability in societies that have been victimized by atrocity crimes. Victims may, indeed almost always do, need restorative justice. But that does not mean that they do not also want retributive justice for the masterminds of the atrocity crimes and, on a very personal level, for the individual on the ground who actually brought such horror into their lives. Armchair advocates of forgiveness and restorative justice rarely know the rage of the victim, and that individual's need for authentic justice to be done. Nor do nonjudicial responses to atrocity crimes do much to deter future illegal conduct. At least with real trials and real punishments there is a hope for deterrence.

By focusing our attention on atrocity crimes, I would hope we could agree that for that magnitude of illegal conduct, the leading perpetrators must face the full weight of judicial accountability. By understanding the character of atrocity crimes and atrocity law, and by rejecting a pagan ethos in the conduct of international affairs, we can establish a credible means to pursue justice within a moral framework that recognizes the power of forgiveness in the proper context and for the appropriate category of criminals.

Notes

1. The following discussion of atrocity crimes and atrocity law is derived from the author's law review article "The Future of Atrocity Law." It is further amplified in the author's article "Genocide and Atrocity Crimes."

2. See Osiel, *Obeying Orders,* 45.

3. Kaplan, *Warrior Politics,* 118; the discussion about Kaplan is derived from the author's review of Kaplan's book in Scheffer, "Delusions about Leadership, Terrorism, and War."

4. Kaplan, *Warrior Politics,* 121.
5. Portions of the following text appear in the author's "Review Essay."
6. Biggar, *Burying the Past.*
7. Ibid., 12.
8. Ibid., 13–14.
9. Ibid., 283.
10. Ibid.

Critical Response
to David Scheffer

DAVID LITTLE

David Scheffer's edifying essay illustrates in several ways the pertinence of international considerations to our discussion of justice and mercy.

First, he calls attention to experiments like South Africa's Truth and Reconciliation Commission, which are efforts to find "nonjudicial" means, as Scheffer refers to them, for handling crimes related to societies with an authoritarian past. Incidentally, of the various arguments usually given in support of such arrangements, which also include political and practical considerations, two of them illuminate with particular clarity the connection to the justice/mercy discussion.

One argument contends that in situations where whole societies are caught up in patterns of widespread abuse, ordinary criminal remedies are at least partially inadequate. Since most of such a society's institutions are systematically organized so as to encourage or shield criminal behavior, rather than restrain it, the normal standard of individual accountability, so central to retributive justice, is compromised, at least for many lesser offenders. There is no doubt still a point to prosecuting top military and political officials, as Scheffer proposes. The degree of their individual responsibility, should they be convicted, is not typically in doubt. But the guilt of lesser offenders is thought to be mitigated up to a point, and thus not readily susceptible to standard judicial proceedings.

The other argument favors overhauling retributivism, either partially or totally, so as to make room for "restorative justice" in the interest of reconciling estranged members of previously repressive societies. The focus would be less on punishing offenders as an end in itself, and more on rehabilitating relations between offenders and victims, as well as between offenders and the rest of society, by means of techniques like amnesty and other acts of mercy, and by otherwise recasting modes of punishment as primarily "reparative" rather than retributive.

A second way Scheffer's essay relates to the question of mercy and justice is in regard to his discussion of international law. As Scheffer develops his imaginative notion of "atrocity law" and urges its implementation, he, by implication, underscores and reaffirms the irreducibly retributive feature of existing human rights law. With all the concern to find extrajudicial means for coping with crimes committed by the members of authoritarian societies (a concern he also shares), Scheffer nevertheless vigorously discourages us from altogether setting retributive justice aside. At least those individuals accused of "atrocity crimes" would, on Scheffer's account, appropriately be dealt with within the framework of conventional judicial procedures. Of course, lesser offenders might still be handled in extrajudicial ways.

Atrocity Law and Retributive Justice

Let us now turn to examine more closely this argument of Scheffer's concerning the retributivist character of atrocity law, keeping in mind our overarching interest in the justice/mercy discussion.

"Atrocity law" is intended to identify a category of crime, namely, gross human rights offenses, which are to be understood, according to Scheffer, in an irreducibly retributivist way. Scheffer is very explicit about this in taking issue with the position of Nigel Biggar, who advocates an extreme version of the argument about restorative justice we just mentioned. As a way of "burying the past" (the title of his edited book), Biggar seems to favor the complete replacement of retributive with restorative justice, recommending "nonjudicial remedies and rehabilitation," including "forgiveness and nonpunitive" measures as the only the appropriate means for dealing with the crimes of previously authoritarian societies. As quoted by Scheffer, Biggar contends that "there are ways of vindicating the victim that do not involve the punishment of the perpetrator: namely, by recognizing the injury, supporting the victim, and discovering the truth."

Scheffer strongly dissents from Biggar's position, claiming that in regard to atrocity crimes at least, the victims can, in fact, "tolerate [nothing] less than maximum punishment for the perpetrator." He goes on: "Judges on international criminal tribunals and on domestic courts (not to mention the victims) may find it a bit difficult, after hearing the evi-

DAVID LITTLE

dence of heinous crimes taking the lives of thousands with unbounded cruelty, to apply this antiseptic formula. Try out the 'take-it-easy' theory on the mothers of Srebrenica, and see how they react."

Scheffer's firmly held assumption on which the bulk of his argument rests is apparently that victims of atrocity crimes, together with those charged with adjudicating such crimes, simply cannot bear, or cannot live with, the idea of annulling or reducing maximum punishment for atrocity criminals, or of replacing conventional punishment with restorative measures such as are recommended by Biggar. Scheffer does not discuss why victims and legal officials might not be able to accept anything less than maximum punishment.

Incidentally, Scheffer suggests in passing a second reason for upholding the retributivist approach to atrocity crimes, and that is its probable deterrent effect. I shall not, however, pursue this point, both because Scheffer refers to it only briefly, and because, as a nonexpert, I have nothing informed to say about the rather large and (I suspect) controversial question as to how much the threat of punishment actually discourages crime.

As to his central argument, I begin by commending Scheffer for his efforts at defining atrocity law. His five criteria, the last of which, interestingly, accentuates the retributivist theme, provide some helpful guidance. According to Scheffer, atrocity crimes are "high-impact crimes that are of an orchestrated character, shock the conscience of humankind, result in a significant number of victims, and . . . [merit] an international response that at least would hold the leading perpetrators accountable before a court of law."

There is something intuitively correct, I think, about Scheffer's retributivist emphasis, but I do not find his argument well enough developed. I do find some hints in his discussion that provide the basis for what is in my opinion a more elaborate and thus more convincing case, and I shall briefly sketch out my argument and contrast it with Scheffer's as I go.

Generally understood, retributive justice presupposes (among other things) two senses in which punishment is justified: (1) as *forcible restraint*, and (2) as *forcible reversal of advantage*. In other words, force (or unwanted inhibition) may be applied (1) to frustrate the further pursuit of certain illicit goals, and (2) to undo a system of "ill-gotten gains." The prospect of a criminal's being allowed to seek prohibited goals unimpeded, or to "go on as though nothing had happened," and enjoy life at the unfair expense of others, is self-evidently intolerable when considered from the perspective of retributive justice.

In the case of atrocity crimes, the special urgency of applying these two standards seems clear. Atrocity crimes are, among other things, "high-impact crimes" that "shock the conscience of humankind" and "result in a significant number of victims." For obvious reasons, one would conclude that there exists a strong and justified incentive to restrain such behavior, and to make sure perpetrators do not continue to profit from it.

Indeed, Scheffer himself correctly advocates the idea of forcible restraint in discussing the justifiability of armed humanitarian intervention. Action of that kind, he says, "might be better understood and more supportable politically if the objective of the intervention were to end or prevent an atrocity crime." Moreover, he accentuates the retributivist theme by recommending that humanitarian intervention be coordinated with the work of international criminal tribunals, whose basic task, on Scheffer's proposal, would be to prosecute atrocity crimes. It can be assumed that an important aspect of the work of the tribunals, as well as of the exercise of humanitarian intervention, would not only be to restrain atrocity crimes but also to reverse any "ill-gotten gains" that committing them produced.

The first point, then, in constructing a more convincing case in favor of a retributive approach to atrocity crimes, is to call attention, as Scheffer himself does implicitly, to how compelling it is, in face of such crimes, to want to apply the standards of forcible restraint and forcible reversal of advantage. Please note: This is not a comment about what victims or legal officials are or are not likely to accept, which is Scheffer's stated concern. It is rather a broader comment about what is *reasonable* for *any* observer (including victims and legal officials, of course) to conclude about atrocity crimes, and it suggests why such a conclusion would be reasonable.

However, there are two other points to be made, as well. One is that since atrocity crimes have "high impact" and "result in a significant number of victims" ("heinous crimes taking the lives of thousands with unbounded cruelty")—that is, since they adversely affect whole populations—it is virtually impossible to design a way to determine whether or not victims would agree to acts of clemency or other forms of restorative justice. "Lesser offenders" typically affect fewer people. It is therefore feasible to consider consulting victims, or victims' relatives, in regard to questions of clemency or other extrajudicial measures. But that is, as I say, not really imaginable in the case of atrocity crimes.

The last point concerns the question of individual responsibility in regard to retributive justice, a point Scheffer himself brings up. Though he might have made more of it, Scheffer rightly suggests that "leading perpetrators" of atrocity crimes are the proper subjects of judicial proceedings because "[w]e are loath to allege collective criminal responsibility; [and] we emphasize the responsibility of individual leaders and military commanders." For that reason we make a distinction between the liability of the leaders and of "mid- and low-level perpetrators."

What is key here is one of what Scheffer identifies as defining characteristics of atrocity crimes, namely that they "are of an orchestrated character," which means that the "crime must have been led in its execution by the ruling or otherwise powerful elite . . . who planned the commission of the crime." In line with my first point, the central idea is that precisely because of their degree of responsibility for initiating and directing such abhorrent crimes, there is a particularly strong reason to restrain leading perpetrators (including preventing any opportunity for recidivism), as well as to reverse any and all advantages they may have derived from their action. Incidentally, to support further this point, one can invoke arguments like the one introduced at the beginning of this essay about the diminished responsibility of lesser offenders because of membership in a system of institutionalized criminality, a system itself presumably "orchestrated" by the principal perpetrators.

Taken together, then, these three points are intended, in the form of a "friendly amendment," to fill out and strengthen Scheffer's belief that "atrocity criminals" (as defined) should be the target of retributive justice.[1]

Forgiveness and Justice

Still another way Scheffer addresses my concerns is in his discussion of "forgiveness and accountability," and he does it in a way that applies to his discussion of retributive justice, just examined.

Contrary to Biggar's position (mentioned above) and what he takes to be the position of Donald Shriver (author of *An Ethic for Enemies*), Scheffer contends that forgiveness is not necessarily at odds with retributivism:

forgiveness and accountability are not incompatible; instead, they reinforce each other. . . . The pathway between forgiveness and accountability
is repentance by the sinner. . . . [W]e can all forgive and yet still hold an
individual accountable under the law. . . . [F]orgiveness by some individuals does not absolve other individuals of taking responsibility for their
action. . . . For [atrocity] crimes, the courtroom remains the great leveler,
addressing both the perpetrators and the victims through the revelation
of the truth and also through the knowledge that consequences flow
from evil actions.

My view is that Scheffer is partly right and partly wrong about the
connection between justice and forgiveness. On the one hand, he quite
astutely observes that the two concepts do overlap in some important
ways—ways, incidentally, that are not often enough noticed. For our purposes here, an act of "forgiveness" may be taken to include the following
features: (1) a transaction between at least two people (forgiver/forgivee);
(2) a common acknowledgment between them regarding, (a) the "truth"
concerning wrongdoing and responsibility, and (b) a fitting penalty for
the wrong done; (3) contrition on the part of the forgivee; and (4) mercy
on the part of the forgiver—namely, the annulment of the penalty (2b).

Scheffer's quoted comments identify the critical points of conceptual
overlap between retributive justice and forgiveness, namely, the various
elements of feature 2 in the list just above. Common to both concepts is a
need to determine the "truth" about the wrong done (last sentence), and
the "responsibility" for having done it (fourth sentence), as well as a need
to determine a "fitting penalty" (the "consequences [that] flow from evil
actions"—last sentence).

Even here, there are some differences between the concepts. In respect
to forgiveness, all of these matters are informally or consensually arrived
at. In the case of retributive justice, they are of course formally (and sometimes nonconsensually!) determined, in keeping with established judicial
procedures. Nevertheless, truth, responsibility, and penalty in regard to a
wrong done apply equally to the notions of retributive justice and forgiveness. Without them, neither notion can work.

This means that Scheffer is profoundly right when he says that "forgiveness by some individuals [forgivers] does not absolve other individuals
[forgivees] of taking responsibility for their actions." Indeed, the whole
idea of forgiveness could not get off the ground unless the person forgiven

DAVID LITTLE

took responsibility for the wrong done, and agreed, in accord with the forgiver, that such a misdeed deserved to be punished in a specified way. Such agreement is, obviously, the logically indispensable basis for both the contrition of the forgivee (3) and the mercy of the forgiver (4). This conclusion is confirmed by Scheffer's incisive comment that the "pathway between forgiveness and accountability is repentance by the sinner." In short, Scheffer correctly perceives that the idea of forgiveness cannot do without the idea of retribution, and this insight is of the greatest importance.

On the other hand, there are problems. Most worrisome is Scheffer's claim that "we can all forgive and yet still hold an individual accountable under the law," if that means, as it appears to, that there is, for Scheffer, no deep difference between forgiving a person and prosecuting that person "to the full extent of the law"—punishment and all. Deep in both the Judaic and Christian traditions, to mention two religions that Scheffer invokes, is our fourth feature of forgiveness, "annulment of punishment." While the Ninety-ninth Psalm, which Scheffer quotes, may support the idea of simultaneous forgiveness and punishment, there are countless passages in Jewish and Christian scriptures that give a very different impression. These picture a merciful, forgiving God as one "who does not deal with us according to our sins, nor requite us according to our iniquities" (Psalm 103)—as one, that is, who forgoes administering fully deserved punishment in the interest of "repairing" and "restoring" relations. It would, indeed, be very hard to picture the central Christian message concerning divine-human relations as involving at its core anything other than "annulment of punishment."

There are, it is true, differences of opinion in the literature over whether or not forgiveness and justice are compatible. As a matter of fact, Donald Shriver, whom Scheffer criticizes, takes a view close to Scheffer's. He contends that, at bottom, forgiveness is not so much about annulling judicial punishment as it is about relinquishing attitudes of enmity and hostility toward the wrongdoer. On this view, one might simultaneously forgive and condone punishment, so long as one's attitude toward the perpetrator was properly benevolent.

The problem is that even if there is occasional support in Jewish and Christian scriptures for this view, it is certainly not the only or by any means the dominant view, and neither Shriver nor Scheffer undertakes to give reasons why this view should be preferred over others. Beyond that, it would be impossible to make sense of the distinction Scheffer himself repeatedly draws between "judicial" and "nonjudicial" means of coping with criminal behavior if forgiveness and justice were as readily compatible as he says.

I must conclude, therefore, that while Scheffer helps us in some important ways in regard to the relation between forgiveness and justice, there nevertheless remains considerable work to be done.

In Defense of International Law

Finally, Scheffer provides some highly pertinent thoughts in his critical response to Robert Kaplan's recent book *Warrior Politics: Why Leadership Demands a Pagan Ethos.* I want fully to endorse and briefly to expand on Scheffer's critique. While there is much to object to in this book (including Kaplan's circuitous and inconsistent comments on religion and morality), let me confine myself, as Scheffer does, to Kaplan's remarks on international law and their bearing on the topics of relevance to this volume, justice and morality.

Kaplan's claim, which Scheffer cites, that international law is increasingly irrelevant to contemporary conflicts around the world because it rests on Hugo Grotius's idea of the inviolability of state sovereignty is mistaken. Grotius was an internationalist, not a statist. The whole point of his famous book, *The Law of War and Peace* (1625), was to develop a set of universal norms that might *restrain* appeals to "national self-interest" when it came to international armed combat. As a matter of fact, Grotius had no qualms whatsoever about ignoring the claims of state sovereignty in extreme circumstances. He explicitly advocated humanitarian intervention in the name of what he spoke of as "the enforcement of rights": "If the wrong is obvious, in case [a leader] should inflict upon his subjects such treatment as no one is warranted in inflicting, the exercise of the right [to intervene] is not precluded. . . . I may make war upon one who is not one of my people but oppresses his own [as a means of] the infliction of punishment, a procedure which is often connected with the protection of innocent persons" (*Law of War and Peace*, 2.25.3.2).[2]

Moreover, Kaplan's additional claim, later in his book, that Grotius's idea of a "just war" "presupposed the existence of a Leviathan—the pope or the Holy Roman Emperor—to enforce a moral code"[3] is equally amiss (as well as contradicting his preceding claim). Grotius was writing, quite self-consciously, in a postmedieval period, characterized by the *absence* of transnational authority. Again, his consuming purpose was to promote a set of international moral and legal standards for regulating state interest and interstate armed conflict in a chaotic world deeply riven by conflicting appeals to "state sovereignty" and "national self-interest."

As Scheffer understands, and Kaplan does not, we still have not entirely escaped from Grotius's world, and many of the urgent issues we face today are to be explained accordingly. At the same time, thanks in part to Grotius's abiding influence, we have begun to make a certain degree of progress in establishing and developing international legal institutions, and to grope our way, by means of such instruments as human rights and humanitarian law, toward a worldwide normative consensus concerning the limits of state interest and the standards of armed conflict. Whatever Kaplan may say, these developments are undeniably a positive achievement, and therefore ought to dispose us to promote, rather than to disparage (as Kaplan does), strengthening and expanding those institutions.

In this connection, it is, frankly, hard to imagine two more appalling assertions than are put forward by Kaplan as central theses of his book: (1) The United States "*and nobody else will write the terms for international society*";[4] and (2) "The moral basis of our foreign policy will depend upon the character of the nation and its leaders, not upon the absolutes of international law."[5]

As Scheffer appreciates, and as he has himself admirably exemplified in his devoted and distinguished contributions to the development of the International Criminal Court during the Clinton administration, cultivating international legal institutions requires, above all, a spirit of common commitment, collaboration, and interaction—the polar opposite, of course, to Kaplan's first assertion. Kaplan's outlandish words would perhaps be less worrisome did they not epitomize the attitude of strident unilateralism that dominates the current Bush administration.

In respect to the second assertion, one will want to know whether Kaplan seriously means to suggest that, on his understanding, "the moral basis" of U.S foreign policy and "the character of the nation and its leaders" should oppose or be indifferent to "the absolutes," for example, of human rights and humanitarian law. If so, then Kaplan will, frankly, be hard hereafter to take seriously. If not (as he here and there cryptically hints), then he ought to stop talking as though American policy and international law were starkly opposed to each other, as he does in this statement, and start developing in *a careful, considered, and consistent way* just what the precise and proper relation between them should be. At present, there is nothing of that sort in Kaplan's book.

The other question that needs to be raised about the second assertion is what reasons Kaplan might have for blindly trusting our leaders to do the right thing, especially in the absence of any reference to international standards. As mentioned, Hugo Grotius was deeply apprehensive in his time about such a policy, and he had considerable evidence to support his apprehensions. Nor, subsequently, do we lack similar evidence concerning the dire consequences of untrammeled national leadership. If, under present conditions, it is no doubt unwise to invest too much faith in international standards, it is, surely, equally unwise to invest too much faith in national leadership that ignores or is indifferent to those standards.

Notes

1. While my "friendly amendment" does support the inescapability of retributive justice in regard to atrocity crimes, I remain unclear as to whether it also supports Scheffer's particular claim that victims and legal officials must favor the "maximum penalty" for atrocity criminals. "Maximum penalty," I would have thought, will need to be defined and then evaluated carefully. So long as the "retributive floor" (forcible restraint and forcible reversal of advantage) is stringently maintained, proposals for creative and innovative sentencing (such have been mentioned by other contributors such as Marc Mauer, Jonathan Rothchild, and Peter Paris) might well be considered.

2. Obviously, this comment is relevant to my earlier remarks about the features of retributive justice, particularly forcible restraint.

3. Kaplan, *Warrior Politics,* 130.

4. Ibid., 146–47 (original emphasis).

5. Ibid., 131.

DAVID LITTLE

PART II

Approaches to
Justice and Mercy

Samaritan Justice

*A Theology of "Mercy"
and "Neighborhood"*

MATTHEW MYER BOULTON

In the United States today, perhaps the consummate "outsiders" are the ones, as we say, "on the inside." The people in many respects most peripheral in American social and political life are those who live incarcerated in prisons and jails, at once outcast to the public perimeter and corralled together in "correctional centers." As political subjects, they are (1) among the most disenfranchised, exiled from the political processes by which state power is determined and carried out, and (2) among the most thoroughly determined by those processes and that power. This stark asymmetry is acceptable to most citizens of the United States—which is to say, to most of the incarcerated's "neighbors"—because the incarcerated have been legally convicted of crimes. By committing these crimes (so the argument typically goes), they effectively forfeit their rightful claims to full political and moral subjectivity, pending the appropriate penalty or rehabilitation. For as long as they are held captive, they live out a liminal, suspended status: they are the being-punished, or the being-corrected. In this sense, they are subjectively postponed.

Accordingly, they are kept out of sight. The act of *facing* them is a difficult act to arrange, even for the family, friends, and specialists with whom face-to-face encounter is permitted and expected. And accordingly, as politically and morally compromised and suspended, their life and activity are commonly named as the mere passage of time itself. They are, as we say, "doing time," or "serving time." In this way, they are officially reduced to two thin dimensions: in space, they are isolated and hidden, and in time, they are commonly thought not to work and live and act, but rather merely to wait. There are more than 2 million such people in the United States today. For most other U.S. citizens, they are the quintessential "them," society's categorical "outsiders," both kept out and waiting to get out.

As the Gospel of Luke has it, it is "a lawyer" who poses what is arguably the central question of the entire text: "Teacher," the lawyer asks Jesus, "what must I do to inherit eternal life?" (Luke 10:25). Jesus answers, first of all, with two questions, well suited for his examiner: "What is written in the law? What do you read there?" The lawyer then supplies— quite correctly, Jesus goes on to say—the answer to his own question, a citation and combination of Deuteronomy 6:5 and Leviticus 19:18: "You shall love the Lord your God with all your heart, and with all your soul, and with all your strength, and with all your mind; and your neighbor as yourself." In this way, Luke ascribes to the lawyer what Christians later call "the Great Commandment," the ultimate and normative paraphrase of Christian life, and in that sense the centerpiece of Christian ethical thought: "do this," Jesus responds, now citing Leviticus himself, "and you shall live" (Luke 10:28; Lev. 18:5).

But this answer, central as it is in the gospel account, is in turn called into question by the lawyer who has just recited it. Not yet satisfied, he asks for a definition of terms: "And who is my neighbor?" Put differently, I know God commands me to love; but exactly which human beings must I love? And so: From which human beings may I withhold my love? This time, Jesus answers the lawyer with a story, a parabolic commentary on "the Great Commandment," and so arguably a parable with special standing in his curriculum—if not "the Great Parable," then certainly a crucial one. "A man was going down from Jerusalem to Jericho . . . "

In this essay, I sketch a close reading of both this story and this narrated exchange, and so propose a theological account of "mercy" not as the lenient remittance of deserved punishment, but as the practice of transgressive care, a practice already pointing toward corollary accounts of both "justice" and "neighborhood." The lawyer's second question, I contend, goes to the heart of our own struggles with criminal justice in the United States, and Jesus's narrative response—which both reframes and finally upends the question—does, too.

In his essay in this volume, "A Place for Mercy," Albert Alschuler equates "mercy" with "mitigating a wrongdoer's punishment," and as such with "an act of grace, not duty. [Mercy] is the paradigmatic example of supererogation." In other words, Alschuler understands "mercy" as the lenient remittance of deserved punishment, and here he represents a long-standing, widespread legal tradition. To impose a lighter sentence than the law demands or allows—that, for Alschuler, is to act "mercifully" in the administration of criminal justice.

But as Alschuler's essay ably shows, this account of "mercy" leads into considerable difficulties, primarily because "mercy," as the remittance of deserved punishment, appears to run against "justice"—and so the definition seems to introduce a cluster of antimonies and conceptual tangles. Both "just" work and "merciful" work are prized and required; but if they are opposed, how do we negotiate their opposition? By what rule do we decide when to be just, and when merciful? Or again, from another angle: If mercy is fitting, is it not just? But if it is just, and justice runs against mercy, then can we still call it "mercy"? Likewise, if justice is sensitive and humane ("sophisticated," as Alschuler puts it), is it not merciful? But if it is merciful, and mercy runs against justice, then can we still call it "justice"? And so on. The further we pursue these lines of thought, the more unsatisfactory they seem. Thus a more fundamental question arises: Are other accounts of "mercy" available?

"A man was going down from Jerusalem to Jericho, and fell into the hands of robbers" (Luke 10:30). Thus Jesus's answer to the lawyer begins with a narrated crime: "they stripped him, beat him, and went away, leaving him half dead." Two passersby arrive on the scene, "a priest" and "a Levite," the consummate insiders of the Jewish religious establishment, a clergyman and a lay leader. Upon seeing the dying man, both "pass by on the other side"—but a third traveler, a "Samaritan," sees the man and is "moved with pity," and so undertakes a choreography of care: dressing and bandaging wounds, lifting the man onto his animal, carrying him to an inn, staying the night with him, paying all costs. In short, Jesus reports, the Samaritan "took care of him" (Luke 10:34).

And yet, from the perspective of both Jesus's Jewish audience and Luke's readers and hearers, this particular episode of care is unexpected, not only because it is extravagant, or because the two prestigious insiders neglect it, but also precisely because "a Samaritan" carries it out. As descendents of colonists brought by Assyrian conquerors, Samaritans in first-century Palestine were considered by many Jews to be unclean apostates, and in any case foreigners with whom intimate contact was typically avoided; and in turn, Samaritans typically took a hostile and critical stance toward Jews.[1] Moreover, as Luke tells it, Jesus and his party had just come through Samaria on their way to Jerusalem, "but [the Samaritans] did not receive him, because his face was set toward Jerusalem"— which is to say, because they recognized his trip as a pilgrimage to the Jerusalem temple for the Passover feast (Luke 9:53). For Samaritans, the Jerusalem temple was an illegitimate sanctuary, and so on Luke's account, they "did not receive" Jesus and his party on explicitly liturgical grounds, not only because they were Jews but also and particularly because they were on their way to worship at a Jewish holy site. As we might expect, Jesus's disciples are furious, and ready to retaliate: "'Lord, do you want us to command fire to come down from heaven and consume them?' But he turned and rebuked them" (Luke 9:53–55). That is, Jesus rejects their call for violence, rebukes them for their zealotry, and then, in Luke's next chapter, as if to drive the point home beyond question, parabolically appoints "a Samaritan" as the one who properly obeys the greatest commandment of all.

The contrastive tension could hardly be more severe. Not only were Samaritans apostates in the eyes of most first-century Palestinian Jews, not only were they paradigmatic religious "outsiders" from a Jewish point of view, they had also just denied hospitality to Jesus and his followers on religious grounds, in effect rendering Jesus a religious outsider from a Samaritan point of view. For the world of Jesus's immediate audience and the world of Luke's most immediate readership, Samaritans were both outcasts and casters out—in a word, they were enemies. Jesus's enemies. They might well have been judged, as his own disciples put it, deserving of "consumption by fire" (Luke 9:54). But to the contrary, Jesus strikingly names "a Samaritan" as one who follows the highest law, who sets the standard for all others to follow. Moreover, he narrates the Samaritan's obedience in direct contrast to the disobedience of two consummate religious "insiders," men most patently within—indeed presiding over—the most exalted Jewish precincts of moral and religious authority.

But this contrast between an obedient "outsider" and disobedient "insiders," understood in the context of Jesus's exchange with the lawyer, is no critique of the Jewish religious establishment.[2] Rather, as part of an answer to a question about the proper form of human life, the contrast serves to underline and heighten the unexpected, boundary-crossing, reconciling character of the Samaritan's care. The fact that the priest and Levite "pass by" the man in effect establishes the act of "passing by" as

MATTHEW MYER BOULTON

typical, as ordinary and so as expected: if even these men, leaders and moral authorities par excellence, neglect to care for the man, then surely such care is, in a word, extra-ordinary. Put another way, at primary issue in the parable as told to the lawyer is not *who* carries out the love mandated in the law, but rather *what kind* of love is mandated. The fact that not an "insider" but an "outsider" carries out this love is crucial to disclosing its character, but the main point of the story is just this disclosure, this portrait of what we are to "go and do," as Jesus finally puts it (Luke 10:37). By setting the Samaritan's actions off against the actions of the priest and Levite, Jesus expounds the "love" in "love your neighbor as yourself" as unexpected and extraordinary love, transgressive of customary sociopolitical boundaries, and restorative for relationships beset by hostility and suspicion. After all, in the cited text—Leviticus 19:18—the "love" in "love your neighbor as yourself" is contrasted directly with both "taking vengeance" and "bearing a grudge"; thus the command to love is explicitly a rejection of "vengeance," and so is an injunction to love precisely in the face of wrongdoing, precisely when vengeance or retribution would be typical, and love unexpected.[3] Indeed, bearing in mind that for Luke, Jesus and his party had just been denied hospitality by Samaritans, we may read Jesus's very narration of Samaritan hospitality as itself an act of this kind of unexpected, transgressive, reconciling care. That is, according to Luke, even as Jesus parabolically recounts one episode of transgressive care, he effectively carries out another, narratively enfranchising a foreigner and apparent enemy—"a Samaritan"—to the status of moral and legal exemplar.

This account of "mercy"—as the lawyer goes on to name it (Luke 10:37)—is a fruitful alternative, I contend, to the widespread account Alschuler takes for granted. Rather than conceive "mercy" as the lenient remission of deserved punishment, this account invites us to conceive it as the practice of transgressive care, the humane and humanizing work of repair and reconciliation in human life. In the first place, this conception of "mercy" is pointedly detached from questions of desert: in the parable, none of the passersby know whether or not the man "deserved" the beating he has apparently received, and they have no way to discover that information before deciding how to respond. In this sense, this account of "mercy" excludes not only "deserved punishment" but "desert" entirely, and so is not based first of all on lenient remission of penalties, but rather on gratuitous provision of benefits.[4] This conception of "mercy" is consistent with a good deal of the English word's contemporary common usage: those who speak of "mercy killing," for example, hardly mean to suggest that the suffering and pain relieved by death are "deserved punishment"; and the familiar call in prayer, "Have mercy!"—or indeed, *Kyrie eleison,* "Lord, have mercy," employing the same Greek word (*eleos,* "mercy") found in Luke 10:37—is often a call for tangible benefits and care, not merely juridical leniency. Indeed, on this view, juridical leniency is a possible form of merciful treatment, one benefit among others, but it is neither normative nor dominant among the range of mercy's gifts.

Far from simply equating "mercy" with "generosity" or "beneficence," however, this account characterizes mercy as not only detached from desert but also transgressive and reconciling. On this view, "mercy" is *transgressive* care insofar as it acts to cross and provisionally overcome sociopolitical boundaries of alienation, hostility, and suspicion. In this sense, merciful acts are acts reconstituting social arrangements and social life, of trespassing conventional lines between "insiders" and "outsiders" by helping to usher outsiders "in," and so of unsettling customary structures of privilege and dispensation.[5] Precisely because of this transgressive character, "mercy" will likely appear as unexpected and extra-ordinary from most prevailing points of view. Superficially, and at times distressingly, it will surprise. In Luke, for example, it takes both the parabolic form of a stranger transgressing lines of religious and cultural antagonism, and the narrative form of a rabbi transgressing lines of outrage and conventional retribution by appointing an enemy to a position of moral leadership.

But just as "mercy" on this view is not "benefit" for benefit's sake, it is not "transgressive" for transgression's sake, either. As transgressive *care,* it is always work undertaken—as much as constraints permit—to help remedy and renew persons, relationships, and communal life. It is, in short, restorative work. It may follow on the Samaritan's tangible work of binding wounds, standing by, and paying costs, or Jesus's rhetorical work of calming fears, countering calls for "vengeance" and retribution, diminishing "grudges" and resentment, naming outsiders "in," and reconceiving enemies as would-be friends—but it is always care, always a work of reconstructive, doggedly hopeful renovation. In Isaiah's terms, it is always "building up from ruins" (Isa. 61:4), a transgressive act, to be sure, but always and finally a generative, reconciling act of binding and "building up."

MATTHEW MYER BOULTON

In this way, understanding "mercy" as the practice of transgressive care provides the term a clear, distinctive grain, and so may help keep it out of some conceptual trouble. Defining "mercy" as the lenient remittance of deserved punishment leaves it open to an unfortunate ambiguity: if mere "leniency" is the measure, then even (for example) an all-white jury's racist favoritism toward a white defendant accused of killing a Latino man may rightly be called "mercy." In this case, the jury might indeed "withhold punishment" from a perpetrator guilty of murder—but surely this is no "merciful" work. Understanding mercy as transgressive care, however, clarifies this ambiguity, exposing and excluding this jury's leniency as not merciful at all, as in fact brutally unmerciful, since it is neither transgressive, insofar as it serves racist "insiders" (whites) over and against an "outsider" (the Latino victim, and nonwhites generally), nor care, insofar as it serves explicitly to dismiss and demean a human being and his people on racist grounds. In short, conceiving "mercy" as transgressive care allows us, in principle, to distinguish it clearly from partisan, hateful prejudice, and so to chart more clearly and consistently the outlines of "merciful" work.

Finally, this account parts company with Alschuler both sharply and suggestively on the matter of whether mercy is, as he puts it, "the paradigmatic example of supererogation," which is to say, the paradigmatic example of "going beyond the requirements of duty." As we have seen, "mercy" in Luke's gospel is not only mandatory, it is mandated in and as the highest law in human life, indeed as divine law, as what Christian tradition later calls "the Great Commandment," and what Luke calls what we "must do" (Luke 10:25). In Alschuler's terms, far from the paradigmatic act of "going beyond" duty's requirements, for Luke "mercy" is no less than the paradigmatic duty. Indeed, from this point of view, the question is not whether or not "mercy" has a rightful place in contemporary systems of criminal justice, but rather whether or not those systems sufficiently afford "mercy" its rightful place.

But perhaps Alschuler's talk of "supererogation" may be understood another way. Though he defines "supererogatory" as "going beyond the requirements of duty," the term may also be glossed, "performed or observed beyond the degree required *or expected.*"[6] As transgressive care, mercy will indeed exceed and subvert conventional expectations, crossing customary lines of hostility and distrust, working to bring outsiders "in," to enfranchise the disenfranchised—and so to "build up from ruins" (Isa. 61:4). In this sense, mercy may be called our "supererogatory duty": our vocation and charge to go beyond what is typically expected in our care for one another, to exceed the familiar, to neither "take vengeance" nor "bear grudges," but rather to stand together again, even amidst our past and present desolations.

On the legal spectrum of options for understanding "justice," this conception of "mercy" as transgressive care finds its place near so-called "restorative justice,"[7] a wide and varied set of proposals and programs that seek to enact the idea that "justice" means neither punishment nor retribution, but rather the constructive work of repairing and promoting communal life.[8] As transgressive care, "mercy" is not only consistent with this approach, it is, I contend, foundational for it, in effect providing the broad framework within which "restorative justice" is understood and worked out. That is, to say that justice is properly "restorative" is to say, bearing in mind the account of "mercy" outlined above, that justice is properly merciful, that justice is properly served when communities are restored and renovated—and so that the work of justice, finally, is work undertaken in the service of mercy, of "building up from ruins." A crime, on this view, is an act of ruin, of demolition. The common pre-emptive task of the state and the neighborhood in question is to diminish social conditions that encourage and allow such acts to take place; but when they do take place, the common responsive task of state and neighborhood, of victims and perpetrators, is to face and assess the ruin, to account responsibilities, and to begin to build anew. Understood this way, "restorative justice" means merciful justice, Samaritan justice, justice framed and founded on transgressive care—which is to say, justice framed and founded on the concrete work of resurrection, of rebuilding and renewing common life among ruins, wreckage, and devastation.

Are "mercy" and "justice" therefore identical on this view? By no means—but they are inseparable, and so they are understood well only together. "Justice," we may say, is the indispensable work of treating persons and communities fairly and equitably; "mercy" is the equally indispensable work of transgressive care for those persons and communities. But among ruins, there can be no fairness and equity—no justice— unless outsiders are continually ushered "in," unless the weak receive special protection, unless lines of hostility and suspicion are crossed and, at least provisionally, overcome. The work of justice thus requires mercy,

MATTHEW MYER BOULTON

and is guided by it at every turn. On the other hand, among ruins there can be no transgressive care—no mercy—without critical attention to social structures and dynamics, to questions of when and where and how fairness and equity are violated, and so to who is left "outside," and who "inside."[9] Transgressive care requires this analysis and presupposes that equitable care for the whole means special care for the marginal and excluded, for those left out and left behind. In this sense, justice is constitutive of mercy.

As we have seen, however, on this view the work of "mercy" is the prior, foundational, and final work. Thus "mercy" properly frames and founds the work of "justice," and excludes both the "taking vengeance" and the "bearing grudges" (Lev. 19:18) that so often masquerade as "justice" between peoples and nations, states and citizens, victims and perpetrators. That is, on this view, for genuine "justice" to be served, persons and communities must be restored—and "vengeance," "grudges," or punitive retribution have no place in that restoration.[10] In contrast, genuine "justice," Samaritan justice, justice framed and founded by transgressive care, plays an integral role in any "building up from ruins." To be sure, the injunction "love your neighbor as yourself" implicates its hearers straightaway in matters of fairness and equity, in the difficult work of justice. But this call to neighborliness, first and last of all, is a call to love.

At the parable's close, Jesus turns again to the lawyer, once more eliciting the decisive word from the questioner himself: "'Which of these three, do you think, was a neighbor to the man who fell into the hands of robbers?' He said, 'The one who showed him mercy.' Jesus said to him, 'Go and do likewise'" (Luke 10:36–37). In this way, Luke reports, the conversation between the lawyer and the rabbi comes to its swift conclusion—but a great deal happens here in the blink of an eye. First, Jesus disturbs and critiques the lawyer's question; finally, he transforms it.

The lawyer had asked, "Who is my neighbor?", or *Which human beings must I love as myself?*; and Jesus's parable, as it unfolds, seems to be preparing the way for the platitude *Your neighbor is anyone in need* (a reading of this passage not uncommon among Christians today!). That is, the lawyer asks Jesus to specify some subset of humanity that counts as the "neighbors" he must "love," and Jesus's story, with its antiheroes who refuse to care for a needy man, and its hero who does care for him, seems to pick out "the needy" as the "neighbors" who deserve love. But to close his discourse, Jesus does not say, "Which of these three recognized the man as a neighbor?" but rather, "Which of these three *was a neighbor* to the man?"

The answer to this question, of course, is "the Samaritan"—and so in the first place, Jesus pointedly puts the lawyer in the position of identifying a foreigner as a neighbor. That is, to an attempt to discover the boundary line between "neighbors" and "strangers," Jesus gives the unsettling reply, *Your neighbors are among the ones you call strangers.* But his critique goes further: with his final remark—"Go and do likewise"—Jesus reframes and upends the lawyer's question once and for all. By asking, "Who is my neighbor?" the lawyer had asked Jesus to mark out a particular group of human beings who must be loved; but now Jesus commands him not to love the neighbor but to be the neighbor, to "do likewise" by "showing mercy" in the Samaritan's footsteps. This reversal amounts to both a rejection and a transformation of the lawyer's question: first, the command "Go and do likewise" is a refusal to identify some people as "to be loved" and so others as "not to be loved." In this way, Jesus exposes and rebuffs the clannishness of the lawyer's question, and so any attempt to identify one's "neighbors" as some select group among others. Second, "Go and do likewise" transforms the question "Who is my neighbor?" back into the lawyer's initial query, "What shall I do?" Thus Jesus seems to say: Worry less about to whom you show mercy, and more about showing mercy. Don't discern "the neighbor" from among your fellows; become one. Show mercy. Go and do likewise. For not only the other's life, but your own depends on it: "Do this, and you will live" (Luke 10:28).

In other words, this account finally names "mercy" as central and constitutive for genuine human life, as not only humane but also in the strongest sense "humanizing" for both beneficiary and practitioner. Go and do likewise—and you will live. Shakespeare puts it this way: mercy is "twice-blessed; / It blesseth him that gives and him that takes."[11] In Luke, however, the stakes of this mutuality are perhaps the highest stakes imaginable: the lives of both parties hang in the balance, the passerby no less than the one dying on the side of road. Acts of "mercy," then, are properly performed out of neither solemn duty nor "supererogatory" whim, but rather as the genuine form of human life and work. Do this, and you will live. Accordingly, "neighbor" here means not someone alongside us, but rather someone for us continually to become, the one who "lives," and so in that sense the true human being, alive and well. The practice of neighborliness—of "neighborhood," of mercy—is finally, on this account, the practice of living human life. In Christian theological terms, we are dealing here, after all, with "the Great Commandment." For Luke, human hope finally rests on this task and this charge: to be the neighbor, to do likewise, to build up from ruins, to live.

On this view, the fundamental question is never *who* deserves mercy, but rather *how* mercy, as transgressive care, is best carried out for all concerned, both victims and perpetrators, within particular constraints and circumstances. Victims need mercy to the extent that crime leaves them and their situation in ruins, and to the extent, too, that crime renders them, as it so often does, stigmatized, caricatured, avoided, or forgotten "outsiders" in their own communities. Perpetrators need mercy to the extent that crime leaves them marked and broken by guilt, grief, and the harm that harming brings, and to the extent, too, that practices of criminal justice define and render them "outsiders" par excellence: accused, incarcerated, hidden, feared, and alone.

To define mercy as the remittance of deserved punishment, and then inquire into who deserves mercy and under what conditions, is doubly problematic: first, as we have seen, because it leads into conceptual tangles and ambiguities, posing questions like "When does a criminal deserve less than he deserves?"; and second, because it invites clannish attempts to decide who deserves mercy and who doesn't, who has sufficiently atoned and who hasn't—and so on. To the contrary, conceiving mercy as transgressive care leaves moral desert and punitive atonement behind, instead framing a different set of questions: How may flourishing common life be protected and promoted? What ruins need rebuilding? What "outsiders" need ushering in? What "insiders" need provocation? And in response to crime: What ruptures have taken place? What victims, what perpetrators, what ruins? What lines of hostility and distrust have deepened or opened up, what "outsiders" and "insiders"? And so, bearing all this in mind: How best to care, to restore, to build up again?

As advocates of "restorative justice" rightly point out, these questions and decisions, though they may and should be asked and made by criminal justice professionals on their own, are often best handled by these professionals in cooperative consultation with social workers, clergy, family members, and other community leaders with key stakes in the conflict and key connections to the victim(s) and perpetrator(s). These consultations are crucial for rightly discerning wounds, patterns of exclusion, and fronts of hostility, as well as for implementing strategies for reconciliation and building up. In many places across the United States, this kind of co-operation is already in play: police and clergy, lawyers and social workers, wardens and community leaders can and do work together to enact more expansive, more restorative practices of criminal justice. These initiatives deserve applause, support, constructive critique, and further development. And in many cases, significant responsibilities for imagining and maintaining such initiatives will fall to some community institutions—schools, voluntary organizations, churches, synagogues, mosques—who have not traditionally understood themselves to be "criminal justice professionals."

But responsibilities will fall to the conventional professionals, too. Institutional practices and patterns must be rethought and retooled, and only those who know them well can finally lead the way. Theologians and ethicists may provide some guidance and groundwork, some conceptual frames and clear rationales for further development; but police, probation officers, case workers, lawyers, judges, legislators, and community leaders will take the helm when it comes, as it must come, to design and implementation.

In the meantime, the "merciful"—those who practice transgressive care, continually working to usher outsiders "in," to trespass lines of hostility and distrust, and to carry forward the work of reconciliation—are often charged (or condescendingly tolerated) with being naïve and insufficiently "realistic." But the charge is out of place: "mercy" need not be coupled with foolish sentimentality, well-meaning gullibility, or even "leniency" as such. As any engineer knows, "building up from ruins" can be work as hard-nosed and realistic, as sophisticated and levelheaded, as any other. Indeed, the work of restoration, with its refusal to succumb to the cycle and downward spiral of retribution, is arguably the most "realistic" work of all. Moreover, the chief hallmarks of criminal justice systems—uses of force, police officers, prisons, courts, and law offices—remain fully operational in any well-considered "restorative justice" system. It is and will continue to be necessary that some citizens of the United States, as part and parcel of the care they and their communities need, temporarily or permanently become wards of the state. The state's coercive use of force, applied within limits, is and will continue to be necessary—again, as part and parcel of the care victims, perpetrators, and their communities require—to apprehend and incarcerate some who commit crimes. Founding institutional practices on transgressive care rather than on retribution or punishment by no means does away with those practices; to the contrary, it properly orients them, strengthens them, and provides a basis for their continual reform.

What is done away with—or at least ruled out in principle—is "taking vengeance" and "bearing grudges" (Lev. 19:18), the idea that any institutional practice is properly conceived and carried out as fundamentally punitive, retributive work, designed and accomplished not in order to "build up from ruins," but strictly in order to punish a wrongdoer. That is, what is done away with is the idea that by perpetrating a crime, even and especially a catastrophic crime, an individual actually and properly becomes an "outsider," an appropriate object of excommunication from community, an expatriate and not a neighbor, someone undeserving of care. Or, more to the point, what is done away with is the idea that by virtue of his crime I become someone relieved of my obligation to care for him; that because of his crime, I cease to be his neighbor. To the contrary, on this view, the one guilty of a crime stands before me—not only despite but also precisely because of his guilt—as one in perilous need of care. And in turn, on this view, I stand before him—not only despite but also precisely because of my relative innocence—under the perilous obligation to face him and to care for him, to become and to be his neighbor.

A crime, we may say, is an attack on neighborhood; but so is punitive retribution as such. A supposed "insider" is ushered "out" (or, as is often the case, a relative "outsider" is ushered even farther "out"). Whenever and wherever calls for so-called "retributive justice" precipitate or presuppose this kind of alienation, they take place over against "mercy," as its adversary and reversal. "Mercy," as transgressive care, in turn opposes and works against the clannish, alienating work of punitive retribution, as indeed its adversary and reversal, as both "rebuke" and constructive counterpoint to all demands, in their various forms and disguises, for "consumption by fire" (Luke 9:54).

Accordingly, criminal justice practices and the rationales that generate and justify them are always open to critique, and on this view, they should be interrogated in particular as to whether or not they are sufficiently "merciful." That is, they should be continually asked—with no less than lawyerly perspicacity—about whether or not they appropriately enact transgressive care for the community, whether or not they help restore and renew common life from the "outside" in, and so whether or not they "show mercy" above all to the marginal and outcast, including the community's consummate "outsiders" defined and in that sense produced by criminal justice practices themselves: the arrested, the accused, the convicted, the imprisoned—and the released, let out but still hemmed in (called, for example, "ex-cons").

The challenging work of being a neighbor, of "neighborhood," means just this sort of transgressive care for "outsiders," exceeding the familiar, surpassing what may appear as ordinary expectations. It may take the form of juridical leniency—but only if and when such leniency can be shown to be properly "merciful," that is, part and parcel of restoring communal life, bringing outsiders "in," overcoming broad social lines of hostility and distrust, reconciling adversaries, and so "building up from ruins." Likewise, "mercy" may also take the form of humane prison conditions, visitation rules, and drug-treatment regimes; or sensitive police procedures, carried out in cooperation with community leaders; or job-placement programs for released prisoners; or church-based networks of care for at-risk juveniles; or new sentencing mandates, reformed so that judges may take some "merciful" account of the cases before them; and so on. Many practical questions remain, of course, and await further conversations between rabbis and lawyers, priests and police, judges and social workers—but in any case, conceiving "mercy" this way means we need not seek out "a place for mercy" in our criminal justice practices, but rather continually seek out criminal justice practices that can and do take place as properly "merciful." According to this view, Micah's injunction to "do justice, love mercy, and walk humbly with your God" (Mic. 6:8) is no dialectical jumble of trade-offs, but rather an integrated whole, calling us into neighborhood, and so into life.

Notes

For comments and suggestions, thanks to E. Myer Boulton, W. Boulton, B. Briggance, A. Kern, G. Mobley, J. Rasmussen, R. Saler, and W. Wright.

1. For Israelite and Johannine records of this antipathy, see, for example, 2 Kings 17:24–34, and John 4:9, 20. Samaritans, needless to say, kept other histories. For a brief account of these complexities, see *The Anchor Bible Dictionary*, 940ff.

2. The tendency in Christian commentary to read this way—both in preaching and in print—is regrettable for at least two reasons: first, because it dominates and obscures the parable itself, cutting readers and hearers off from other understandings of the text; second, and preeminently, because it may issue from

and in any case participates in an often undetected (by Christians) and so particularly insidious form of anti-Judaism: namely, an all-too-eager readiness to read Jesus as critical of Judaism, or rather, a readiness to read a simplistic and objectionable modern critique of Judaism (as, say, rule-oriented and hypocritical) into Jesus's words.

3. Leviticus 19:18: "You shall not take vengeance or bear a grudge against any of your people, but you shall love your neighbor as yourself: I am the LORD." The question of just who comprises "your people" is precisely the question the lawyer puts to Jesus; this scriptural background thus makes even clearer both the clannishness of the lawyer's question ("And who are my people?") and Jesus's rejection of all clannishness in his answer. And with this rejection, please note that Jesus does not critique but rather follows Leviticus: "When an alien resides with you in your land, you shall not oppress the alien. The alien who resides with you shall be to you as the citizen among you; you shall love the alien as yourself, for you were aliens in the land of Egypt: I am the LORD your God" (Lev. 19:33–34). As so often in the Gospels, Jesus is portrayed here interpreting Jewish texts as a Jewish exegetical virtuoso, not a non-Jewish critic or innovator.

4. This way of understanding "mercy" is perhaps more consistent, too, with the English word's etymological origins: deriving from the Latin, *merces*, "reward," it would seem to orbit more closely around "benefit" than around juridical "leniency" or "withheld penalty." Similarly, the English word "alms" (benefits) derives from the Greek *eleos*, the very term translated as "mercy" in Luke 10:37.

5. Cf. the Hebrew *chesed*, often translated as "mercy," which in many biblical narratives—the Book of Ruth is representative: "your people will be my people" (Ruth 1:16)—means treating one who is not a family member with the same loyalty and affection conventionally due to a family member. Here, too, customary expectations are subverted, and "outsiders" are ushered "in." For this insight, I thank Gregory Mobley.

6. See *The American Heritage Dictionary* (rev. ed., 1982), 1220 (emphasis added).

7. For overviews, see Braithwaite, "Restorative Justice"; and Zehr, *Changing Lenses*.

8. And please note, as transgressive care, mercy is not unrelated to the internal state of mind of the mercy-giver, but it finally has to do with concrete practices carried out, and so in that sense in principle may be detached from "internal states" altogether. In other words, nonmerciful people (motivated by, say, vainglory) can still carry out "merciful" acts, acts that actually do provide transgressive care for individuals and communities. In these cases, the acts may be called "merciful," and the actors, "vain."

9. The thoroughly sociopolitically embedded character of any concrete act of "mercy" on this view may indicate that the *narrative forms* in Luke 10 (parable and historylike report) are theologically constitutive to the account of "mercy" there, not strictly ornamental or pedagogical. In other words, while nonnarrative abstractions or "general rules" may be useful as clarifying supplements, "mercy"

may best be understood by way of particular narrated acts of transgressive care in particular historical contexts (e.g., concrete acts by "Samaritans" and "Jews" in first-century Palestine)—which is to say, "mercy" may best be understood by way of narrative forms of discourse, including parable (Jesus) and historylike report (Luke).

10. This is not to say, however, that anger, resentment, fury, and even confrontational rage have no place in practices of restorative justice; on the contrary, these and other emotions may well be indispensable for moving toward communal restoration. But these dynamics, however intense, can and should be distinguished from "vengeance" and punitive retribution.

11. *Merchant of Venice,* act 4, scene 1.

The Way of the Cross as
Theatric of Counterterror

MARK LEWIS TAYLOR

Since writing about systems of criminal justice and injustice in *The Executed God,* one of that volume's major notions, organized terror, has become more pertinent than I could have anticipated at that time. The book argued that U.S. practices of policing, imprisonment, and the death penalty form a system that disseminates terror among poor communities, and further, that this system often functions to reinforce exploitative patterns of political, economic, and social power. This terrorizing function, and its importance to U.S. public order, is hidden, for many people, behind the claims of moral legitimacy that police and other criminal justice officials claim as wielders of state-sanctioned force, and behind the public's granting of moral legitimacy to them out of a concern for security amid fear of crime and disorder. Consequently the public rarely reflects on the way institutional practices that terrorize (prisons, death penalties, and police use of excessive force) have become an important part of social control in the United States. This terrorizing function is more readily seen by the more than 2 million residents now in U.S. jails and prisons, by those daily intimidated by police brutality, by those among the 3,300 on U.S. death rows—*and* by the families and communities whose members suffer, often for generations, from the effects of the prison industrial complex in the United States.[1] In the more constructive part of *The Executed God,* I developed proposals for how Christian life and practice can be understood as a way to counter this organized terror, particularly by construing Christian practice as a life-giving dramatic performance, a "theatric of counterterror."[2]

In this essay, I argue more broadly that being a Christian means participating in creative, popular movements against organized terror. Such participation, of course, is not the only meaning of being a Christian, but it is *a* central meaning. I will be rethinking the notion of "the way of the cross," understood as the lifeways of Jesus that led to his death, which orient Christians to participation in movements deploying a "theatric of counterterror" against organized terror. In light of recent events[3] since the September attacks on the World Trade Center and Pentagon, particularly considering U.S. attacks in Afghanistan and Iraq, it is necessary now to refer to "organized terror" in a still more multidimensional manner.

The essay has four major parts. First, an introductory part clarifies my use of the notion "organized terror," as well as of the notion of "movements" with which Christian theology as a public theology in our time has such an important interest. The second part begins the heart of the essay with an account of organized terror today as a "theatric." Third, Christian practice, its way of the cross, is presented as a "countertheatric," embodied in sustained movements for countering organized terror. Then, in a fourth and final section, I provide some examples of movements within which a Christian theatric of counterterror might find its place today.

Introducing Organized Terror and a Public Theology of Movements

If Christian practice involves participation in creative movements against organized terror, as I will argue in the essay, I need to introduce two particular notions. Here, I will discuss first the notion of organized terror and its modes, and then movements as crucial to public theology.

MODES OF "ORGANIZED TERROR"

I suggest we speak of organized terror as operative in four related but distinguishable modes.[4] There is, first, the organized terror that arises from U.S. systems of criminal (in)justice, which was dealt with in my book and which I discuss in more detail below. It is terror as disseminated throughout "lockdown America," that is, America's citizens imprisoned and subject to surveillance within their own nation. I shall refer to this form of organized terror as *domestic disciplinary terror.* This may be an action as blatant as a "shock-and-awe" tactic of a paramilitary policing operation in an urban city that uses sudden deployment of helicopters and grounds officers to carry out a nighttime raid on an entire neighborhood block, or those more subtle but disquieting actions of surveillance, like those recently exposed as having been carried out without warrants against hundreds, perhaps thousands, of U.S. residents by the U.S. National Security Agency.[5]

There is, second, another kind of organized terror discussed in my book.[6] It is that to which powerful nations, especially the United States, routinely accommodate themselves, and that is assumed to be a necessity for the functioning of the global order. I refer to this as *imperial maintenance terror*,[7] the regular use by the most powerful nations, of covert and overt use of military force against even civilians. This use of force is what Thomas Friedman of the *New York Times* approvingly referred to as "the hidden fist" that assures that "the hidden hand" of the global market functions smoothly.[8] One example of such imperial terror is presented by the other September 11, that of 1973, when the United States used economic and military power to force from office the democratically elected president of Chile, Salvador Allende, thus inaugurating, under military strongman August Pinochet, a reign of terror more deadly for innocent civilians than the September 11 attacks of 2001.[9]

There is, third, now, that terror experienced by the U.S. public on and since September 11, 2001, when major symbols of its official political and economic order, the World Trade Center and the Pentagon, were attacked. U.S. children, families, a whole citizenry were terrorized by this attack in New York City and Washington, D.C. I will refer to this as *blowback terror*. It is as unjustifiable and barbaric as any organized terror, but it is distinguished by its being performed by those who consider themselves to have grievances against the powerful nations.[10] Often the grievances, even if real, are cover for other agendas (political, religious, social) that perpetrators of blowback terror also seek to advance through their actions of organized terror. Nevertheless, blowback terrorists thrive and grow stronger when they can point to grievances they have against greater powers. These grievances allow them to grow stronger within the populations subject to imperial powers, and from the ranks of those populations will come the planners of blowback terrorism.

Fourth, there is also the organized terror experienced by ever larger numbers of world communities today as a result of U.S.-led, -sponsored, or -supported activities in its "war on terrorism." This mode of organized terror is *imperial retaliatory terror*. Primary here would be the actions resulting in the deaths of large number of civilians in Afghanistan, which now exceed in number those lost at the New York World Trade Center,[11] and whose suffering is compounded by continuing political strife, poverty, and natural disaster.[12] This imperial retaliatory terror comes with all kinds of duplicities and exploitative agendas, often unannounced. The war and occupation of Iraq was presented to the U.S. public as necessary to protect the United States and allies from Saddam Hussein's weapons of mass destruction, when, in fact, operative were other interests: securing control of oil and water rights in the area, maintaining key military bases in the region, and strengthening the general geopolitical advantage of the United States in the Middle East vis-à-vis emergent powers of the European Union, Russia, and China. This organized terror is imperial *retaliatory* terror, then, even if the retaliation is made for a host of announced and unannounced reasons.

I cannot here treat fully each of these four modes of organized terror. Nevertheless, in formulating Christians' way of the cross as a theatric to counter organized terror, I will work in a way that acknowledges these four modes and their frequent interrelation. Even though my primary focus is on the terrors of lockdown America—domestic disciplinary terror—a Christian theatric of counterterror must also take account of the other modes.

It may also be necessary to point out that to interpret each of these modes as modes of organized "terror"—having in common a traumatizing of entire populations and communities—does not mean that the modes are identical in form, effect, or cause. Each mode of organized terror has its own complexities and distinctive structures and textures of formation. That having been said, analysis of any one of these modes of organized terror often requires careful reflection on the other modes due to their mutual interdependency.

MOVEMENTS IN PUBLIC THEOLOGY

Since the Christian theatric of counterterror entails participation in creative, popular movements, I need to address the role of movements within the public discourse of theology.

Allow me to locate my own sense of public theology in relation to one statement of it, namely, that of David Tracy, in his book *The Analogical Imagination: Christian Theology and the Culture of Pluralism*. Tracy has

MARK LEWIS TAYLOR

developed his own notions further, in light of diverse criticisms and later rethinking, but his 1981 formulation has remained influential enough that it can serve as a rubric for locating my own approach.

Tracy distinguished theology's public discourse in terms of "three publics," three communities of accountability to which theology was responsible and with which it interacted.[13] Its engagement with these communities of accountability generates, for Tracy, distinctive theological subdisciplines. There was, first, theology as largely accountable to the canons of the university or academic traditions, which yielded a subdiscipline of "fundamental theology." Second, there was theology as largely accountable to the church and its traditions of symbol and belief, yielding "systematic theology." Third, there was theology as accountable to, and variously interacting with, what Tracy called "the society," or sometimes, "the wider society." This latter public prompted theology to formulate its interpretations, studies, and claims as a third subdiscipline, "practical theology." This rubric yielded no easy compartmentalization of theology's tasks, and Tracy himself acknowledged various modes of complex interplay and overlap among the publics and subdisciplines he identified.

A reservation I have had with Tracy's formulation is that it could be read as interpreting the publics of academy and church as being of the same magnitude or scope as the public he names "the wider society." As the comparative vagueness of the latter phrase suggests, however, "the wider society" is better understood less as a distinctive public alongside academy and church and more as an encompassing realm inclusive of them both. The wider society, to stay with that phrase, is more like a large background field of all possible publics, against which we might distinguish the publics of academy and church.

Moreover, I suggest placing an additional "public" against that background field, one that interacts with academy and church but that is not identical to either one of those two. It is that of "movements." Theologians do not all belong to the same movement, or to all movements, any more than they could belong to the same academy or church, or to all academies and churches. Nevertheless, some movements constitute a distinctive community of accountability, a distinctive way a theologian has a "public," and often in ways that impact and structure theological discourse.[14] In sum, I see public theology as having to orchestrate three always interacting publics: academy, church, and movement. All three of these publics can be seen against the background of "the wider society" within which they interact in different ways.

Why add the notion of movement as an additional public? As a first, perhaps more subjective, response, I would say that over the years I have found and built for myself a social life in relation to movements. I have found myself in positions of accountability to them, and in ways that seem distinct from the ways I am positioned in relation to the communities of the academy and the church. I find this experience of mine to resonate also with experiences of other theologians.

Less subjectively, I would say that both the canons of scholarship in the academy, and also the symbols and beliefs of the church, usually, if not always, entail certain ideals of transformation (a moral dimension that implies certain actions held to be good or preferable). If and when those ideals are pursued by theologians in the context of "the wider society," that pursuit often involves them in modes of sociality that have their own distinctive complexities, and these often do not fit precisely (or, sometimes, at all) with those generated by academy and church. In short, my adding the notion of movement as a public for public theologians is no mere subjective addendum; it emerges from the various ideals of transformation implicit in the canons of scholarship[15] and church belief.

The kind of sociality that a movement involves is signaled by the definition of it given by Sidney Tarrow. He defined a movement as "a collective challenge, based on common purposes and social solidarities, in sustained interaction with elites, opponents, and authorities."[16] Integral to this definition is the idea that the movement's effort to realize some ideal or ideals is (*a*) a collective challenge, arising from (*b*) a shared common purpose and (*c*) sense of solidarity, issuing in (*d*) sustained, usually contentious, interaction with opponents and conditions that mitigate against realization of some ideal(s).

The modes of sociality involved in movements are complex and now analyzed in a growing body of scholarly literature,[17] to which theologians do well to attend in greater detail than I can do in this essay. Here, however, I only briefly introduce movement and movements in order to render more complete the understanding of the publics that shape the work of public theology and to make clear why this essay takes movements so seriously. This focus on movements is not meant to replace, certainly not to jettison, the concerns with academic canons of scholarship or of church belief. To the contrary, while giving perhaps unusual stress to movement-

MARK LEWIS TAYLOR

oriented discussion, this exercise in public theology presupposes also the still-relevant roles of academy and church.

The Theatrics of Terror

While my notion of a Christian theatric of counterterror may be unique, the idea of a theater of terror, or of criminal justice systems involving a "theatric of terror," is hardly new. The phrase has been applied often to the ways official force is deployed to combat crime and to the ways proscribed punishments are applied to wrongdoers.[18] I clarify the notion of "the theatrical" in relation to terrorism and summarize the senses in which terror (primarily domestic disciplinary terror) is operative in U.S. criminal justice systems.

THEATRICS OF TERROR

What are "theatrics," and what happens when we think about theatrics in relation to what we call terror? We may derive a first understanding of the notion of "terror" by noting its origins from the Latin *terrere*, "to cause to tremble." This is an important etymological point, because it accents how the term takes its meaning from the kind of impact it engenders. According to sociologist Mark Juergensmeyer, the term came into common usage in "the political sense, as an assault on civil order, during the Reign of Terror in the French Revolution at the close of the eighteenth century."[19] "Terror" takes its primary meaning from the effects it has on a victimized audience that is made to feel the tremors of the attack. It is an audience-defined term, and the resultant effects of trembling and being in terror define the act more than do the intentions, rationales, ideologies, or identities of their perpetrators. Afghanistan civilians suffered organized terror in October 2001 as much as did those of New York City in September 2001. The fact that there were different forces bringing the terror, and with different rationalizations, does not negate the fact that both are exercises of organized terror. What the U.S. military announced as its "shock-and-awe" strategy in the 2003 attacks on Iraq was a mode of organized terror. Audiences were "caused to tremble" and afflicted with all the effects of organized terror.

To speak of "theater," or of a "theatric" (i.e., the art of theater), in reference to power and terrorizing power is to acknowledge that those powers do not have their way with people simply because of mechanisms of force or physical violence; but that they also use symbolic performance for terrorizing or to intensify other terrorizing actions. Such performance may narrate stories, set up rituals (such as body-cavity searches in prison, the last meal, or the final walk of a death-row prisoner), offer certain symbols, and construct various pageants and spectacles (opening and closing curtains for the revealing *and* hiding of stages of a person's execution). They steep audiences, especially through the mass media, in experiences of awe, enchantment, fascination, and fear.

Theatrics occur through just and unjust social forms in many ways. Systems of inequality, for one example, often excel in making themselves enchanting, as anthropologist Clifford Geertz explained in his study *Negara: The Theatre State in Nineteenth-Century Bali*.[20] Conversely, systems of rebellion often realize their more effective transformations when they resist power not just with counterforce but also with "enchanting" strategies that delight and charm, as in the contemporary Mexican Zapatista movement.[21]

THEATRICS OF TERROR IN LOCKDOWN AMERICA

The powers of the theatrical are evident in today's U.S. criminal justice system, and with considerable self-awareness they are described by some architects of that system. Police, for example, have written about seeking dramatic impact when cordoning off neighborhoods for drug raids, when using the spectacular moves of SWAT teams, or with their surveillance helicopters, which can light up whole urban areas for special operations. One California police sergeant remarked, "They [targeted neighborhoods] see our big gray SWAT bus, and the weapons, and they know we mean business."[22] The use of "Robocops," police dressed in full riot gear, designed for both protection of police and maximum intimidation at scenes of antiglobalization demonstrations, offers another example.

Prisons have grown with a startling rapidity, representing a dramatic impact on our society, again, especially for communities of color, which now contribute 70 percent of the imprisoned population. The total population of more than 2 million has *quadrupled* just since 1980, representing the largest, most frenetic growth of prisons seen in the history of world cultures.[23] Prisons have become a kind of spectacle, a theatric, in themselves, now referred to increasingly as an entire "industrial complex."

MARK LEWIS TAYLOR

Moreover, prisoner life inside is replete with the dramas of high-tech surveillance and control, combined with high exposure of inmates to violence and rape (some 290,000 men per year, often raped daily).[24] These are the material of theater and drama indeed.

The "now-you-see-them/now-you-don't" approach to executions in the United States, which are ritually staged and scripted by "execution protocols,"[25] makes them theatrical events. Witnesses and the wider public are steeped in terror and fascination when the state implements this ultimate penalty. The terrorizing effect of the death penalty, throughout officials' deliberation on that maximum punishment, has been a mainstay throughout the history of the death penalty in the United States.[26]

The theatrical use of terror today, by criminal justice systems specifically, was rather boldly acknowledged in a revealing comment shared in an interview with Jonathan Kozol by a prison educator at Rikers Island, New York City, the largest penal institution in the world: "Without this island [Rikers] the attractive lives some of us lead in the nice sections of New York would simply not be possible. If you want to get your outcasts out of sight, first you need a ghetto and then you need a prison to take pressure off the ghetto. . . . *Short-term terror and revulsion are more powerful than long-term wisdom or self-interest.*"[27] This prison worker was revealing a hard truth: "short-term terror and revulsion" are now organized so that terror and revulsion result to reinforce control and social governance.

I will not here rehearse what I document at length in my book, i.e., that organized terror is operative in our criminal justice systems. Suffice it to say here that this terror includes 2 million people being subjected to what is a life-destroying "spirit death," stemming from exposure to routinized time spent in cages for years, months, days, hours, minutes, seconds.[28]

It includes also the experiences of those among the 70 percent of the U.S. prison population who are from "communities of color" and who thus are subjected to the indignities of what many studies, including Marc Mauer's in this volume, have documented as the "cumulative racial bias" in the U.S. policing, judicial, and correctional systems.[29]

There is the hushed-up reality of the 290,000 annual cases of male-on-male rape, all in a way that reinforces sexual violence and sexism not only in the prison but also throughout the wider society (noted in Lois Gehr Livezey's essay in this volume).[30]

The theater of terror also includes the over 3,300 people who are kept on death rows in spite of studies proving that the capital punishment system is so broken that over 100 people have had to be released from death row for later findings of innocence just since 1976.[31] It includes the assignment of excessively long sentences for nonviolent crimes, which pour a bitter and poisonous gall of injustice into those who are made to suffer a terror that is more than their error.

The theater of terror includes our country's youth (especially those of African, Latino, Indigenous, Arab, and Asian descent), who live in a constant sense of terror while navigating the harassments and brutality of neighborhood cops.[32] Youth, and especially those in families of Arab descent, have endured a veritable nightmare in the wake of September 11 and the U.S. government's new "security" measures.

To confirm the magnitude of the violation under way in the United States, we might note the studies of Amnesty International, usually a rather mild critic of U.S. policies, which charged in 2000 that the United States stood in fundamental violation of its own citizens' human rights because of the patterns of injustice operating in its prisons, its treatment of immigrants, its police brutality, and its dependency upon executions.[33] As U.S. leaders have been increasingly implicated in approving harsh interrogation and torture, Amnesty International USA, in 2005, even called upon the other nations who signed the Geneva accords to consider detentions, arrests, and prosecutions of America's highest leadership.[34]

But are all these examples of brutality, organized force, and punishment rightly called "terror" in the same sense that the attacks on the World Trade Center (WTC) are designated "acts of terror"? Maybe the mother who showed up for the rally to stop retaliatory war after the WTC attacks was involved in a category mistake when she carried a sign that read: "What about police terrorism in the USA?"

From the perspective of the terrorized, there is no category mistake. Those who suffer the startling rise of prisons, and police intimidation and brutality in our country have been and are suffering a tremor and loss daily that is like that known by New Yorkers and their families now, in a more focused way, after the attacks on the WTC. The fear, the psychological coping, the sense of loss, the exposure to unpredictable killing force, the erosion of felt senses of safety, the daily dis-ease and lack of trust in the world by children survivors—all this is experienced terror, and it does not really matter if the perpetrator is an al-Qaeda extremist, a paid prison warden or police officer in the United States, or a bomber pilot from Nebraska flying above Afghanistan or Iraq to drop cluster bombs or

MARK LEWIS TAYLOR

launch cruise missiles. Their actions all produce terror, however different may be the means of creating the terror, however sophisticated may be the rationales that are offered.

A Christian Theatric of Counterterror

It is in such a context that I propose that Christians would do well to offer a "theatric of counterterror." The basic idea is that Christians, amid the terror of criminal justice systems today and other modes of organized terror, can forge their own dramatic counterresponse in relation to concrete popular movements. Even though issues of organized terror are not always understood as being at the core of Christian faith, they are integrally pertinent to the Gospel, especially when viewed in relation to the context of the historical emergence of early Jesus movements.

Jesus's ministry in the land of Galilee and Judea was undertaken during a Roman occupation of his people's land. He violated legal stipulations and expectations of the religio-political order, unsettling authorities. Before suffering imperial execution, he was arrested, confined, interrogated, beaten, tortured (some historians say he probably was also "sexually abused"),[35] and put on a forced march. The founder and confessed Lord of Christians knew what it meant to suffer not only as a criminal but also as one singled out for a political punishment in the imperial regime's theater of terror.

Moreover, even the apostle Paul's contribution to the Jesus and early Christian movements—for all of Paul's tendency to make of Jesus a resurrected figure transcendent beyond the historical martyr-figure of Galilee—still insisted on a "savior" whose power challenged the emperor/savior cult of Rome. The mere designation of Jesus as "savior" was a religio-political challenge to the Caesar thought to be savior. Paul struggled for alternative communities to mobilize resistance and survival for people under conditions of Roman imperial subjugation.[36]

Paul's anti-imperial praxis was especially evident in the way he fashioned a message of the cross. The cross already had a strange "dramaturgy" (a working through the powerful effects of its terrorizing spectacle) in Roman and Hellenistic milieus. Like executions in the history of the United States, crucifixions had an ambiguous, sometimes contradictory, dramaturgical effect: they could produce in their beholders not only a numbed callousness regarding the cruelty displayed but also the fear that Roman officials hoped would deter insubordination and anti-state behavior.

One way to view Paul in the fashioning of his message of the cross is to see him as a kind of conjurer, one who added strange new potions to the dramaturgy of imperial executions so that its ambiguous effect was intensified. Indeed, one might say, he conjured the cross so that its effect turned out to be the opposite intended by crucifying authorities. Paul knew that the daily intimidating effects of visible bodies broken on the crosses along the highways of empire not only intimidated and shamed subordinate peoples; they also potentially united those peoples into a new community of grievance and resistance.

Terror became hope when the cross was used as a symbol that bridged the cultural differences between the various subject peoples of the empire. Grim resignation became joyful anticipation when the grotesque method of execution used by the Romans became an omen of the impending salvation of the righteous and destruction of the wicked.[37]

Paul's conjuring amid the dramaturgy of imperial execution was possible given the theatricality and spectacular nature of Jesus's crucifixion. I suggest that our own forging of movements vis-à-vis systems of organized terror today might take cues from the theatricality of Jesus's death, and to this theatricality I now turn in more detail.

THE DEATH OF JESUS AS THEATRICAL EVENT

One of the contributions of recent Jesus movement research to Christology is its reminder that the death of Jesus was an execution. Within most U.S. Christian communities, the meanings of the death of Jesus are usually abstracted from its historical setting as an imperial execution. Often Jesus's death is interpreted mainly as a step in a sublime plan of divine love and personal redemption, while the earthly politics leading to and involved in Jesus's exposure to torturous execution go unreflected upon, or are reduced to mere historical mechanisms by which providence's sublime plan of redemption was implemented.[38] When that is done, we omit giving adequate attention to what might be called the politics of Jesus, and we omit also a study of how Jesus's death was experienced by those associated with him. In the process, I suggest, we also alienate the Gospel from that politics which is at its heart. This is all the more unfortunate, especially if we want a Christian theology that engages the contemporary vicissitudes of criminal justice and injustice today. John Dominic Crossan's words in *The Birth of Christianity* are timely: "instead of the death of Jesus, we must speak of the imperial crucifixion of Jesus." [39]

When the politics of Jesus's imperial execution are considered, then a very significant aspect of his death's "theatricality" comes to the fore. Drawing from diverse contributors to the very complex and burgeoning Jesus movement research in our time, [40] I want to suggest that Jesus's death by execution was theatrical in four senses.

First, the type of execution Jesus endured was in its very nature part of a theatrical event. Rome used executions to create terrorizing spectacle. As New Testament scholar Paula Fredriksen points out in her book *Jesus of Nazareth, King of the Jews*, crucifixions were a "public service announcement" that said, in effect, "do not engage in sedition, as this person has, or your fate will be similar." [41] Crucified victims were frequently set on display. Their deaths were theatrical in the sense that they formed state-authorized spectacles, making examples of the executed, to teach a lesson, especially when the offender was a slave in rebellion. Even when crucifixion was used against dangerous criminals and seemingly nonpolitical offenders, their special punitive suffering was intended to be seen as punishment appropriate for those viewed as enemies of the standing political order. [42]

Second, the theatrical display made of Jesus on the Roman cross was, in part, due to his own theatrical "acting up" in opposition to Roman and religious leadership in his day. He might have stayed away from Jerusalem at Passover, a time of crowds gathering and surging, wondering about any future liberation for Jewish peoples. Roman security forces were unusually vigilant, looking out for sedition at this time. Not only did Jesus apparently position himself, intentionally, in that turbulent festive milieu, but, as Mark renders the drama, Jesus entered it with a bit of street theater, coming in on a donkey and parodying the whole idea of a military king's grand entry into a city. He marched on the temple, symbolically challenging the legitimacy of the entire Temple State, in which local religious elites routinely complied with Roman political domination and made life miserable, especially for the poor and the marginalized.

Thus, his death was theatrical also in the sense that it was partially a result of his own theatricality, a theatricality that acted up and took aim at some of the most symbolic theaters of the religio-political order. Jesus's theatricality, as portrayed in Mark, involved marching on and challenging the heart of the Temple State system, the Jerusalem temple where the corruption of money changing and the forgetfulness of the just ways of the great Hebrew prophets drew forth the Jewish Jesus's rage. This was to challenge and act up dramatically against a whole social network of accommodations that local and political officials had made with Roman occupation and religion, most notably, perhaps, by temple officials' rendering of a daily sacrifice for the well-being of the Roman emperor. In short, this Jewish prophet and sage, Jesus, was dramatically acting up at the heart of what with some accuracy could be called the "World Trade Center" of the region, "a huge bureaucratic organization arisen at the central cult place, maintained by a vast civil service of scribes, administrators, accountants, service personnel, Temple officers, and high priestly families who were dependent on the Temple revenues for their support."[43] Ultimately they were dependent upon and subservient to Roman power, symbolized not only by the daily offering to the emperor but also by the very real Roman military force ensconced in the Antonia Fortress at the northwestern corner of the Temple enclosure.[44]

Here arises the third sense in which Jesus's death was theatrical. It is not unusual for those of prophetic spirit[45]—whether of Hebrew, Christian, Muslim, or other traditions—to focus their resistance and dramatic acts of opposition at centers of world trade that are built on exploitation of dependent peoples.[46] Yet unlike the zealous assassins of the first century, the *Sicarii,* who deployed terrorizing killings and kidnappings, and also unlike those who deployed violence against the New York City World Trade Center in 2001, Jesus did not use violence. While certainly the Jewish Jesus spoke and acted as an adversary to Roman and local religious powers, he deployed no violence against his antagonists' physical bodies, nor against those of innocents. This marks the *third* sense in which his death was theatrical. He nurtured theatrical drama by intensifying a contrast between the organized violence of the state/religious powers, on the one hand, and the actions that emerged from his own ways, on the other. His nonviolent ways (still active, confronting, and productive of change, as we'll see below) were theatrical by reason of their otherness, their dramatic contrast, to the habitual use of violence by his enemies and by many others.

To have mobilized violent force or terror, to counter the force and terror with more force and terror, would have introduced nothing new. Rather, it would have been more like another point in the chronology of events (*Chronos*), and not a turning point, not the *Kairos* event it has become. To die as he did, often mute on the way to a brutal and quick death, abstaining from retaliatory force and terror, and dying at the hands of the very ones he vigorously and creatively charged with injustice and unfaithfulness to his God—all this only intensified the drama of his life and teaching.

Jesus is certainly not alone in the historical record for expressing adversarial practice through direct actions marked by nonviolence. Archbishop Arnulfo Oscar Romero and Mahatma Gandhi are just two of many that come readily to mind.[47] They nurtured the contrast in an especially startling way, in that they did not spend large amounts of time denouncing insurrectionary violence, even allowing for a certain necessity of it under certain conditions of injustice.[48] Rather, in a surprising practice of nonviolent opposition's higher way, they displayed its contrasting powers for transformation. Similarly with Jesus—for all the vaunted contrasts between Jesus and "the zealots"—we have few if any extensive critiques of zealots and rebel groups of Jesus's day. He simply lived an alternative way.

Fourth, Jesus's death showed its theatrical character in the way it galvanized an audience and set it in motion. The previously mentioned contrast—between his adversarial stance for justice against the many effects of Roman and religious elites' practices, on the one hand, and his nonretaliatory, nonviolent resistance of love, on the other—seared his teachings and witness into the minds of many, and in a way that generated a mobilizing and catalyzing power. Many others would, of course, be greatly offended. The whole idea of anything good coming from one who had been put to the shameful fate of the cross would have been seen as the antithesis to any good religion, not only to that of the elite Jewish authorities but especially to the Hellenistic spiritualities and religions who needed their gods to be quite above the shameful stuff of crosses and history.[49]

The dramaturgy of Jesus's death, its way of composing the drama, included an impact of rising and spreading movements that remembered and celebrated his life and teachings. Jesus's death was a kind of seed, one that dramatically could grow like the small but feisty mustard plant and could take on greater powers, not just the power of death in general, but the powers of Rome, of corrupt laws and corrupted piety. If political theorist Michael Doyle is correct, early Christian movements helped sap the military and civic power of Rome's imperial and conquering aspirations.[50] Sociologist Rodney Stark described the rise of early Christianity as "one of the most successful revitalization movements in history."[51]

In short, with Jesus's death, a figure is shown to have suffered the worst of Roman theater, which was designed to stifle and quash Jesus's own theatrical acting up in Galilee and Jerusalem, and to deter any acting up by others. Rome's theatrical execution, however, was theatrically upstaged (Jesus and the Jesus movement "stole the show," as I say in *The Executed God*), precisely through refusing to act up violently in spite of his opposition to the religio-political powers of Pax Romana and its supporters.

THE SHAPE OF A CHRISTIAN
THEATRIC OF COUNTERTERROR

This theatrical reading of Jesus's death might provide a new model of Christian practice, one that I think is especially necessary if, today, theaters of terror are to be challenged effectively. Christians might exhibit a "theatric of *counter*terror," the shape of which is like a cord that weaves together three kinds of always-present strategies. The strategies I summarize here constitute one interpretation of the "way of the cross" for Christian practice vis-à-vis imperial settings. Let us consider each practice in turn.

First, a Christian theatric of counterterror is marked by an *adversarial* practice. Here, there is opposition. We cannot dodge the fact that Gospel themes and historical accounts indicate that the way of Jesus entailed an adversarial stance toward religio-political systems of terror. This was especially evident in Jesus's opposition to the practices of the Temple State, which were not only antithetical to his religious views but also constituted a system inconsistent with the political and economic dimensions of the great Hebrew prophets' vision.[52]

I doubt there will be any effective Christian practice to take on organized terror unless Christians understand themselves to be in resistance to the structures that defend, maintain, or compromise with organized terror. The Jesus who was put to death on the Roman cross, with the support of religious officials and crowds, is a Jesus who marks an adversarial relation between himself and his followers, on the one hand, and official powers, on the other. This is not to say that there is no discourse of love and forgiveness in Jesus's message and life; both were noticeably extended even to the advocates and defenders of imperial systems. Love and forgiveness lose their meaning, though, if we lose sight of the adversarial

MARK LEWIS TAYLOR

situation of imperial contestation within which Jesus extended love and forgiveness.

Second, a Christian theatric is also *mimetic*.[53] I choose this word to signal that Christian practice employs a full range of artistic representations, ranging from creative storytelling, to creative actions and dramatic events. The parables and street theater of Jesus are perhaps exemplary here. It is with its deployment of the arts, seeking out creativity and drama, that Christian practice marshals a poetics of power, to challenge the powers at work in the theaters of organized terror. It is with the mimetic concern that the "theatrical" nature of Christian practice, as participation in the way of the cross, is developed most fully.

A theatric of counterterror challenges violent mechanisms of power, and it unleashes a countervailing power from nonviolent action through dramatic creativity. A theatric of counterterror challenges violent mechanisms of power with an aesthetic creativity. In so doing, it offers up far more than a violence-renouncing pacifism. In fact, I don't think "pacifism" is a good word at all. It does not allow adequately for reading Jesus's nonviolence *as* a mode of contestation and adversarial practice. It certainly does not do justice to the modes of creative, adversarial practice that Gandhi, King, and others have forged as "nonviolent creative *direct action*," and that we must forge today.

Third, a Christian theatric of counterterror is *kinetic,* i.e., it is moving and dynamic. It embeds its adversarial and mimetic strategies in concrete movements for change in history. I have already noted how Jesus's death was theatrical in its catalyzing of movements and of followers. A Christian theatric that would really counter the terror of an age is not content with mere personal stances (of an adversarial sort or any other), nor with occasional actions of creative nonviolent drama. No, it presses further and attempts to embody these in the organizing of movements that seek to sustain life-renewing activity and communal work. This third aspect of a theatric of counterterror is crucial. It is this movement-oriented character of the theatric that prevents the way of the cross from becoming mere aestheticism. Christians, along the way of the cross, constitute themselves as a social movement in history and incarnate their witness and practice in relation to other movements where the spirit of Jesus may be seen at work.

In summary, we might say that by means of this threefold theatric of counterterror, Christians "participate" in the theatrical quality that Jesus's death had in the Roman theater of terror. The notion of theatricality is important for any future interpretations of the notion of Christian "participation in Christ's sufferings," this latter notion being one that has endured from the Gospels, through Paul's writings, and throughout the history of Christian faith and practice. If theologians want to emphasize the kind of suffering that "participates" in the kind of suffering Jesus underwent—a kind that avoids pious masochism and also has positive, transformative effects toward life, justice, and restored peace—then the notion of *suffering theatrically with public effect* is indispensable.

From a descriptive point of view, such theatrical suffering—born of the fusing of adversarial practice, dramatic action, and organizing of movements—is the public function of the way of the cross. A contemporary public theology interested in serious change will trace and render ever more clear the revolutionary transformations being worked by a theatric of counterterror.

I need now to comment on a potential misreading of the phrase "Christian theatric of counterterror." It should be clear from this section, especially, that when I write of this strategy of "counterterror," I am not prescribing an alternative campaign of terror, a mere contrasting type of terror to throw up against reigning modes of organized terror. On the contrary, my portrait of the way of the cross—as adversarial, as mimesis of nonviolence, and as movement-oriented—is a social formation and process qualitatively different from the modes of organized terror rending the body politic today. If some were to say that there is still something disturbingly confrontational, maybe even threatening that engenders fear for elites and the powerful—something awesome in these senses—that is appropriate. It is about time that Christians and peoples of conscience learn to practice adversarial, creative nonviolence in movements so effective that the holders of unjust power and wealth anticipate our counterpractice with some awe. We need to ask, now, where are the sites in any contemporary theater of terror in which this Christian theatric of counterterror is most at work, and perhaps needs to grow stronger.

Christian Theatrics of Counterterror Today

Let me close by identifying sites of struggle where a theatric of counterterror is at work. Before I do so, however, I want to offer another clarification. The reinterpretation I have offered here of the way of the cross, as a response to organized terror, does not mean that Christianity is the only or best faith tradition to fuse with activism today. Quite to the contrary, the spiritual practices most demanded by today's political crises must be interfaith ones that are presented as points of dialogue with all peoples of conscience as well.

If this essay gives primary emphasis to Christian reinterpretations of Jesus's death and the way of the cross, it is because I am seeking to move Christian traditions into a closer and more effective solidarity with those forces of an interreligious spirituality that are working for justice today. Given that Christianity remains such an important religious influence in the United States, revisioning its heritage is a significant contribution to ecumenical, interreligious, and broader public movements for justice. If U.S. Christians were to move in this direction, they would find themselves in direct coworking relationships with other cultural and spiritual communities of conscience that for decades, often centuries—among Muslims, Jews, engaged Buddhists, the Yoruba, Caribbeans, and others—have been pursuing a theatric of counterterror against imperial formations.

In the examples I cite in closing, I lift up those that I see displaying the three elements of a theatric of counterterror: adversarial practice, theatrical action (nonviolent mimesis), and organized movement (sustained kinesis). My examples involve many Christian participants, but the organizations are of diverse religious institutional affiliation and are often seen as "secular." Honoring and being oriented by the way of the cross of Jesus guides us to broad human work like what I identify in this final section.

What I am identifying in this closing section as a "theatric of counterterror" is "Christian," therefore, not because only Christians perform it, or because it is performed in the name of Christianity, or as some disguised Christianity. The sites to which I point here are "Christian" mainly in the sense that they are sites of advocacy/mimesis/kinesis where Christians can position themselves to experience consonance with their founders' gospel and to contribute to the liberation and flourishing of the larger human project. What sites do I mean?

1. First, let us consider the blowback terrorism suffered by citizens in the United States since September 11. Unfortunately, in the United States there has been precious little display of a theatric of counterterror in the ways I have described. Political leaders and the media have promoted a nationalistic fervor of revenge and retaliation as policy, one that, I be-

lieve, will ultimately serve the public poorly. Nevertheless, there are some more positive examples.

Before the official mass rallies of lamentation that were televised nationally, people throughout the stricken metropolis of New York were giving needed, theatrical expression to their grief and shock in numerous ways. I saw Union Square at Fourteenth Street in the city just days after the attack. It was one grand altar of candles, sounding forth with spontaneous rituals of diverse faiths, with graffiti of remembrance scrawling out cries for peace—mixed, to be sure, with calls for vengeance. These creative pressures for peace received little coverage, but many New Yorkers marched through the streets from late October through November and later, saying no to retaliatory war, and organizing against it, as in "New Yorkers against the War."

People did begin to find voice in the funeral marches and services, in the stadium rallies in New York, and in the television artist concerts and more. All these creative expressions are crucial to a theatric that counters terror. But it was in the small groups, I suggest, where the theatrical impulses were not only more creative but also more usually fused with an adversarial resistance to imperial power and to all organized terror, and surely more connected to the organizing of sustained movements against all organized terror.

2. What about a theatric of counterterror regarding what I referred to as the terror of lockdown America, domestic disciplinary terror? Amid the burgeoning U.S. prison industrial complex, police and prosecutorial misconduct, draconian sentencing practices, and the death penalty, where can we turn for a theatric of counterterror?

One of the most impressive sites in this regard is the national and international movement that has been forming around the journalist Mumia Abu-Jamal. He has been on death row in Pennsylvania for twenty-one years, after a trial that almost all human-rights observers and people of conscience have found fraught with error and violations of due process and constitutional rights. The strength of the movement, in large part, stems from a small community of activists in Philadelphia and throughout the nation who have been working to reverse the scars done to that urban body politic since the days of the mayoral regime of Frank Rizzo. The corruption of Philadelphia's police forces brought an unprecedented suit from the U.S. Department of Justice.[54]

The U.S. movement—in part because of Abu-Jamal's journalistic skills in radio and print journalism[55]—has linked itself with other movements such as the alternative globalization movement and the Zapatista movement of Mexico. In his writings, Abu-Jamal regularly commented on the rising "war on terror" of the Bush regime and on the wars in Afghanistan and Iraq. In another key symbolic move, Jamal has been made an Honorary Citizen of Paris, an honor the city has not bestowed on anyone since Pablo Picasso. These links, as well as its own focused energy and themes, have made the movement around Abu-Jamal not only adversarial vis-à-vis the criminal justice system but also theatrical and resiliently organized.

Part of its theatricality is nourished by its strong ties to the politically conscious hip hop movement in the United States. Artists in that musical genre routinely hold benefits for that movement, and the focus is not just on Jamal's case—about which he himself rarely writes—but on the many voiceless and unnamed people who suffer in lockdown America in communities of color. Notable here are the Activism tours sponsored by the Prison Moratorium Project (PMP), a youth-led grassroots organization dedicated to halting prison expansion, encouraging alternative thinking among youth regarding criminal justice issues. I won't detail their projects here, but they include declaring a moratorium on the runaway boom in prison building over the last several decades, redefining the police function as we know it, and ending the death penalty.[56]

Since alternative globalizers' 1999 protests in Seattle against the World Trade Organization, which brought out over fifty thousand persons, the interaction between the Abu-Jamal movement and globalization protestors has been more intense. From the alternative globalization protestors, the Abu-Jamal movement has imbibed much of the extraordinary creative puppetry, miming, and other creative drama that are crucial for an effective, nonviolent theatric of counterterror. The Abu-Jamal movement, therefore, has become a centerpiece of movements adversarial to the organized terror in lockdown America, which so many persons and families know through the prison, policing, and execution practices of present U.S. policies. Although the efforts of activists working against U.S. wars and practices of torture have taken them in many different directions, the movement remains strong to this day.[57]

Christians have been slow to join these movements or any sustained structural challenge to the emergence of lockdown America, but their pastors and people have had a significant presence at times, such as in the drives against police brutality in New York City and in the movement for Abu-Jamal.[58]

3. As I read the current situation, most of the participants in the movements against the organized terror of lockdown America are also at work in those movements challenging the imperial maintenance terror and imperial retaliatory terror.[59] That is to say, they trace out with their actions the many connections between the repression they experience on the domestic front within the United States and the imperial reach maintained by U.S. military force abroad.[60]

In the United States and abroad, there long have been movements critical of U.S. imperial force and terror, whether over U.S. involvement in Vietnam or over U.S. support for Pinochet in Chile, for perpetrators of the Dirty War in Argentina,[61] for the Somozas in Nicaragua, for Lucas Garcia and Efrain Rios Montt in Guatemala, for the Duvaliers in Haiti, for Ferdinand Marcos in the Philippines, for Suharto in Indonesia, for Savimbi in Angola,[62] for apartheid and the imprisonment of Mandela in South Africa, and on and on. Indeed, some of the best theorists of current U.S.-based imperial power root the U.S. tendency for imperial abuse, in part, in its past legacy of forced Indian removal and slaughter (compounded by disease) and of years of reliance on the African labor of institutionalized slavery.[63] Resistance movements to these forms of imperial terror in general have long been in place, even if often consigned to a relatively beleaguered status.[64]

I want to draw my final two examples, however, from the way a theatric of counterterror can be observed in movements against the more recent imperial *retaliatory* terror, which is currently orchestrated by the United States in its so-called "war on terror." Two sites are notable in the present moment.[65]

First there is the organized effort of a San Francisco–based organization, Global Exchange, which linked the grieving families of the September 11 WTC disaster to Afghan civilian families who have now lost loved ones to U.S. bombing missions. The adversarial character of this work is evident in the group's willingness to challenge U.S. policy in Afghanistan. One woman, who had lost a husband in the September 11 attacks, said this: "I have heard angry rhetoric of some Americans, including many of our nation's leaders, who advise a heavy dose of revenge and punishment. To these leaders, I would like to make clear that my family and I take no comfort in your words of rage. If you choose to respond to this incomprehensible brutality by perpetrating violence against other innocent human beings, you may not do so in the name of justice for my husband."[66]

This kind of action occurring between grieving families was not only adversarial but part of sustained movement activity. In fact, it was preliminary to organize for relief and reparations from the U.S. government for the suffering borne by Afghan civilians. On April 7, 2002, Afghan civilians traveled from throughout their country to a conference in the capital, Kabul, in order to report on damage and loss of life. It was also surely theatrical, full of so much human drama that perhaps it would have rivaled the dramatic lines of drama on television that tended to prefer the heroics of U.S. war actions against ever-elusive terrorists.

As a second example, I point to movements under way amid current Israeli incursions into Palestinian territories, especially in the West Bank, in Ramallah, Jenin, Bethlehem, and elsewhere, where Israel continues its illegal occupation, one clearly contrary to international law.[67]

Israel's recent rampaging through refugee camps and cities of the West Bank, a version of its own imperial retaliatory terror, serving back terror severalfold upon Palestinians for the blowback terror suicide bombings of extremist groups. (This retaliatory terror is also a means to consolidate Israel's plans to occupy land that had been legally assigned to the Palestinians.) Israel was a perpetrator of systematic and structural violence against Palestinians long before the recent round of suicide bombings that Israel suffered.[68] The suicide bombings are barbaric and unjustifiable acts, as were the attacks on U.S. soil of September 11. But both are the expected acts of blowback terror that are usually committed by groups that yield to rage and violence under conditions of imperial terror and occupation.[69]

What is needed in order to break the cycling between imperial terror, blowback terror, and then imperial retaliatory terror is a theatric of counterterror, in which there is a marked adversarial organizing against imperial exploitation (here against the Pax Americana–Israelica),[70] but in ways that deploy theatrical nonviolent action. Precisely this, however, has been what the Israeli occupiers have long feared. They have, therefore, moved fiercely to deport, imprison, or kill leaders with the capacity of organizing the kind of nonviolent movements capable of creating moral force and effectiveness for Palestinian justice and flourishing.[71]

Yet the emergence of a genuine theatric of counterterror may be emerging in our time, in spite of Israeli repression of it, and amid the recent reign of terror during the Israeli incursions in the West Bank. Often such efforts have the support of Israeli justice and peace movements within Israel.[72] Toward the end of 2001, a Palestinian, Dr. Mustafa Barghouthi, launched a new nonviolent movement of European activists (around 550) to enter Palestine with Palestinians to orchestrate nonviolent resistance. When he entered Israel, he was apprehended by Israeli authorities and interrogated and beaten, suffering a broken knee from rifle blows and damage to his head.[73]

Nevertheless, hundreds of other nonviolent activists, from Europe, the United States, and elsewhere, have entered Palestinian territories, situating themselves, quite literally at times, between Palestinians and Israeli forces, constituting what is known as the International Solidarity Movement (ISM). In it are such groups as the Christian Peacemaker Teams, the Israeli Committee against Home Demolitions, Bustan Shalom, Haluzay Shalom, and Rabbis for Human Rights. Some international activists have been shot and beaten by Israeli forces at checkpoints and elsewhere.[74] The activists remain, however, working to resist Israeli and U.S. efforts to evacuate them.

One who remained for an extended period, who has received a bit of coverage in the media, and who has taken theatrical action to the global cable networks is Adam Shapiro, a young activist in the ISM who was interviewed several times on CNN and MSNBC. He is Jewish and from the United States, and his parents live in New York, where he hopes to return and marry. His family has received numerous death threats for his principled, nonviolent resistance to Israeli occupation and incursion. His presence, along with the dramatic action of many of the others in ISM, has had catalyzing effect on many of the demonstrations and protests throughout the world, and especially in the Palestinian solidarity movement in the United States. His Jewish background has highlighted also what is often obscured, namely that many Jews within Israel and the United States are uniting with Muslims, Christians, and other persons of conscience to resist the Israeli occupation and deadly incursions.[75] International activists in the West Bank are, at this writing, planning ways to harness some of the energy of the alternative globalization movement's theatric, youth involvement, and global organization for deployment in Palestine on behalf of peace and justice there.[76]

In conclusion, I offer these sites as exemplary of the way of the cross in our time, as sites where a theatric of counterterror is being forged. On these sites, people are weaving together adversarial practice to imperial power, creative nonviolent theater, with organized movement action. These may be the neighborhood New Yorkers remembering their victims from 9–11 *and* marching for peace against the U.S. bombings. They may be the theatrically mobilized supporters of Mumia Abu-Jamal taking on the criminal (in)justice system. They may be the ones who dare to link U.S. families with Afghan civilians in lamentation and protest of U.S. bombings that recycle organized terror. They may be the courageous, nonviolent protestors in the West Bank of Palestine today, laying their lives on the line, resisting both the terror spread by suicide bombings and also the terror of the Pax Americana–Israelica that violates international law and decimates human living.

These all may constitute a beleaguered few, but I submit that they are beacons, marking out the best road forward we have, through the conflicts and wars of organized terror today.

Notes

1. The prisons now constitute an entire industry in the U.S. political order, with expenses of $25 to $35 billion annually and officially employing more than 523,000 people, more than any Fortune 500 company, save General Motors. The number of other citizens affected, beyond the 2 million incarcerated, includes the 1.5 million U.S. children of incarcerated mothers and fathers. See B. Bloom, "Why Punish the Children? A Reappraisal of the Children of Incarcerated Mothers in America," *IARCA Journal* 6 (1993): 14–17. Cf. "The Next Generation: Children of Prisoners" by John Hagan, available at www.doc.state.ok.us/DOCS/OCJRC/Ocjrc9619.htm.

2. Taylor, *The Executed God,* 70–191.

3. This essay was originally penned in February 2002.

4. Failure to distinguish these types of organized terror, institutionalized violence, or orchestrated terror lies behind the difficulties scholars and politicians have in defining "terror" and "terrorism." When one scrutinizes definitions of terrorism in light of all actions of planned violence, often the only trait that sets an al-Qaeda action apart from a U.S. cluster-bombing mission is that the former is done by what the U.S. State Department calls, in its definitions of "terrorism," a "subnational group." See Whittaker, *The Terrorism Reader,* 3, 9. Cf. Crenshaw, *Terrorism in Context,* and Said's comments on the word "terrorism," in Said, *Power, Politics, and Culture,* 331–32.

5. For a summary of the NSA action, and a critique of it, see the American Bar Association memos and resolution at http://www.abanet.org/.

6. Taylor, *The Executed God,* 48–69.

7. The notion of the "imperial" refers to "economic exploitation of other peoples buttressed by military and political domination." See Felix Greene, *The Enemy,* 96. See also Doyle, *Empires;* and Hardt and Negri, *Empire,* 166, 314–16.

8. Thomas L. Friedman, "What the World Needs Now: A Manifesto for the Fast World," *New York Times Magazine,* March 28, 1999.

9. On consequences of the U.S. involvement in the Chilean coup, see Kornbluh, *The Pinochet Files.*

10. Here I follow Johnson, *Blowback,* who argues that organized terror often "blows back" upon the citizens of powerful countries that commit themselves to various "imperialist escapades" like those engaged in by the United States (see esp. 3–33).

11. BBC News, "Afghanistan's Civilian Deaths Mount," January 3, 2002, http://news.bbc.co.uk/1/hi/world/south_asia/1740538.stm.

12. Herrold's figures show 3,767 civilian deaths, just through the date of December 6, 2001. See Marc W. Herrold, "A Dossier on Civilian Victims of U.S. Aerial Bombing of Afghanistan: A Comprehensive Accounting," at www .cursor.org/stories/civilian_deaths.htm. Herrold is a professor of economics at the Whittemore School of Business and Economics, University of New Hampshire.

13. Tracy, *The Analogical Imagination,* 3–31.

14. Tracy might include my discussion of movements within his category within the wider society, which he discusses as "polity" (see 7, 9–11).

15. On the ways that empirical discovery, critical reflection, and judgment march toward and necessarily invoke ideals of moral transformation, the philosophical work of Lonergan is still difficult to transcend. See Lonergan, *Insight.*

16. Tarrow, *Power in Movement,* 4–5.

17. In addition to Tarrow and his own numerous other published studies, see Hilary Wainwright on women's movements in postcommunist Eastern Europe, *Arguments for a New Left;* Tilly, *From Mobilization to Revolution;* Banaszak, *Why Movements Succeed or Fail;* and Melucci, *Challenging Codes: Collective Action in the Information Age.*

18. Parenti, *Lockdown America.*

19. Juergensmeyer, *Terror in the Mind of God,* 5.

20. Geertz, *Negara,* 1980. For Geertz's discussion of an aesthetics or "poetics of power" and the powers of inequality to enchant, see 121–36, esp. 123–24.

21. Gilly, *Chiapas.*

22. Parenti, *Lockdown America,* 135.

23. Donziger, *The Real War on Crime,* 31.

24. Parenti, *Lockdown America,* 184–87; Gilligan, *Violence,* 164ff.

25. Trombley, *The Execution Protocol.*

26. Banner, *The Death Penalty,* 39, 51, 69, 70, 74, 109.

27. Kozol, *Amazing Grace,* 142 (emphasis added).

28. Abu-Jamal, *Live from Death Row,* 65.

29. Mauer, "Developments in the Law."

30. In addition to the sources in note 7 above, see Sabo, Kupers, and London (authors inside and outside of U.S. prisons), *Prison Masculinities.*

31. James S. Liebman, Jeffrey Fagan, and Valerie West, "The Broken System: Error Rates in Capital Cases, 1973–1995," http://www.law.columbia.edu/news/PressReleases/liebman.html.

32. Miller, *Search and Destroy.*

33. Amnesty International, *United States of America,* 87–98.

34. William Shultz, Director of Amnesty International USA, "Director's Statement," http://www.amnestyusa.org/annualreport/statement.html.

35. Tombs, "Crucifixion, State Terror, and Sexual Abuse."

36. Horsley and Silberman, *The Message of the Kingdom,* 145–62.

37. Ibid., 161.

38. Sobrino, *Christology at the Crossroads,* 72.

39. Crossan, *The Birth of Christianity,* 411.

40. By contemporary "Jesus movement research," I am especially thinking of the works by Crossan and Horsley. Horsley has also edited a number of collections by many more scholars throughout biblical studies and Ancient Near Eastern studies. Elisabeth Schüssler Fiorenza's studies (from *Bread Not Stone* and *In Memory of Her,* to the more recent *Miriam's Child, Sophia's Prophet,* and *Jesus and the Politics of Interpretation*) also can be grouped with Crossan and Horsley, as can the work of Paula Fredriksen, author of *Jesus of Nazareth, King of the Jews.* Each of these scholars, whose works sometimes differ markedly from one another, has criticisms of the others' works. From the perspective of theological interpretation of this research, valuable as I take it to be in this essay, there remain two problems: (1) the historians who excel in developing the often-neglected political and imperial meanings of the historical situation of Jesus's life and work and of the texts about him often do not reflect in depth on the ways their own political situatedness relates, for better and worse, to their extraction of political meanings from historical research; and (2) the focus on politics and empire, while a needed and important corrective for theological use of biblical materials, has tended to date to focus on class and gender issues and not those of race and ethnicity. In this regard, these researchers still need to attend more adequately to the Asian and African cultural presences in relation to the context of the Jesus movement and early Christian developments.

41. Fredriksen, *Jesus of Nazareth, King of the Jews,* 233.

42. Horsley and Silberman, *The Message of the Kingdom,* 75, and, for background on the Temple, 75–80.

43. Ibid. 75–76.

44. Horsley, *Jesus and the Spiral of Violence,* 40–42.

45. On "prophetic spirit," see Mark Lewis Taylor, *Religion, Politics, and the Christian Right,* 9–12, 96–109.

46. Various groups struggling on the underside of the U.S. international imperium have used their arts to depict the destruction of major edifices of large

city centers, and even structures like the World Trade Center in the United States. See http://www.truthorfiction.com/rumors/c/coup.htm.

47. Romero, *Voice of the Voiceless*, 144–45; Gandhi, *Gandhi on Non-Violence*, 36.

48. For a list of nonviolent strategies of adversarial resistance, forged in the context of violent repression, see the list in Wink, *Engaging the Powers*, 243–56.

49. Hengel, *Crucifixion*, 6–10.

50. Doyle, *Empires*, 98.

51. Stark, *The Rise of Christianity*, 9.

52. For one summary of the literature on the Temple State, see Myers, *Binding the Strong Man*, 78–87.

53. On the notion of "mimesis," see Auerbach, *Mimesis*.

54. See Daughen and Binzen, *The Cop Who Would Be King*.

55. For the first and most influential of his books, see Abu-Jamal, *Live from Death Row*.

56. For summaries of these strategies, see Mark Lewis Taylor, 147–54.

57. For most recent updates on Abu-Jamal's case, see the Web site titled "Educators for Abu-Jamal," http://www.emajonline.com.

58. See the April 5, 2000, edition of the *Christian Century*, "Call for a New Trial for Mumia Abu-Jamal", 396; and the African Methodist Episcopal denominational publication, the *Christian Recorder*, April 17, 2000, 9. For more examples, see Mark Lewis Taylor, 141–42, 153.

59. See notes 1 and 2, above.

60. For a political theorist's reflections on the logic linking the building of domestic coalitions through force and the carrying off of imperial enterprises abroad, see Doyle, *Empires*.

61. Feitlowitz, *A Lexicon of Terror*, 9–10.

62. Gleijeses, *Conflicting Missions*.

63. Hardt and Negri, *Empire*, 170–71.

64. Often such movements of resistance were much stronger than many knew. Regarding the resistance to the Persian Gulf War inside the United States in 1991, see Zinn, *A People's History of the United States*, 600, 619–29.

65. These two sites were selected for this article in March 2002. Since that time, and throughout the war and occupation of Iraq and the continuing conflict in Israel/Palestine, many other sites might now be considered.

66. Kim Sengupta, "U.S. Jittery about Symbolic Meetings of Grieving Families," *Independent* (UK), January 15, 2002.

67. Particularly violating UN General Assembly Resolutions 181, 194, 3236, and UN Security Council Resolutions 242, 338, 298.

68. For an excellent history, see Farsoun with Zacharia, *Palestine and the Palestinians*.

69. Again, on the notion of "blowback" suffered by imperial powers, here by the Pax Americana–Israelica, see Johnson, note 10 above. More recently, see Paper, *Dying to Win*.

70. One-third of all U.S. military and economic aid goes to the tiny country of Israel. Sixty to 70 percent of all aid to Israel is military in nature. This is just one—perhaps the most dramatic—sign of the linkage between the United States and Israel, which makes the U.S. ability to mediate between Palestine and Israel difficult, if not impossible. See Stephen Green, *Taking Sides*, 250–51.

71. On Israel's efforts to interfere with nonviolent organizing among women and labor union movements, see sociologist Joost R. Hiltermann, *Behind the Intifada*, 104–6, 138–41.

72. Carey and Shainin, *The Other Israel.*

73. Edward Said, "A New Current in Palestine," *Nation*, February 4, 2002.

74. *New York Times*, April 2, 2002. Cover photo and caption.

75. Marc Ellis has been a long-time Jewish ethicist and theologian developing criticism of Zionism and Israeli nationalism and its policies. See Radford Ruether and Ellis, *Beyond Occupation;* and Ellis, *Revolutionary Forgiveness.*

76. Mark LeVine, "Bring the Turtles to Ramallah," *AlterNet*, April 4, 2002. (The reference to "turtles" concerns the costumed sea-turtle marchers who were so memorable as part of the effective alternative globalization march in Seattle in 1999, against the World Trade Organization.)

Critical Response to Mark Lewis Taylor

SARAH COAKLEY

Mark Taylor writes a very powerful and passionate essay, in which he has gone significantly beyond the central themes of his recent book *The Executed God*[1] by bringing the notion of "organized terror" in the American prison system into relation now to other forms of (so-called) "imperial" terror and reactions thereto. In what follows I shall be raising four specific questions about the *advisability* of his particular strategies for critical response to the current prison system in the United States; as I do so, however, I hope it will be clear that I share with utter conviction Taylor's horror at the institutionalized violence and racism of much of America's penal system, and his fervent desire for reform. (Since I have recently served for a brief term as an assistant prison chaplain in the South End of Boston, I have an extremely visceral sense of the accuracy of Taylor's portrayal of the current state of American goals and prisons.) I am also broadly sympathetic—though one might argue about particular explicative and hermeneutical details, as I do briefly below—with the use Taylor makes of recent "historical Jesus" research in his assertion that Jesus's death should be seen as an "execution," a "terrorizing spectacle" utilized by Rome to make a point about threats to the *Pax Romana*.

However, I am much more worried, critically, about the following four issues, with which this response will concern itself: (1) the "tactics" (in Certeau's sense)[2] for reform that Taylor encourages us to adopt, and the sociopolitical categories of analysis that undergird these; (2) a certain lack of *theological* analysis in Taylor's account of the dominant system that he is attacking; (3) the apparent smudging in the course of his essay of the very distinctions between *different* types of "terrorizing" violence that Taylor initially sets up—a smudging that then, in my view, causes the opposite practical effect for his project from that which he intends; and finally (4) a certain *rhetoric* of violence in Taylor's own proposals, which threatens then to infect his own project of "counterterror."

Let me then attend briefly to each of these four issues in turn.

1. A critique of the "tactics" of "theatrics." At the end of his essay, Taylor declares that what he has described "mark[s] out the best road forward we have," that is, the use of the "theatrics" of "counterterror" as an adversarial response to "organized terror." My first point of question here is one somewhat parallel to a justly controversial (and indeed intemperate) critique of the political tactics of Judith Butler by Martha Nussbaum, in her now-notorious 1999 *New Republic* article "The Professor of Parody."[3]. There, Nussbaum chides Butler for her "performative" proposals for the subversion of gender binaries, thus: "For Butler", she writes, "the act of subversion is so riveting, so sexy, that it is a bad dream to think that the world will ever get better. What a bore equality is! No bondage, no delight. In this way [Butler's] pessimistic erotic anthropology offers support to an amoral anarchistic politics."[4] Now clearly the parallels to Mark Taylor's project are far from exact; but I am bound to ask Taylor whether the very "act of subversion" is equally "riveting" for him? And if so, does it tend to divert attention from the fact that such minor "theatric" explosions, such performative acts of resistance on the edges of dominant society, are highly likely (or so I fear) to *leave everything as it is?* In other words, does Taylor's pessimism about the "system" actually assume its continued maintenance?

Another way of stating this first problem is to look more closely at the sociological theory that may be sustaining it. If we go back to the founders of modern sociological theory, Weber and Troeltsch, we note that for them sectarian "movements" always initially define their identity precisely as "oppositional"; for them to move in turn into positions of authority and dominance, complex changes have to occur in their sense of consciousness and purpose. I am bound to ask Taylor, then, how— beyond the immediate delightful *frisson* of subversion—the "movement" against organized terror can hope to gain political ground and itself assume dominance? What are Taylor's plans for such a transformation? A book like Christian Smith's *Disruptive Religion*,[5] which I am somewhat surprised that Taylor does not cite, tells a complex story in this regard. Not every religious/sectarian "movement" is successful in its political goals (least of all, one suspects, if only "theatrics" are involved); but if a "movement" is successful, it has to undergo extraordinary changes if it is to sustain its distinctive momentum and not become negatively bureaucratized and corrupted when it does achieve power. Thus, if it does come by power through legitimate democratic means, it must still then face the new challenge of envisaging its own different future as a now-dominant force in society. One thinks here, on the one hand, of the subversive religious "movements" in the former (Communist) "East Germany," which did indeed involve ritual activity (candlelit vigils in the Nicolaikirche in Leipzig, for instance), but which were also sustained by hard-nosed political planning that ultimately proved effective; one thinks, in contrast, of the fate of Solidarity in Poland, once so sterling a religious resistance movement, now having somehow lost its impetus once catapulted into a situation of democracy.

I am not myself a political scientist by training, but rather a theologian profoundly influenced by the work of Ernst Troeltsch;[6] and it is precisely this training and influence that make me aware of the correlations and alignments that tend to adhere between particular theological "tactics" or "strategies" and particular sociopolitical circumstances. Thus, when such circumstances change (as the above example proves that they can, even "miraculously"), new theological and political visions have to be ready to meet such an era of "success." The mere sloganizing of "No more prisons," I submit, does not provide a sufficient vision for such a potentially changed political environment. In short, we need to hear not only of the immediate "theatrics" of subversion but of a long-term vision of societal and political change, beyond the delicious subversions of a sectarian revolt. To this task, then, I challenge Mark Taylor.

2. My second point is more explicitly theological. At the start of Taylor's chapter we are told that "being a Christian means participating in creative, popular movements against organized terror." That, of course, is Taylor's interpretation of "Christianity," though it is admittedly the perspective of "the beleaguered few," as he puts it toward the end of his essay. But this analysis markedly does not proffer an explanation of why the dominant "Christian" culture of this country not only accepts a prison—and police—system of systemic violence but actively defends it. As a fellow theologian, then, I invite Taylor to hazard an explanation for this profound riddle; for without an answer to it, I doubt whether we can begin to effect the sort of social and political transformation we both desire. Let me at this point present a speculative hypothesis.

As an English person, I constantly reflect on an interesting (sociological) paradox: that the more "secularized" Northern Europe has become, and the more alienated from its state churches (where such exist), the less it has thirsted for the death penalty. In contrast, in North America, famously "religious" in its commitments, the death penalty is in many states not only tolerated but actively supported. What then is the ostensibly uniting spiritual heritage of North America that makes punitive violence not only so acceptable but even coherently intrinsic to a whole theological outlook? Generalizations here are doubtless crass; but since the modern prison system that we have inherited was—as we hear elsewhere in this volume—itself founded in theological reflections on punishment and atonement, it is worth pushing this theological question to the fore. And my tentative hypothesis here is that an excerpted misreading of Calvin might be at least partly to blame, a form of Calvinism in which the crucial (and unrepeatable) atoning effectiveness of Christ's penal substitution (discussed with rich depth in book 2 of *The Institutes*) has somehow become overshadowed by the more general picture of the threat of divine wrath in book 1. Is this a debased, "Christless" Calvinism that we are up against, which somehow misses the profound reversals of chapters 15–16 of book 2 of *The Institutes,* where Christ "takes away all cause of enmity" and wipes out all "need for further punishment"? Or is it a reading of this section that retains the idea of the "expediency" of undergoing "the severity of God's vengeance," yet seeks to fill up the sufferings of Christ (itself a Pauline theme, of course) with ever-more instantiations of punishment?[7] To clarify these questions theologically would require a painstaking analysis of the rhetoric of contemporary American religious defenses of capital punishment, and especially of the implicit reading of Calvin (and Paul) within them. But it seems to me that Taylor's position as a theologian would be greatly strengthened if he could attempt such an analysis, and at the same time indicate what, for him, is achieved *once-and-for-all* by Jesus's ordeal and death at the hands of Roman imperial power. Otherwise, again, we leave the dominant (religious) culture *as it is.* What then is Taylor's own analysis of the theological pathology of the American political scene he criticizes, and can his own alternative go beyond a mere victimology?

3. My third point is closely correlated to this second one. It is part of Taylor's rhetorical ploy in his essay to shock us a little by resmudging the

initial distinctions he makes between "organized terror," "imperial terror," "blowback counterterror," and "imperial retaliatory terror"; as far as the victims are concerned, Taylor avers, it makes little difference which of these forms of terror is in operation. But in seeking to disturb us by such "resmudging," I think Taylor makes a strategic mistake of some seriousness, which draws our attention away from a deeper pathology that needs addressing. For the really "obscene" dimension of the organized terror of the lockdown system in this country, in my view, is its invisibility, its wholly successful and complacent commodification of an "industry" of systemic racism, sexism, and violence to which white American citizens implicitly and mutely give their assent. To lift the lid on this system is to expose not just a soft underbelly but an underground sewer. My suggestion here to Taylor, then, is that—*pace* his point about victims' similar responses to "terror" wherever they find themselves (as if all "terror" were equally morally culpable)—Taylor needs more urgently to concentrate on the miraculous invisibility of the lockdown system, and thus the utter difference of this form of "terror" from others known to us. For while no one living in New York could have failed to notice the public "terror" events of 9/11, a marked majority of New Yorkers (or indeed of "respectable" Americans, *tout court*) apparently operate with little consciousness of the prison system that empties significant proportions of its minority populations into incarceration at any one time. In my second point, I have urged Taylor as a theologian to give some explication of the spirituality that sustains such a system; now I am inquiring: what are the other factors—cultural, social, political, anthropological—that collude to safeguard this "secret" status quo? While "the system" just remains as the undifferentiated and unexamined "enemy," can one hope that it be dislodged?

4. My fourth, and last, point raises a problem about keeping "peaceful" responses to violence peaceful, especially when couched in a verbal rhetoric that itself suggests the opposite. Here I worry—as I do similarly also over the work of John Milbank, a theologian at a very different end of the theological spectrum from Taylor[8]—that the politics of peace should be announced with the language of violence. Perhaps there is not explicit violence as such in what Taylor writes; but there is certainly the language of forceful resistance ("adversarial" theatrics), that can so easily tip over in to a *mimesis* of that which it holds up for mockery. A case from the life of Jesus—and here I part company from a particular piece of exegesis in

Taylor's account that may be significant—may help to focus this point both symbolically and christologically.

For the synoptic account of the triumphal entry of Jesus into Jerusalem (Mark 11:1–10 and pars.), Jesus is indeed engaged in conscious "theatrics," planning ahead as a form of peaceful demonstration inspired by Zechariah 9.9, and then "acting out" in the temple (Mark 11:15), as Taylor might put it; but for the Johannine account (John 12:12–19) the story is interestingly different in tone and instigation—and seemingly reflects a different strand of tradition behind it. Here the so-called "triumphal entry" is not something planned and intentionally "acted out" by Jesus at all;[9] nor is it connected with the 'cleansing of the temple' that is placed much earlier in John (John 2:12–22). Rather, the entry is an event that is instigated by an excited crowd, unfolds spontaneously, and rapidly gets out of hand; here, the exuberance of the crowd results in actions and events well capable of construal as a will to violent insurrection. So, similarly, in John 6, as the end of the feeding of the five thousand, the Johannine author adds that Jesus fled to the hills, "seeing that they were coming to make him king" (John 6:15); again, an event intended as peaceful excited the expectation of messianic rebellion. I mention this Johannine strand of reflection not only because I myself am persuaded it may have some basis in the facts of Jesus's life,[10] but because it well illustrates my point of worry with Taylor, that of the difficulty of constraining a "subversive" "theatric" movement such as he envisages within ordered and necessarily peaceful confines. The recent antiglobalization demonstrations are a worrying case in point, although notably Taylor does not comment on their record of violence.

I thus ask Taylor in closing: what are his proposals for maintaining a politics of peace in resistance to organized violence? He cites Gandhi; but is his own proposal for "acting up" in any way akin to Gandhi's theory of *ahimsa?* To be so akin, there would have to be spiritual disciplines for this movement, repeated practices aimed at the inculcation of the costly maintenance of nonviolence. And thus I am bound to ask: can "acting up," as such, provide such a demanding asceticism of disciplined resistance?

To sum up: I have raised, first, some questions about the long-term effectiveness of the "theatrics" tactic, and inquired of Taylor about the social and political theory for change that accompanies it. Second, I have called for a thoroughgoing analysis of the (sometimes covert) theological arguments of a "Christian" culture that maintains, and sometimes benefits from, a prison system of "organized terror." Third, I have called into question the wisdom of blurring the distinctions between different sorts of "terrorization"; instead, I have urged the critical exposé of the quiescent acceptance of the form of "terror" hidden in our midst (the prison system), for this is significantly different from other forms of "terror" in virtue of its "invisibility." And finally, fourth, I have inquired about the difficulties of sustaining a "peace"-seeking movement in which rhetoric often slips toward the violent, and in which followers may easily be caught up—in the heat of the "theatrics" to which Taylor enjoins us—into activities of violence ironically imitative of that which is denounced. What are the moral and ascetic guards against such a danger?

These questions notwithstanding, I thank Mark Taylor again for a challenging, suggestive, and (above all) provocative essay.

Notes

1. Taylor, *The Executed God.*
2. See Certeau, *The Practice of Everyday Life,* 34–39; here Certeau distinguishes between a "tactic," which is an "art of the weak," a form of surprise "*legerdemain*" (37), and a "strategy," which is "the calculation—of power relationship that becomes possible as soon as a subject with will and power—can be isolated" (35–36).
3. Nussbaum, "The Professor of Parody."
4. Ibid., 44.
5. Smith, *Disruptive Religion.*
6. The strong influence of Troeltsch's *Soziallehren* can be seen in my first book, *Christ without Absolutes.* I take some trouble there to dispel the oft-repeated critique that Troeltsch's use of social "typology" is necessarily a religiously reductive tool of analysis.
7. Calvin, *The Institutes of the Christian Religion,* vol. 1, bk. 2, 15–16, 494–528.
8. See my brief comments on Milbank's important *Theology and Social Theory* in my *Powers and Submissions,* xx.
9. Here I take John 12:14b-15 as a *vaticinium ex eventu,* as verse 16 itself acknowledges (from the disciples' perspective).
10. I must admit here to being affected by domestic theological discussion: for this line on the possible historical significance of the Johannine reading of the "triumphal entry," see Coakley, "Jesus's Messianic Entry into Jerusalem: Jn 12.12–19 par."

Criminal Justice and
Responsible Mercy

WILLIAM SCHWEIKER

Introduction

The American public is increasingly aware of problems in the United States criminal justice system as well as the massive social ills—poverty, racism, abuse—that motivate and yet are concealed by the system. More and more individuals, especially young men from ethnic and racial minorities, populate the prison system. In 1999, 1.5 million children in the United States had at least one parent in prison. What is more, even those who complete their sentences are marked for life: background checks, employment problems, family difficulties, and the like. Cities and states continue to build prisons in the hope of stemming crime, but also of vitalizing their economies. Businesses, like telephone companies, enter the prison system as a new market. Private prisons, poor conditions in many complexes, and economic failure also stalk the criminal justice system. Politicians and a range of social agencies labor to address the spread of crime and violence among us. Yet the politicization of the problem rarely lessens the increasing criminalization of our society and, in fact, often aids it. In sum, the American criminal justice system is characterized by stiff sentencing, the spread of criminalization through initiatives like the "war on drugs," and the manifest inequalities in the prison population, where it seems that we have one system for whites and one for the rest.

All of this is well known. Thankfully, there are voices of criticism and change, especially coming from poor, ethnic, and racial communities. Moreover, the troubling facts of the criminal justice system have provoked renewed reflection on justice and mercy. This is part of a wider global movement in political thinking. For much of Western thought, the theme of reconciliation, especially in the form of mercy or forgiveness, was outside of politics; it was seen as a suprapolitical human act best spoken about in religious and moral terms. Yet things began to change with the twentieth century and its horrible violence and suffering.[1] Theologians, religious thinkers, philosophers, and political theorists started to reconsider the place of mercy in debates about justice. War crimes tribunals, the United Nations, commissions on truth and reconciliation in South Africa and elsewhere, and the World Council of Churches heighten the awareness that suffering and conflict must be addressed in new ways.

Some years ago the philosopher Hannah Arendt offered a basic insight about forgiveness and justice as political and not religious acts. Arendt argued that forgiveness, which she defined as the ability to begin anew after ruinous human action, is basic to politics. She even insisted that the "discoverer of the role of forgiveness in the realm of human affairs was Jesus of Nazareth."[2] Of course, Arendt quickly acknowledged that acts of forgiveness, the sparing of the vanquished, and even the right to commute a death sentence are found in other traditions, say, among the ancient Romans. The biblical message, she insisted, is unique in that the power to forgive is a "human power" in which God forgives those who show mercy (cf. the Lord's Prayer). Arendt understood this discovery in purely philosophical and political terms and thus without reference to the divine. Yet she was not the only one to insist on the importance of reconciliation in politics. The great movements of liberation in the twentieth century inspired by Gandhi, Martin Luther King Jr., and Nelson Mandela insisted on reconciliation as a political act. Perhaps we must think about social life differently in light of the realities confronting people around the world.

In what follows, I want to explore these matters of justice and mercy with respect to matters of criminal justice from the perspective of work in Christian theological ethics. I intend to do so mindful of the wider, global debate about the relation between justice and reconciliation in political existence. Let me begin by clarifying the central claim and direction of my argument.

What Will Be Argued and How

My intention in what follows is to develop a conception of mercy, what I call "responsible mercy," in relation to the demands of justice. I will do so by drawing on the resources of one specific religious tradition, realizing that other arguments could and should be made out of other traditions. It might immediately be thought that drawing on the resources of one

WILLIAM SCHWEIKER

religious tradition in order to make general, public arguments about justice and mercy in political life is a logical as well as social impossibility. Is it not the case, someone might ask, that religious claims are irreducibly private, and, furthermore, do not admit of public assessment about their moral and political veracity? Most contemporary social and political thinkers working with highly differentiated, democratic, and pluralistic societies believe that religious claims have no rightful place in public debate.[3] That judgment, it seems to me, confuses two things that ought to be held logically distinct, namely, the question of the *sources* of one's argument as distinct from the question of how an argument is validated or shown to be true.

On my understanding, every thinker, as a time-bound creature, draws on the *sources* of some religious or cultural or philosophical tradition in making arguments. Yet the fact that one necessarily deploys ideas and concepts drawn from some *source* does not ensure the validity of an argument. Establishing the truth or validity of an argument is another matter. It requires showing within the rough and tumble of public debate that an argument is more comprehensive, coherent, and illuminative or error-reducing than its actual rivals.[4] In other words, the fact that a theologian draws on the sources of a tradition in her or his moral thought is just what we would expect from any thinker. A challenge to the very idea of open, public debate enters if the theologian insists, as some in fact do, that her or his tradition is self-validating in its claims about social existence. By self-validating I mean those arguments that claim that a religious text or idea in and for itself constitutes the necessary and sufficient condition(s) for its validity, say, in certain claims about revealed truths or the command of God. For these kinds of theological and religious positions to ask about the truth-conditions of a religious claim is simply to ask about the meaning of those claims. Any other supposed necessary or sufficient binding conditions—say, the rough and tumble of public debate or coherence with other ways of knowing—do not per definition pertain since the very meaning of the claim specifies its truth.[5] That a theologian or anyone else must in fact insist on the self-validating character of a tradition's public claims in order to remain within that tradition is a judgment that I find no compelling philosophical or theological reason to adopt.[6]

Theological ethics, as I conceive it, seeks to provide guidance for human life and conduct armed with a variety of resources, including those of a specific religious tradition's moral wisdom and insights (in my case, the Christian tradition). However, the theological ethicist does not speak only to fellow believers. The claim—a claim that must be validated in actual argument—is that a tradition's resources can shed light upon and provide guidance for anyone seeking to live responsibly. This is to insist that religious sources—say, the symbols, beliefs, narratives, and practices of the Christian tradition—speak not only about a certain faith but also address widely shared human concerns and problems, like the complex and confusing relation between justice and mercy. The same could be said about other great religious traditions. That is why we can rightly speak of Jewish or Buddhist or Christian moral philosophy. It is another matter, and one I will not address in this essay, to explore the internal life and self-understanding of the religious community. My intention is to make a specific case for mercy in relation to justice rooted in the Christian, biblical, and philosophical traditions. However, the kind of argument I forward, while it draws on those religious sources, is intended to be a version of Christian moral philosophy, a theological ethics, and so it is engaged in a fully public argument about the validity of its claims.[7]

In order to advance the idea of responsible mercy, we need to acknowledge the sources of reflection and the criterion of validity but also reach some conceptual clarity. Specifically, one needs some distinctions too often overlooked in the present worldwide discussion about justice and political reconciliation.[8] Clemency, or commuting sentences, must be distinguished from mercy, that is, forbearance by one in power despite a lack of a (justified) claim to kindness, a forbearance that may (or may not) involve commuting actual punishment. Clemency and mercy should also not be viewed as synonymous with forgiveness. Forgiveness entails specific subjective conditions on the part of the one granting forgiveness (say, a willingness to identify with the wrongdoer) in ways missing from mercy or clemency properly defined. One can easily imagine how an individual might forgive another and yet deny clemency; an act of mercy might or might not entail forgiveness. Generally speaking, Christians must practice mercy and forgiveness. That is the case because mercy and forgiveness are bound one to the other in a Christian conception of love.[9] For the sake of this argument, I want to forego any exploration of "forgiveness" in its proper sense and concentrate instead on the political question of the relation of justice and mercy.

Like many other thinkers, I believe that mercy cannot violate justice. Like them I also do not believe that acts of mercy are understandable only in terms of subjective feelings or instances of discretionary judgment. That is, again, to confuse mercy with forgiveness and clemency, respectively. Yet while philosophical and political theorists have helpfully distinguished mercy from forgiveness and clemency, what remains lacking is a clear and robust account of the political meaning of mercy. This essay is an initial attempt at providing such an account. The idea I seek to elucidate and sustain is that acts of mercy enact or disclose the necessary, if not sufficient, condition of any system of justice and yet a condition that cannot be created or ensured by that system itself, namely, that human beings bear intrinsic worth.[10] Acts of mercy have disclosive power. As a phenomenon, what an act of mercy makes manifest, what it lets appear, is the worth of persons as the object of justice. In this sense, mercy is a necessary precondition for any account of justice. Mercy is a human analogue to the divine act of creation; it makes possible claims of justice.[11] The importance of this attribute of an act of mercy cannot be doubted. A system of justice must presuppose human worth and seek to respect and enhance it; the system cannot create the worth of persons. Doing justice to mercy is thereby to grasp this complex connection between the appearance of human worth and that social system designed to protect and promote human purposes, namely a system of justice.

What I will call "responsible mercy" is, then, nonnecessitated action, a forbearance, that enacts or discloses the worth of persons within a system of justice when that system has gone awry and threatens to eradicate or efface human worth. Responsible mercy might be marked by certain feelings of solidarity, sympathy, and empathy; it may, that is, be marked by forgiveness. Yet those feelings do not capture the real meaning and force of the action. Likewise, responsible mercy may be displayed in discretionary judgments of clemency, but it need not since it is quite imaginable that in a specific legal case such a judgment could demean or destroy a recognition of human worth and undermine real justice. And, finally, an act of responsible mercy cannot violate justice since it enacts the distinctly human good that any system of justice is designed to protect and promote. Now, I tend to think that this account of responsible mercy arises from but is not limited to the insights of the biblical religions. It probably finds analogous sources in claims about compassion or self-sacrifice within other great religious and moral traditions.[12] My task is to sort through these claims within Christian and also Western discourse and show their continued importance for political existence.

How then to proceed in order to make my case for responsible mercy? The rest of this essay will move in three broad steps. First, I will isolate the deepest conundrum we face on the question of doing justice to mercy and also note the unique causality of some kinds of human actions. These ideas—one about the context of human social action and the other about the power of some human acts—form the conceptual framework for developing the idea of responsible mercy. Second, I isolate briefly three basic types of responses to this human conundrum, including the present criminal justice system in the United States. Here my argument is diagnostic. I want to grasp the options in the debate about justice and mercy. In order to do so, I develop a typology of positions, and that will require a very brief statement of how and why one carries out typological analysis. The typology specifies a range of positions in relation to which my account of responsible mercy must demonstrate its truth. In this respect, the typology not only clarifies the shape of the current debate about justice and mercy. It also denotes the public truth conditions for my argument. Finally, I advance thoughts about "responsible mercy" as an idea needed to face the deepest conundrum of social life in a realistic way.

On Human Wretchedness

Theologians and philosophers throughout the ages have noted that justice, including retributive justice, and mercy cross and meet in the core of moral experience and the interworking of social systems.[13] This is why, for instance, justice and mercy can be seen as human virtues, excellencies of character, but also as predicates of a fair, that is, just, social system or merciful kinds of actions within social relations, say, acts of clemency. In the Christian tradition, the very being of God has been understood to spin around these ideas. The living God is a God of covenantal fidelity and justice, a God of righteousness (*tsedeq*). Yet God is also the God of steadfast love and mercy (*chesed*). And this means, as the theologian Paul Ramsey once noted, that theologically considered "[j]ustice (*mishpat*) means what we today call justice permeated by the character of God's righteousness (*tsedeq*)."[14] Mercy in the domain of human affairs must also be understood with reference to the divine. In other words, the connection between excellence of character and predicates of political action is rooted, theologically speaking, in divine being and action.

Of course, honesty is required here. Ambiguity abounds in claims

WILLIAM SCHWEIKER

about the divine within the Christian and Jewish scriptures. It hardly seems obvious that the God of the Bible always acts by common standards of virtue! That ambiguity found in Holy Writ about divine action has driven theological reflection on the being of God. If we take instances of divine mercy and wrath found in the book of Genesis, the cosmogonic myth of the Bible, we see that God shows mercy on Cain for the act of murder by banishing him but not taking his life, and, yet, God's wrath is evoked by human injustice bringing about the great flood and the destruction of all life on earth. Moreover, God liberates and defends Israel in acts of justice and mercy.[15] The question of the relation between God's justice and God's mercy has also been basic in much Christian thought. This is because, on some accounts, Christianity can best be characterized as a religion of love. The cross and resurrection of Christ, the proclamation of God's free grace for all, and the insistence that all human beings are created in the image of God are defining features of the Christian tradition. Accordingly, the drive of Christian thought, begun in the letters of St. Paul, is to see God's righteousness as itself God's mercy. Christian existence is nothing else if not lived between cross and resurrection, woe and joy, humility and exaltation, and, what is more, lived in love for the sake of others. In other words, Christian existence is defined by those actions and relations that respect and enhance the integrity of life before God. It does not overcome, but rather renders productive, fundamental tensions in existence. This vision of Christian faith and life is not a rejection of political existence but a way of political existence.

Of course one can hardly claim that Christians have consistently ordered social life by the norms of justice and mercy. The legacies of hatred and violence that characterize too much Christian history are well known. The point here is a conceptual one. The whole texture of Christian thought could be written from the perspective of the debates about and formulations of the relation of God's justice and God's mercy in the very being of God. And the whole of Christian morals can be seen to revolve around the relation of justice and mercy. Writing that history about Christian ideas of the divine is not my task in this essay, let alone guarding against the problems that arise in religious life when ideas like "justice" and "mercy" become leading abstractions that actually blind us to the complexity of life.[16] At issue is the terrain of questions demarcated by the relation of justice and mercy: (1) primal moral experiences, (2) the functioning of social systems and human excellencies (virtues), and

(3) basic ideas about the divine. As stated, my intention is to focus on social relations and human, as opposed to divine, capacities. This is an essay in Christian *moral philosophy;* religious claims are factored in and through the strictures of moral argumentation.

I can now clarify the focus of my position by citing a passage from St. Augustine's *City of God,* even though at many points my argument is decidedly non-Augustinian. In the famous book 19, Augustine, reflecting the complexity of human judgments about innocence and punishment, notes this:

> ignorance is unavoidable—and yet the exigencies of human society make judgment also unavoidable. Here we have what I call the wretchedness of man's situation. . . . How much more mature reflection it shows, how much more worthy of a human being it is when a man acknowledges this necessity as a mark of human wretchedness, when he hates that necessity in his own action and when, if he has the wisdom of devotion, he cries out to God, "Deliver me from my necessities." [17]

Human wretchedness—to use this powerful but no doubt unfashionable term—is that our lives are always marked by ignorance and yet also by the necessity to make judgments. It is this particular kind of "necessity" basic to practical existence that is at the core of the argument to follow. I contend, again, that the purpose of the moral life is not somehow to overcome tensions that permeate existence but to render them productive rather than destructive. The necessity of existence, we must note, is not the denial of freedom. It is, rather, a claim about how human freedom is encumbered by the fact of human finitude and the pressures of real choice. The necessity is apprehended as "wretched" when it becomes clear that human beings long to escape the ignorance and limitations that mark finitude and to flee the burden of judgment and yet can never do so.

Two distinct but related issues about justice and mercy flow from this ineradicable necessity of human judgment: one is about social cohesion; the other issue is about how to understand and respond rightly to our plight. I cannot deal with the political question of social cohesion in detail. Suffice it to say that insofar as social life is always marked by the kind of wretchedness Augustine isolates, then any society is open to disintegration when it cannot secure social coherence in spite of the failures of justice that are bound to transpire. Societies enforce coherence, we know too well, in a variety of ways, ranging from outright tyranny and terror to enlisting common consent in and through ideological, economic, religious, and other means. In this light, the criminal justice system (its aspirations and horrid abuses) is one response to the problem of social cohesion, a very ambiguous response indeed. The system seeks to secure social harmony but often in ways that require the punitive use of threat and even terror.[18]

The second issue about justice and mercy that flows from the wretchedness of the human lot has to do with moral responsibility. Any judgment we make will always be open to the possibility of fault; yet to avoid judgment in human affairs is to invite not only chaos or the loss of social cohesion but also injustice. The wretchedness of our condition is the twofold unavoidability of ignorance and judging, the unique form of "necessity," as Augustine put it, of social existence. Acknowledging this *necessity* does not mean accepting the status quo. There must be a relentless push to minimize ignorance and also to minimize the need for punitive judgments. But making this acknowledgment of necessity does require a certain realism and humility in thinking about social life.

Justice and mercy, on this account, are complex and necessarily related responses to human wretchedness. Justice is demanded insofar as judgment is unavoidable, and our judgments, if they are to have any validity in the political domain, must be just—that is, manifest a fundamental commitment of fairness and equality to treat similar cases alike. However, justice must always be tempered by mercy because we can never judge infallibly, individual cases may call for unique responses, we can never know the full consequences of any action, and the victim may—in an act of grace—forgive.[19] Only God, according to Augustine's reasoning, escapes wretchedness because only God weds infinite knowledge with perfect judgment in absolute freedom. This too is a paradox. The Christian must consent to the divine judgment as merciful and just even when it does not appear so from our limited perspective. The idea of election was developed by Augustine and other theologians to address this paradox, an idea that no longer is persuasive to many people. The point, however, was that divine mercy and forgiveness transcend our capacity for knowledge. Our human lot is wretched, in this sense.

One last observation is needed about Augustine's depiction of human wretchedness. His account is open to contrary evaluations. For some thinkers and movements, the plight of our condition leads to moral cynicism and the assumption that, in the end, human life is just a war of competing powers, all sound and fury. One sees this in thinkers as diverse as Hobbes, Schopenhauer, and modern advocates of Realpolitik. For others, it is possible for some people some of the time to escape this necessity of human life and to present an alternative to human wretchedness. Some Christian particularists and revolutionary Marxists have made these astonishing claims.[20] I tend to think that we need a frank realism about our plight, including confronting the kinds of deception and destruction too often found in social existence, while having a radical affirmation of goodness and good people. Human actions and relations always take place somewhere, in some *context*. Augustine's claim about wretchedness is most fundamentally a specification of an unavoidable feature of the *context* of social existence.

Importantly, what is left out of Augustine's analysis is a claim about the efficacy or power of some human actions as another basic feature of social existence. The actions enable one to attenuate the grip of necessity on human existence by disclosing the goodness, the worth, of human existence. The insight was partly caught by Arendt and her ideas about new beginnings. More recently the Polish poet and essayist Czeslaw Milosz has made the point in ways helpful to the present argument. He writes: "Evil grows and bears fruit, which is understandable, because it has logic and probability on its side, and also, of course, strength. The resistance of tiny kernels of good, which no one grants the power of causing far-reaching consequences, is entirely mysterious, however . . . human beings have a role in something like what could be called superterrestrial causality, and thanks to it they are, potentially, miracle workers."[21] Some human actions can break legacies of hatred and retribution and thereby reestablish social bonds. This mysterious power of (some) human action factors in my reflections on responsible mercy. Stated otherwise, I intend to advance a conception of responsible mercy that is at one and the same time marked by an Augustinian realism about human wretchedness and also a Miloszian activism and humanism concerned with the power of some human actions.[22] This is merely to acknowledge that any account of human political realities entails claims about the moral space of life, that is, the *context* of existence that sustains but limits human purposes, and also some specification of the capacity or *power* of human beings as agents.

Importantly, conceptions of justice and mercy as well as the many positions for relating or radically separating them are different ways to respond to human "wretchedness," the necessity that constrains social life.

WILLIAM SCHWEIKER

For diagnostic purposes, I can isolate three main kinds of responses on this matter. My idea of responsible mercy must not only be realistic about social necessity and specify the power of human acts of mercy, but it must also account for these positions while avoiding their problems. Only in this way can I establish the validity of this argument.

Responses to Wretchedness

I now turn to the second step of these reflections and in doing so isolate some accounts of mercy and justice in light of the necessity that bedevils human social life. I will explore these options, what I call (1) the classical realist, (2) the amelioristic, and, finally, (3) emancipatory positions. Some of the insights of these options will inform my own reflections. This part of my argument is typological. For heuristic purposes, I want to isolate the main "types" of responses to human wretchedness in terms of justice and mercy.

A cautionary note is in order. Everyone who deploys typologies admits their limitation. One is isolating logical options and not providing a detailed analysis of any one position. The theologian Paul Tillich once noted that developing types "is always a dubious enterprise. Types are logical ideals for the sake of discerning understanding; they do not exist in time and space, and in reality we find only a mixture of types in every particular example."[23] Not only does typological thinking seem to rigidify or to freeze each position into a "static" rather than dynamic reality, but it also gives the illusion of clarity in a very complex and messy world. Further, every typology is conceived from some standpoint and so necessarily isolates logical options with respect to the perspective of the thinker developing the typology. If one is not careful, typological schemes become self-justifying. Finally, a typology, as a form of dialectical thinking, can be construed not as a means to retain the tensions between positions, but—as in the case of (say) Hegel or Marx—as enacting a logical progression to a nontensive, comprehensive synthesis of every position. One needs to be mindful of these limitations in typological thinking.

Now, I have already admitted the standpoint of my argument, namely, it draws on the *sources* of Christian thought. However, I have anticipated the problems of typological reflection by insisting that a *source* of reflection does not validate claims. By isolating the necessity, the wretchedness, of the human condition, I also denied the possibility of providing an all-encompassing synthesis of positions. In fact, part of my argument is that we cannot escape the tension between ignorance and judgment in political reflection. My claim above about the aim of the moral life as rendering productive tensions in existence rather than trying to overcome them is mirrored, methodologically, in the insistence now that a typology cannot somehow give us a once-for-all synthesis of all positions. In this way, typological thinking is of a piece with my substantive argument about justice and mercy in the face of human wretchedness.

With these reservations about typological thinking in mind, recall that this typology, as all typologies, serves heuristic purposes. Hopefully, the one sketched here will help to clarify the terrain of reflection about the relation of justice and mercy in social existence. Reaching clarity about the range of positions is, after all, a virtue for constructive thinking.

CLASSICAL REALIST POSITIONS

Reflection in light of the "necessity" of social existence characterizes a certain strand of Christian and philosophical political thought. The first type of response I will call the *classical realist position*. Some thinkers in the Christian tradition have been realistic about the demands on human social and political existence so that the weak and the innocent and the vulnerable might be protected. Martin Luther supposedly stated that while in the Kingdom of God the lion and the lamb lay down together, in this world if the lion and the lamb lay together the lamb must be repeatedly replaced.[24] In other words, we ought not to flinch at the realities of power in the name of mercy. The warrant for this stance is strictly theological. Partly by reference to Romans 13:4, realists claim the state has the right to use retributive justice. The deeper assumption, one voiced by Luther and many others, is that the state, or civil authority, exists in order that people may have security in their lives and their property. As the Protestant Reformers put it, the purpose of civil authority is to promote peace and restrain wickedness.[25] In a world of human sin, coercive force is often needed and even the threat of such force works as a sanction for abiding by the law. Mercy is therefore an extra- or suprapolitical reality.

There is a long legacy of "secular" theories of civil authority that make the same point. They too are versions of what I am calling the *classical realist position*. Hobbes, for instance, while denying a Christian conception of sin presupposed by Augustine and others, insisted that the state, the

WILLIAM SCHWEIKER

Leviathan, arises as a rational means to stop the war of each against each that defines the state of nature. The Leviathan holds the power needed to ensure some measure of peace and protection of life and property.[26] For these theories—theological and nontheological—it is the fact of human wretchedness, the necessities of social existence or the reality of sin, which constrain the use of mercy in acts of justice. Beliefs about forgiveness ought not trump or weaken a proper realism about political existence. Again as Luther would put it, one should never try to rule the "world" with the Gospel of Love. That realism is rooted in an acknowledgment of the "necessity" of social existence or the reality of sin, giving rise to the wretchedness of our condition. The twist from a Christian perspective is that one's political realism and insistence on love travel together in order that the innocent, the weak, and the oppressed might yet flourish. Out of Christian love, one may need to dispense justice in strict, speedy, and even lethal ways.[27]

Of course, it may be possible to show clemency in the execution of justice—say, in sentencing or actual punishment—but that cannot trump justice as a rightful response to the wretchedness of the human lot. As Reinhold Niebuhr, a Christian realist, famously put it, the individual person can be moral, in the sense of transcending brute self-interest, in the way a community cannot. The Law of Love is the transcendent but never attainable norm of justice.[28] Our wretchedness is inescapable and therefore we must seek to fashion institutions that protect the innocent and the weak even from our own best, if too often erroneous and self-serving, intentions. The demand of justice, stated otherwise, must always stand under the critical judgment of the ideals of mercy and love. Justice can at best approximate those ideals. The constant demand and possibility of moral and political existence is to labor toward ever and ever closer approximations of ideals.

THE AMELIORISTIC OUTLOOK

The second type of position on the relation of justice and mercy in the face of human wretchedness is *amelioristic* or, in more popular jargon, pragmatic. This type is most readily seen in the current U.S. criminal justice system. A main feature of the system, it seems to me, is a pervasive unwillingness to confront human wretchedness as a fact that cannot be eliminated. One sees in our current situation various attempts to address the horns of the dilemma by overcoming ignorance and also clarifying judgments thereby to eradicate our wretchedness. The deep background to this type of position is probably the great English Utilitarians, like Jeremy Bentham, and their attempt to reform society under the greatest happiness principle (the principle of utility). The assumption is that reform will naturally follow once we clarify the right principle of social concord, shape human affections to strive for that good, and apply rigorous technical reasoning to social problems, especially, for Bentham, the reform of the prison system.[29] Even the idea of the "panopticon," a prison built with a tower for the constant observance of the "criminal," while rightly criticized in our day, was believed by Bentham to be a humane advance in criminology.[30] This type of response is the exact opposite of the classical realist position. Attempts to lessen the necessity of social existence are of course important and should in fact be furthered. These attempts, the realist notes, will never finally overcome human wretchedness.

While ignorance is unavoidable in human affairs, there are attempts to lessen this in the criminal justice system via the use of manifold forms of testing (e.g., the Federal Sentencing Guidelines), gathering of evidence, collaboration of testimony, sentencing boards, and the like.[31] The advances in matters of sentencing and growing awareness of the horrific racial biases of the system are important in trying to minimize bad judgments and social injustice. But we also see how the drive to overcome the kinds of ignorance that stalk human existence has led to increasing invasion of civil rights, the almost constant surveillance of ex-criminals, and the technologizing of the system. A similar ambiguity bedevils attempts to reduce the *necessity of judgment.* Laws like "three strikes and you're out" and other mandatory-sentencing laws seek to remove the travail of judgment and its vulnerability to bias and favoritism. There is a growing awareness of the connection between poverty and crime, and programs meant to address poverty are intended to lessen the necessity of judgment in society. Yet the proliferation of law is leading to the criminalization of society where some—-gangs, those in the drug trade, the sex industry—see incarceration as a necessary "business tax" on their economic behavior. Ironically, the very means aimed at lessening judgment has created an explosion of activity in the criminal justice system.

The *amelioristic* outlook is a pragmatic response to the necessities of social life more than a theory about justice or mercy and how one may or may not relate to the other. If successful, the ameliorist's agenda would

WILLIAM SCHWEIKER

mean that ideas about justice and mercy could be retained in social discourse but simply as museum pieces. The work these ideas did within the confines of social necessity would no longer be needed. The kingdom of God would have come to earth. We would have delivered ourselves from our necessities! It is hardly surprising that this outlook is found among those interested in institutional reform in a nation with a deeply pragmatic spirit. If commentators from Alexis de Tocqueville to the present are right, many Americans see religion as the helpmeet of this pragmatic work of social transformation. Little wonder that there is renewed interest in various prison ministries found throughout the country with promises of better treatment for attending religious studies and educational classes. While the amelioristic type in its various forms (religious or not) indicates important reforms that must be undertaken, it cannot displace or finally overcome the wretchedness of the human lot. At best, it hopes we grit our teeth and forge ahead.

EMANCIPATORY THEORIES

This brings us the third type of position on justice and mercy. The strategy of this type is neither realistically to parse out the relation of justice and mercy with respect to the inescapability of social necessity, nor is it to ameliorate ignorance and the demands for judgment and thereby to escape the horns of the dilemma. Rather, the strategy is to isolate the extent to which justice and mercy specify utterly different phenomena at different levels of existence, the one (justice) definitive of human wretchedness, and the other (mercy) re-creative of human existence. I call these *emancipatory theories*. They try to show how mercy frees us from the necessity of social existence and strict reciprocal justice.

This type is widespread and has various versions. Consider just three. Hannah Arendt saw the importance of "forgiveness" in that it is the power of natality, the power to begin anew, when the social system has broken down. Forgiveness escapes the necessities of our social life, our human wretchedness. Arendt writes: "Forgiveness, in other words, is the only reaction which does not merely re-act but acts anew and unexpectedly, unconditioned by the act which provoked it and therefore frees from its consequences both the one who forgives and the one who is forgiven."[32] Some theologians look to Jesus's extravagant acts of mercy and healing as the way to break the logic of social necessity. Others extend the idea of the Jubilee Year found in the Pentateuch and elsewhere in the Bible to make the same point.[33] Recently there are philosophical and social scientific arguments, pro and con, about the place of forgiveness, or restorative justice, in social life. Contemporary thinkers like Jacques Derrida and others use the language of "gift" as a way to confirm or contest the "necessity" of social life and the logic of strict justice.[34]

Emancipatory theories are extremely popular now, especially among European and American thinkers. However, the contention that mercy or forgiveness is a sui generis act is extremely difficult to sustain and hardly answers our problem. To be sure, one can suspend the demands of justice—as, say, in truth and reconciliation commissions—or transcend the necessity of social processes in the name of social cohesion. At some point one must return and face those necessities and therefore the demand for procedures of justice and judgment. Further, as thinkers like Donald Shriver have shown, the work of forgiveness in political existence is not a single, disruptive act; it is a difficult and long process that cannot thwart the demands of justice.[35]

CONCLUSION

We have now isolated three basic types of argument about justice and mercy that spin around an awareness of the necessity that infests social life and human judgment, the wretchedness of the human condition. One line of argument, found among some classical realist thinkers, insists that appeals to mercy ought not to mitigate the demands of justice in a world in which the innocent are at risk. One can plead to God for deliverance, as Augustine put it, but in this world the work of justice must be done. The realist position, whether in Luther or Augustine or Hobbes or Niebuhr, can lead to quietism, that is, an acceptance of the status quo while hoping for heavenly deliverance.

Another type of argument found in our current political and social situation tries to eradicate the horns of the dilemma, that is, to overcome the ignorance that infests all human judgments and to relieve the conditions that give rise to judgment. While important, this is ultimately doomed to failure because of the inescapable wretchedness of our condition. The third argument—found among as diverse thinkers as Arendt, some current Christian theologians, and poststructuralists like Derrida—tries to isolate the way in which mercy or forgiveness or the "gift" escape the ne-

WILLIAM SCHWEIKER

cessity, the logic, of our social wretchedness. Even if there is some radical counterlogic of forgiveness, an upending of necessity of consequences in social action, the question remains how that is related to the actual problems of criminal justice. It is hardly surprising, then, that when advocates of the "gift" turn to actual political existence, they quickly resort to rather standard pictures of distributive justice.[36]

This brings us to the final step for the present inquiry. I turn to some reflections on justice and mercy in the light of the wretchedness of our condition, the power of human action, and typical positions just isolated.

Responsible Mercy

The reflections in this essay have been framed in terms of the power of human action to have a near-miraculous causality, as Arendt and Milosz observed, but also with respect to Augustine's somber and realistic claim about the necessities of social life.[37] I have so framed the inquiry in order to avoid two fundamental errors that beset much thought on these matters.

One error was famously called "cheap grace" by the theologian Dietrich Bonhoeffer. The claim is that grace comes without a cost; the demands of justice and responsibility no longer hold. I worry that too much high-sounding rhetoric on the part of Christian thinkers and philosophers about forgiveness and the "gift" is just cheap grace. It is important to insist on realism about the wretchedness of the human condition and that mercy not violate justice. The other error, in my judgment, is to believe that "wretchedness," social necessity, is the first and last word about our condition. It is to adopt a world-denying pessimism or to assume that only the machineries of power are what social life is all about. Here realism too quickly banishes mercy from social life.

By the term "responsible mercy," I mean to avoid those two errors. Much more, I mean to identify an assumption shared by Augustinian realism and Miloszian activism, namely, that human beings, no matter how wretched our condition or miraculous our actions, are endowed with irreducible worth. Augustine grounded human worth in God's good creation; Milosz articulates this worth in his own brand of Roman Catholic humanism. My purpose in this argument has not been to undertake a philosophical or theological defense of human dignity, its grounds and scope. On that point I am content here to draw on the sources of the

Christian tradition and its claims about human worth.[38] This is where a Christian perspective rightly informs the argument. However, the validity of this assumption about human worth can be established only by showing its importance for public debate about justice and mercy within social existence. The question then becomes, how is human worth manifest as the object of justice?

In response to this question, we must note something of a paradox, the full weight of which is just now being grasped by thinkers around the world. There must be some fundamental perception of human worth that is to be respected and enhanced by any system of justice in order for that system to be just. Paradoxically enough, systems of justice—just like other social subsystems—rest on goods they do not create and cannot entirely protect, namely, the irreducible worth of human beings. An economic system, for instance, can lead to the condition in which persons are willing to sell their bodies and their time and so undercut the system itself. As many thinkers have noted, any economic system can endanger the "human capital" that is its presupposition.[39] A system of justice, and especially criminal justice, can endanger the very human beings it is meant to serve by effacing or denying the irreducible worth of their humanity. This seems to be the paradox of most of our social subsystems: they can neither create nor ensure that which is the condition of their existence. The depth of this paradox is beginning to dawn on people around the world. Social systems are self-endangering, even so-called successful ones.

In this light, acts of mercy enact, testify to, the worth of persons precisely when that worth is endangered and effaced by the structures of justice. Mercy is meant to humanize justice by manifesting, making apparent, the object and end of just actions. An act of mercy is doubly disclosing: it reveals in the mercy-giver the mysterious causality of human beings to reestablish justice after the chaos of social breakdown; it reveals in the recipient the nonreduciblity of human beings to social systems. This does not qualify the demands of justice or the right of individuation as essential to justice. Quite the contrary is the case. What an act of mercy does—if it is true—is to enact human dignity, both of the giver and the receiver, which is the good that political rights to fair, equal, and individuated treatment are to respect and enhance. The crucial point thereby has two sides. On the one hand, we ought not to make the rights of persons in a system of justice contingent on specific acts of mercy. Those rights (and responsibilities) are intrinsic to the idea of

WILLIAM SCHWEIKER

a system of justice. What that system cannot ensure or create is, on the other hand, precisely why people matter at all, why they bear worth and have irreducible importance. A system of justice requires, paradoxically, what it cannot demand under the strictures of justice, namely, acts of mercy aimed at constantly humanizing the justice system.[40] All too easily a system of justice seeks consistency, fairness, of judgment at the possible cost of the recognition of the specificity of cases and the individuality of persons. Put in the terms of moral theory, responsible mercy is about the *good* of political existence (human worth) that all political and social demands about the right or justice presuppose and must serve. The relation between the *good* and the *right* is of course constantly debated within ethics and politics. On my account, the meaning and purpose of claims to political rightness, to justice, are necessarily dependent on the political good, the worth of persons and human communities. By the same token, the worth of persons is always vulnerable, and therefore this unique good demands the strictures of political rightness or justice.

I take this "two-sidedness" of the argument to articulate the real force of Jesus's acts of mercy. It formulates better than Arendt did the real insight of the early Christian movement. An individual is snatched from the necessities of a system of judgment, shown to be a child of God, and thereby empowered to live justly. "Woman, where are your accusers?" Jesus asked the woman charged of adultery after having dispatched the crowd by saying, "he who has not sinned cast the first stone." With no accusers, the woman is ennobled and redeemed. "Go and sin no more" (John 8:1–11).[41] The same insight into the power of mercy seems to be true of claims about restorative justice. That was the power and brilliance of the South African Truth and Reconciliation Commission. By allowing the accused to speak as individuals free from outright retribution, justice becomes possible within the social necessity of judging. And consider Jesus's other radical act: "Father, forgive them for they know not what they do" (Luke 32:34).[42] Here human dignity is announced even amid violent and perhaps unavoidable ignorance. Christ's actions upend human wretchedness without negating the possibility and demand of justice. It is not a gift that somehow must then be supplemented by an independent conception of justice. One is thereby thinking at the nodal point between mercy and justice.

Can we formulate a concept for this "two-sided" insight that renders productive, not destructive, the necessity of human social existence? "Responsible mercy," as I call it, is the affirmation of human worth amid a realistic vision of the wretchedness of our condition. It is hard, slow, and demanding labor. Responsible mercy is not, strictly speaking, a moral obligation even if it is the deepest fulfillment of the moral aim, namely, to respect and enhance the integrity of life before God. Responsible mercy, if I am right, has a unique causality, as Milosz noted. It enacts the condition for any system of justice, but it cannot itself be created or secured by that system. And I think it best to speak of "responsible mercy" to ensure that we are clear that the demands of justice endure within systems of human power, the contexts of responsibility.

What then of the criminal justice system? As we know from data and research, this system, despite its aspirations and despite the work of right-intending "ameliorists," is in fact too often and too easily dehumanizing. An action—say a sentencing policy—is not responsibly merciful if it merely mitigates punishment without reaffirming human worth as the condition and end of justice. Actions and policies that seem merciful might not be; actions and policies that on some readings might not appear merciful might well be. The measure of this is not simply the amelioration of social tensions. The measure of responsible mercy is the affirmation of human worth that enables and empowers persons to be agents of justice. An act or policy is only responsibly merciful, then, if it enables all involved—criminals, those who execute justice, and the victim—to manifest their unique worth in and through the labor of justice.[43] Surely the increase of harsher forms of punishment and also the use of the death penalty eclipse the claims of responsible mercy if and when those forms of punishment cannot in principle enact, manifest, a person's dignity qua human being.[44] The overwhelming evidence seems to be that the use of lethal punishment not only demeans the executed but the whole of social life.

This account of responsible mercy commits one to many of the concerns of ameliorists, even as it is absolutely realistic in its assessment of the necessities of social existence. And like the "emanicipatory theory," as I called it, mercy is seen not simply as a version of justice or merely a consoling illusion. Yet unlike emancipatory positions that tend toward "cheap grace," responsible mercy enacts human worth, testifies to human dignity, in a way that does not negate but in fact establishes the demand for justice. Stated theologically, responsible mercy is the human analogue to the divine act of creation, and even re-creation, as the condition for covenantal justice. In acts of responsible mercy, human beings manifest the integrity of life as the good that justice can and must serve. Through these actions, human beings, incompletely to be sure, imitate the divine action despite our wretchedness.

Conclusion

I am suggesting, in the end, that what is needed in our context, and indeed in wider movements around the world, is a realistic acknowledgment of the necessities of human existence coupled with ways to enact and testify to the irreducibility of human worth. I have called such a perspective on criminal justice "responsible mercy." I tend to think that this idea is part of a religious vision of life, one that endorses in the face of wretchedness the goodness of created beings and the integrity of life. I am even bold enough to claim that "responsible mercy" is a fair approximation of ideas about divine righteousness. Those matters, along with a host of other legal and political details, will have to await reflection and discussion at another time.

Notes

1. For a remarkable account of some of these events, see Glover, *Humanity: A Moral History of the Twentieth Century.*

2. Arendt, *The Human Condition,* 238.

3. For the most articulate representative of this position in the United States, see Rawls, *Political Liberalism.* For an argument for the fully public character of religious claims to truth and thus the need for their presence in public debate, see Gamwell, *The Meaning of Religious Freedom.*

4. On this account of the task and method of theological ethics, see Schweiker, *Responsibility and Christian Ethics.* I agree with a host of thinkers who explore public, dialogical forms of validation while also admitting the historical nature of human understanding. See, for example, Charles Taylor, *Sources of the Self;* MacIntyre, *Three Rival Versions of Moral Enquiry;* and Tracy, *Plurality and Ambiguity.*

5. One sees this kind of argument among Christian theologians like Karl Barth in the mid-twentieth century and currently by some so-called postliberal theologians who argue that the truth of Christian convictions can only be specified within the language of the church. On this position, see Lindbeck, *The Nature of Doctrine.* For a very different position, see Gustafson, *An Examined Faith.*

6. I have made the distinction here between the public and communal claims of a tradition in order to leave open the question of whether or not claims about

the internal life of a community can be seen as self-validating. It would be odd, for instance, for a Christian to believe that the truth of the Eucharist had to wait on public debate and consensus!

7. The point I am making is that one needs to distinguish the kinds of moral reflection that do and do not engage religious matters: (1) a form of moral reflection that serves the life of a specific community (say, Christian or Jewish ethics), (2) a moral philosophy that denies any relation to a historic tradition and any connection between religion and morals, (3) an ethics that develops a general conception of "religion" and its relation to the moral life, what can be called "religious ethics," and (4) theological ethics or Christian (Jewish, Buddhist, etc.) moral philosophy. This last option, what I practice in this essay and elsewhere, works with the concrete and historically specific sources of a living religious tradition, but it does so in order to speak of the problems and possibilities facing human beings, including, but not limited to, members of a specific community. One can say that a theological ethics is hermeneutically indebted to a specific tradition but through the critical interpretation of those sources seeks to provide meaning and guidance to the lives of moral agents.

8. For a helpful discussion of these ideas as well as options in the debate about justice, mercy, and forgiveness, see Murphy and Hampton, *Forgiveness and Mercy.*

9. The discussion of love, or *agape,* in Christian thought is of course massive and complex. I cannot enter here into a discussion of the "forms" of love and the distinctiveness, if there is any, of Christian love. It is sufficient for my argument to note that, whether distinctive or not, Christian ideas about love bind together claims about actions toward others (mercy) with some dispositional relation to the other (forgiveness). In this respect, a fully theological account of responsible mercy would explore dispositional demands in a way I am foregoing in the present argument. On this, see Schweiker, Johnson, and Jung, *Humanity before God.*

10. Human worth is a necessary but not sufficient condition of a system of justice insofar as the recognition of human worth, a basic good, does not in itself determine the norm or norms for deciding about the distribution of other goods or reaching a just judgment in situations of conflict between goods. Yet, on this point about human worth itself I agree with those authors who find some basic religious or even metaphysical claim behind a principled insistence on human rights. For a helpful discussion, see Perry, *The Idea of Human Rights,* and also his "The Morality of Human Rights: A Nonreligious Ground?"

11. My argument is phenomenological and hermeneutical in character: phenomenologically speaking, an act of mercy allows human worth to appear within systems of justice while the meaning of that event is interpreted through the religious symbolics of creation. I have made the case elsewhere for kinds of actions that are "mimetic," that is, enactments of the most basic power and worth of human existence imitative of the divine. See Schweiker, *Mimetic Reflections.*

12. For a discussion of this point in various religious traditions, see Schweiker, *The Blackwell Companion to Religious Ethics.*

13. Classical examples of this claim are Plato and Aristotle as well as Thomas Aquinas. In each case, "justice" is both a virtue of individual character and a predicate of right political relations. In our day, thinkers like John Rawls have noted that justice is the first virtue of political community. The differences in positions, then, stem not from the use of the idea of justice as personal and political virtue, but in the theory of justice offered.

14. Ramsey, *Basic Christian Ethics*, 10.

15. For a fine examination of Jewish engagements with various myths of divine action, see Fishbane, *Biblical Myth and Rabbinic Mythmaking*.

16. For an account of the importance and danger of such abstractions in all thinking, see Whitehead, *Science and the Modern World*. Whitehead is surely right that philosophy, or critical reflection, must explore, critique, and revise leading abstractions (the "isms") operative in a culture with the intent of providing a robust view of the world. In exploring the relation of justice and mercy, one is in fact isolating two basic ideas or abstractions in the moral cosmology of Western cultures.

17. Augustine, *The City of God*, 860.

18. On this point, see Mark Lewis Taylor, *The Executed God*.

19. This is a long-standing admission about the weakness of human judgment found among Christian thinkers. See, for instance, Thomas Aquinas, *Summa Theologiae* 1–2.91.4, where the fallibility of judgment in fact leads to the need for divine law.

20. I am thinking here of Christian theologians like Stanley Hauerwas; see his *Christian Existence Today;* and Milbank, *Theology and Social Theory*.

21. Milosz, *To Begin Where I Am*, 327.

22. To be honest, the blending of realism and activism is a characteristic of my own religious community, United Methodism, with its roots in the work of John Wesley and others. It is not the purpose of this essay to enter an examination of those resources. It is sufficient simply to note that my argument is characteristic of certain historic options in Christian thought and life.

23. Tillich, *Christianity and the Encounter of the World Religions*, 54–55. There is a long, if contested, use of typological thinking among social theorists and theologians interested in the interrelation of religions and diverse cultures. This is seen in Weber's arguments about "ideal types" and also in theologians like Ernst Troeltsch, in his *Social Teachings of the Christian Churches and Groups;* Tillich's own writings; H. Richard Niebuhr, in *Christ and Culture;* and most recently the work of James M. Gustafson, in texts like *Christ and the Moral Life*. Such thinking is not without its critics, of course. While my position differs substantively from these other theologians, I still judge the use of typological reflection important for the work of theological ethics. On this, see also William Schweiker, "Ernst Troeltsch's The Social Teachings of the Christian Churches," in Meilaender and Werpehowski, *The Oxford Handbook of Theological Ethics*, 415–32.

24. There is some debate about whether or not Luther in fact said this as well as other pithy claims about political existence, like, it is better to be ruled by a

smart Turk than a dumb Christian. Whether or not Luther made these claims, they are certainly consistent with his thought. I want to thank my colleagues Martin E. Marty and Jean Bethke Elshtain for discussion of these matters.

25. For classic statements of this point, see Luther, "Secular Authority: To the Extent It Should Be Obeyed," in Dillenberger, *Martin Luther,* 363–402; and Calvin, *Institutes of the Christian Religion,* bk. 4, chap. 20.

26. There are, of course, long debates about how to understand Hobbes's political philosophy and the forms of political realism that flow from it. See Hobbes, *Leviathan.* For a decidedly different account, see O'Donovan, *The Desire of the Nations.*

27. The theologian Paul Ramsey, as noted above, made this argument and even justified some instances of war on the grounds of *agape.* On this, see Ramsey, *The Essential Paul Ramsey.*

28. See Niebuhr, *Moral Man and Immoral Society;* and *An Interpretation of Christian Ethics.* See also Lovin, *Reinhold Niebuhr and Christian Realism.*

29. Bentham, *Introduction to the Principles of Morals and Legislation.*

30. For the most recent and thorough analysis of this, see Foucault, *Discipline and Punish.*

31. See Stith and Cabranes, *Fear of Judging.*

32. Arendt, *The Human Condition,* 241.

33. For a recent example, see Erickson and Jones, *Surviving Terror.*

34. See Derrida, *Given Time* and *The Gift of Death.* For a general discussion of the relation of gift and sacrifice (and so systems of necessary reciprocal action), see Jill Robbins, "Sacrifice," in Mark C. Taylor, *Critical Terms for Religious Studies,* 285–97.

35. Shriver, *An Ethics for Enemies.* See also his essay "The Taming of Mars: Can Humans of the Twenty-first Century Contain Their Propensity for Violence?" in Stackhouse and Paris, *God and Globalization,* 1: 140–83.

36. See, for instance, thinkers like Derrida but also the work of Emmanuel Levinas (*Otherwise Than Being or Beyond Essence;* and also *Levinas Reader*) on the relation of the "ethical" and justice.

37. Elsewhere I have called this approach "hermeneutical realism" and tried to show its importance for responding to the expanse of human power. See Schweiker, *Power, Value and Conviction.*

38. As noted above, I judge, but do not defend here, that some theological and even metaphysical claims are required to sustain beliefs about human worth. I have made part of that argument elsewhere and also designated the position I endorse as "theological humanism." See Schweiker, *Theological Ethics and Global Dynamics.* For attempts to provide nonreligious accounts of human worth, see Gaita, *A Common Humanity;* and Todorov, *Imperfect Garden.*

39. One finds this in thinkers as diverse as Karl Marx and Max Weber. But see also Troeltsch, "The Essence of the Modern Spirit," in his *Religion in History;* and Grelle and Krueger, *Christianity and Capitalism.* See also William

Schweiker, "Responsibility in the World of Mammon: Theology, Justice, and Transnational Corporations," in Stackhouse and Paris, *God and Globalization,* 1: 105–39.

40. For a similar concern, see Murphy's "Mercy and Legal Justice," in Murphy and Hampton, *Forgiveness and Mercy,* 162–86.

41. One should note that John 7:53–8:11 is lacking in most ancient authorities. Some place it after 7:52 or 7:36 or after 21:25 or even Luke 21:38. There are also variations in the text. This is a case where, theologically and ethically speaking, the wisdom of a developing tradition is seen in isolating a fundamental truth not present in an earlier stage of development.

42. Ironically, this verse is also missing in many ancient manuscripts, and is not found in the other synoptic Gospels, namely Mark and Matthew. Again, I judge that we see an actual advancement of moral and religious understanding by the insertion of this line in the text.

43. This claim has profound implications for ideas about punishment and especially the demand for forms of reformation in criminals. I cannot pursue those arguments in this essay.

44. It is interesting here that many classical Christian thinkers, like Augustine, argued for capital punishment as an act of mercy—it kept the person from further sinning and thus endangering his or her soul's eternal destiny. The insight here, although I think the final position faulty, is that punishment must serve the worth of the one punished and not just the ends of social cohesion and retribution.

Fallibility and Fragility
A Reflection on Justice and Mercy

KEVIN JUNG

Niccolò Machiavelli writes: "[O]ne can say this generally of men: that they are ungrateful, fickle, pretenders and dissemblers, evaders of danger, eager for gain."[1] To deal with this kind of human nature, he argues that a political ruler needs to know how to use force as well as laws, all according to necessity. He also advises that it is important for the ruler to appear merciful to win the hearts and minds of people, while the ruler should remain feared by people.[2] Such a seemingly dark assessment of human nature finds echoes in the political thought of many thinkers in many different quarters of political thought before and after Machiavelli, although his more political doctrines have not been without severe criticisms.

It is probably general common sense, even without invoking theories of criminal justice, that individuals expect their public authority to deal with the dark side of humanity by punishing evildoers or restraining them from harming the innocent, whether for the sake of moral equity or social utility. The fact of the matter is that there are always those in human society, unfortunately, who in various ways would take illicit advantage of others against their will. In turn, many expect and desire some measure of restitution or protection for themselves in the event of such crimes. Thus, despite the long and undecided philosophical debate on the precise nature of justice, for example, from Plato to Aquinas to Nietzsche, it would be fair to say that people generally recognize the necessity of justice.

Yet when another concept, mercy, enters the picture of criminal justice debates, our commonsense notions of justice do not seem sufficient to give any clarity to the meanings of these two terms.[3] Despite frequent references to both justice and mercy, the meaning of these terms often remains hotly debated and not clearly defined. I will not dwell on an in-depth examination of how the two concepts have been used in philosophy. Instead, I intend in this essay to engage the task of both distinguishing and relating the two concepts in a philosophically coherent way.

In order to set up my argument, however, I will challenge two contemporary theses about justice and mercy: (1) mercy *tampers with, or even violates* justice, and (2) mercy should be *unconditional* in order to escape the economy of justice. In both theses, the meaning of mercy remains discontinuous with that of justice. According to the former thesis, justice, conceptually speaking, makes mercy redundant because the function of mercy as that which gives full attention to all relevant moral circumstances of one's action is what is already included in the notion of justice as *suum cuique* (giving each person his or her due). What is worse is that mercy could interfere with and obstruct valid demands of justice by bargaining with justice and placing a limit upon it. According to the latter thesis, any attempt to qualify mercy with justice loses the uniqueness of mercy as a noneconomic act. In contrast to these views, I construe justice and mercy as belonging to independent but systematically related spheres of human action necessitated by the human condition of fallibility. By "fallibility," following the Ricoeurian sense of the term, I refer to the unavoidable condition of a "disproportion" within the human being, characterized by the potential conflict between our tendency to strive for wholeness and perfection and our fragile limitations in consciousness, will, and passion. Whereas justice presupposes and addresses human capacity for evil in the primordial constitution of the fallible person, mercy affirms the opposite side, the human capacity for good. Just as Ricoeur finds in the fallible person a synthetic unity in the finite and infinite structures of human existence, a synthesis that may fail, I submit the view that human society must unite justice and mercy in order to make it genuinely human.

Mercy as Tampering with Justice

Jeffrie Murphy, in his philosophical reflection on the topic of justice and mercy, argues that mercy is at best a private virtue because the public use of mercy may tamper or interfere with justice duly understood.[4] He worries that mercy can be either a vice or a redundancy, if it happens to hamper justice or to do exactly what justice is supposed to do. If justice is understood as giving one's due, a merciful act that seeks to "temper" justice by demanding what is less than required is an apparent "tampering with" justice, since mercy undermines justice.[5] Likewise, if mercy means the careful consideration of all external and internal circumstances that led to the act of a crime, this also seems hardly being opposed to justice, since justice demands nothing more or less than finding one's exact due. If justice fails to account for all the particularities of each individual and each action that should go into finding one's exact due, that seems to be a failure of justice, not an endorsement of mercy, logically speaking. Put otherwise, if someone says that imperfect justice calls for mercy as that which complements justice, this is precisely a case of mercy playing the role of justice, namely, finding one's exact due. Can mercy have its own independent nature from justice? How do we speak of mercy, avoiding any harm to justice or duplicating the meaning of justice?

Murphy's answer lies in a subtle distinction he makes between private and public (institutional) law paradigms. According to this distinction, a private person, who is not bound by the rule of law to impose punishment on anyone, can show mercy to his or her offender. But when society relegates to a person a power to exercise justice to a fellow human being, this person acts as a public officeholder who has a fiduciary duty and responsibility to obey the rule of law and not limit its full application. It follows that a private individual can show mercy to an offender, but a public officeholder cannot. Out of personal virtues, religious or moral, a private individual can offer mercy. For Murphy, mercy is strictly a private matter, and, as such, it is permissible as long as the act of mercy can give some meaning to the person who offers mercy. Murphy argues that civil suit cases, which he believes operate according to the "private law paradigm,"[6] could provide examples of this private notion of mercy. This distinction between public and private law paradigms also means that a public officeholder such as a criminal judge ought not to practice mercy, for they would act, a fortiori, contrary to the rule of law and perpetrate a violation of justice. These public officeholders not only have clear institutional obligations to uphold the rules of justice but also are in no position to waive the right that others deserve and demand by rights.

In restricting mercy to the private sphere, Murphy nevertheless still holds that mercy may be more than a matter of personal preference. It may be an important moral virtue that checks the "narrow and self-involved tendencies present in each of us,"[7] and in this sense mercy may have some dispositional impact on the law. Yet he checks and qualifies this efficacy of mercy by saying that "it is a virtue to be manifested by private persons using the law—not by officials enforcing the law."[8] If Murphy is right, mercy faces a real challenge in establishing and justifying its legitimate place alongside justice, especially in the public sphere.

Murphy's discussion of mercy as a private virtue, however, seems to be problematic on at least two levels. First, if Murphy is right in saying that mercy tampers with justice because it interferes with the demand of justice, why is mercy still allowed as a private act of virtue? His separation of private and public realms in which mercy can and cannot be used seems to presuppose that the private individual is less subject to the rule of justice than the public institution or that the private individual can ignore the rule of justice in a way the public person cannot. While it is true that any person invested with a public duty should not dispense mercy at will, it is not clear therefore that the private person should. If we accept the view that justice is a moral concept with its own intrinsic value, not simply a means to social utility, it is dubious that this separation can still hold. It would seem that justice as an intrinsic value imposes its demand on both the private and public realms alike, irrespective of the sanctions and enforcement of law. Second, Murphy, as many other legal theorists do, tends to locate mercy on the same plane with justice. That is to say, he sees a kind of bargaining process taking place between the opposing requirements of justice and mercy. What results is a tug-of-war of mercy with justice, each canceling the force of the other to find some state of equilibrium. While this may be true in appearance, picturing mercy in this way does not take into account other possible ways of viewing the coexistence between justice and mercy.

One such possibility can be found in the next discussion of mercy as an inherently noneconomic concept. After analyzing and rejecting this possibility, I will then introduce another paradigm that allows both justice and mercy to find their coexistence and that pays due attention to the fallibility of human freedom and responsibility. In this, I seek to give human nature its due and thereby to do justice to the relation between mercy and justice.

Mercy Overriding Justice

In *Cosmopolitanism and Forgiveness*, deconstructionist philosopher Jacques Derrida submits the view that forgiveness should have no limit because any attempt to understand or give a purpose to forgiveness cannot but fail. As I will explain below, on this conception, the act of forgiveness only makes sense as the forgiveness of the unforgivable, for otherwise it simply repeats justice. Only the unforgivable can be forgiven. Take the example of the so-called "crimes against humanity," discussed, for example, by David Scheffer earlier in this volume. How can anyone provide a rational justification for the monstrous crimes such as ethnic cleansing, mass rape, or systematic torture? Worse, how can we even find a measure of justice that can compute or undo the loss and the sufferings of victims? So cruel and massive are these crimes that no semantic expression or juridical-political system will make a proper description of or a remedy to the crimes. There is only the unforgivable in the sense that they are irreparable and irrecusable. Forgiveness, thus Derrida argues, is impossibility itself. It seeks to do what appears to be the impossible to reason. What it attempts to do can never become intelligible to reason, since it wants to forgive what cannot be forgiven.

However, it seems that people often do give a meaning to forgiveness. They provide justifications as to *why* they want to forgive perpetrators. Will such justification preserve the character of forgiveness? Derrida thinks not. At the core of his objection, there is this reason: Any attempt to rationalize forgiveness indeed distorts the very nature of what it wants to forgive. That is to say, upon the moment we explain why we should forgive, the unforgivable becomes forgivable, whereby the irreducible events of horror appear reducible to the horizon of human reason. The unforgivable loses its indescribable and imprescriptible burden of guilt due to the rational justification of forgiveness. Here forgiveness crosses the boundary of amnesty and enters the land of amnesia.

At a deeper level, Derrida is opposed to a particular way of thinking, or what he calls a conditional logic of exchange, in which forgiveness functions as an exchangeable value in economic transaction.[9] He takes issue with the view that forgiveness must be preceded by the acknowledgment of fault or a confessional of sin by the perpetrator.[10] The problem with this view, in Derrida's view, is that forgiveness becomes not only *conditional* but also bound to an *economic transaction*. Once the guilty one acknowledges fault to its victims, the victim now finds himself or herself in a strange situation of now having an implicit obligation to forgive the unforgivable. This condition of repentance puts the victim back at the same level as the unforgivable, which is utterly unacceptable in view of the crimes committed. The guilty, as he meets the demand of repentance,

KEVIN JUNG

is somehow expecting forgiveness that he or she does not deserve. This process of forgiveness then reduces forgiveness to the level of economic exchange. Forgiveness ceases to be a gift; forgiveness must be paid back to the repentance. It is for these reasons that Derrida says the following:

> I shall risk this proposition: each time forgiveness is at the service of finality, be it noble and spiritual (atonement, redemption, reconciliation, salvation), each time it aims to re-establish a normality (social, national, political, psychological) by a work of mourning, by some therapy or ecology of memory, then the "forgiveness" is not pure—nor is its concept. Forgiveness is not, it *should not be*, normal, normative, normalizing. It *should* remain exceptional and extraordinary, in the face of the impossible; as if it interrupted the ordinary course of historical temporality.[11]

Without any grand telos or a slogan of utility, "forgiveness forgives only the unforgivable," says Derrida.[12] Forgiveness is like a "madness" that forgives the unforgivable without any prior conditions.[13] It is doing what is impossible.

At a macroscopic level, Derrida's argument for unconditional forgiveness appears consistent with his overarching project of deconstruction. Just as his deconstruction aims at destroying the promise of the Enlightenment that guarantees the possibility of objective knowledge, and just as he critiques Husserl's structure of consciousness where intention is given to intuition, true understanding of forgiveness is impossible because it can never be fully given to consciousness. Forgiveness cannot but escape the light of human reason. It cannot appear. This absence of knowledge or the fact that we cannot really understand forgiveness is what makes forgiveness actually and strangely possible. To use Derrida's language of gift, in the face of the impossible, one gives a gift of forgiveness that does not belong to the circle of exchange. It is the gift of extraordinary act where neither the donor nor the donee can know what is going on. The gift should be "totally heterogeneous to theoretical identification" or "totally foreign to the horizon of economy, ontology, knowledge, constantive statements, and theoretical determination and judgment."[14] If Derrida is right about the nature of forgiveness, maybe forgiveness should be freely offered no matter how unworthy the receiver is.

This raises a question whether mercy should be granted without any constraints, even without due process of justice. Before answering this question, let us step back and reflect first on the location of mercy in

Derrida. Unlike Murphy, Derrida places mercy outside the circle of economic exchange, and his move apparently protects mercy from any claims of justice. While justice operates on the plane of calculation and measurement, mercy runs perhaps on a higher plane of self-giving and consciousness irreducible to the ordinary logic of justice. This move thus appears to free mercy from justice or from the necessity to calculate who merits mercy and how much. In other words, Derrida's move seems to reject the kind of tug-of-war process between justice and mercy and basically declare that mercy now has the power to trump or nullify justice.

It is here that we must pause and recall Murphy's main concern: Does not mercy tamper with or violate justice? Derrida's account of forgiveness may explain how mercy is distinct from justice, but it fails to address whether it is acceptable or permissible to exempt an offender from the requirements of justice. Granted that we should not subsume or contain mercy within the cycle of justice, we should also think about problems of inequality and unfairness that mercy might inadvertently cause to victims. The issue then is not really about whether mercy should claim a special privilege over justice but whether it is possible to talk about justice and mercy at the same time and how we can justify these two concepts simultaneously.

Human Freedom: United Yet Fallible

Earlier I criticized Murphy's account of mercy partly because his distinction between the private person and public person does not remove the fact that in principle justice applies to both types of persons. Simply put, if it is wrong to do X, it is wrong whether or not the agent is a private individual or a public officeholder. I also faulted his account for his tendency to read mercy as a bargaining concept in the totality of measuring one's due to other persons. Derrida's account of forgiveness was then introduced in order to show that it is possible to see mercy as a nonbargaining concept. Yet his particular way of construing mercy seems to have a potential to override or obstruct our ordinary sense of justice.[15]

To overcome the difficulties concerning the problem of justice and mercy, I suggest that we look at these concepts from a perspective that gives due attention to the nature of human action, and more specifically the human capacity for doing wrong or, to use a weightier term, "evil." After all, both justice and mercy may be viewed as human actions that address moral evil. But it is not immediately clear to us in what ways they differ or agree. To understand justice and mercy from a different perspective, allow me to take a little bit of a detour into some contemporary work in phenomenology and theology.

In his early series of philosophical treatises known as the Philosophy of the Will, Paul Ricoeur reflects on the structures of human existence-in-the-world. More specifically, he is interested in the analysis of "man's structures or *fundamental possibilities*" that could open and limit the complex activities of the will. In *Freedom and Nature,* his first book in this series, he shows how our mind and body, or "the voluntary" and "the involuntary," are tenuously unified in our being. He finds a reciprocal relationship between the voluntary, i.e., our free will, and the involuntary, i.e., our body that is at once a source of our motives, an organ of our movement, and a locus of our necessity. At first, our free will seems unlimited in its intentionality. Like the Kantian idea of the immortality of the soul, our consciousness can intend or produce an object that is free from and exceeds possible empirical verification. At the same time, we do not simply intend such objects—or any object of the will—for any reason. Rather, our willing is directed by different motives in our body such as its needs and desires. Against Sartre, Ricoeur contends that involuntary desires and needs form the infrastructure and starting point for the will. Likewise, our willing takes place only in our body as the very organ of movement. The body both makes possible movement and resists it, such as in experiences of fatigue or old age. Here, our willing meets and is tempered by the emotions and habits in our body. Our willing is also tempered by what Ricoeur calls necessity, "the absolutely involuntary with respect to decision and effort . . . whether in the form of character, of the unconscious, of biological life."[16] Inversely, the voluntary has the power to regulate and transcend the involuntary to the extent that we do not just follow our bodily needs and desires. The will chooses, accepts, or rejects particular needs and desires over others. The will activates or deactivates our emotions and habits. The will must acquiesce to necessity in the form of consent. In Ricoeur's own words: "freedom is not a pure act, it is, in each of its moments, activity and receptivity. It constitutes itself in receiving what it does not produce: values, capacities, and sheer nature."[17] His point is that our freedom is at once a motivated, incarnate, and contingent freedom. Only in this freedom that is transcendental and limited do we find genuine human freedom. We are inserted into the world with a certain perspective, a limit that both orients us and that we can transcend. To understand and accept this freedom is to understand and accept who we are as human beings.

In his next volume, entitled *Fallible Man,* Ricoeur extends his essential description of the will into a description of actual conditions of the will, thereby moving from "eidetics" of the will to "empirics" of the will. If his earlier interest in *Freedom and Nature* was to find and describe the formal conditions of human freedom as a pure possibility, *Fallible Man* seeks to analyze how, in the actual experience of this freedom, the human being fails to actualize freedom, in what he calls a "pathétique of misery." Not seeking to explain away conceptually why individuals fall or commit moral evil, Ricoeur wants to understand what makes it possible for one to fall. Making a distinction between "fallibility" and "fault," Ricoeur deepens reflection into the possibility of moral evil. In this book, the unity of the voluntary and the involuntary in his earlier work is replaced by the synthetic structures between infinite and finite where we experience a "disproportion" within ourselves. In three modes of human consciousness and freedom—imagination, character, and feeling (or knowing, willing, feeling)—he claims that we come to know ourselves as being finite. We are finite because we can only have a fragmentary, perspectival view of ourselves, the world, and others, whether we are talking about the "objects" of our own consciousness, our own character, or our own feelings. For instance, our self-consciousness is only temporal and transient; our character is always changing or changeable, thereby revealing a finitude in our scope of knowledge and character. Yet this finitude also affirms our existence as belonging to the infinite; we can transcend our finitude by acknowledging and desiring other points of view with respect to the self and others. In fact, the very idea of perspective and limit requires us to think and imagine that which transcends these limits. This means that we are always in between finite and infinite, both aiming at the infinite but also being limited by the finite.

In short, Ricoeur believes that it is this disproportion or noncoincidence within ourselves that provides the structural possibility of evil. He calls this possibility "fallibility." It is important to note that this fallibility is not coterminous with fault; it is always a possibility, not a destiny—even if it seems no human being escapes it. Perhaps, more importantly, this fallibility is nothing other than who we are as human beings. As he puts it: "This limitation is man himself. I do not think man directly, but

I think him through composition, as the 'mixture' of originating affirmation and existential negation. Man is the Joy of Yes in the sadness of the finite."[18] On this account, the human being is a fragile mediator of both finite and infinite elements, where its "fragility designates the *occasion,* the point of least resistance through which evil can enter into man."[19]

One can also find a similar description of human existence in theology. Like Ricoeur, Karl Rahner also understands human existence in terms of its finite and infinite structures, though his use of these terms is somewhat different from Ricoeur's. We can understand ourselves from particular objects that are in relation to us, say our bodily organs or things that are made and shaped by us, just as empirical sciences account for human beings from their own particular points of view, say biological, psychological, or sociological. Just as a computer with self-diagnostic tools can analyze its own functioning state, we can also derive some information about ourselves from the empirical data available to us. Yet we also experience ourselves as a whole in terms of both our freedom and self-consciousness. Unlike a programmed computer, we experience ourselves as free beings that can choose and act for ourselves, and our self-consciousness even raises questions about the meaning of our existence, as if we are foreign to ourselves. In other words, while human beings, like other finite beings, understand themselves in relation to the parts that belong to them, human beings can also confront themselves by transcending their finitude and can even acknowledge their finitude in ways other finite beings cannot.

Another interesting twist about human existence is the fact that we do not seem to be able to fully answer all the questions we can raise to ourselves. There appears to be an infinite horizon, as Rahner calls it, that grounds or makes possible our being as a transcendent being but that cannot be ever thematized by us. As a theologian, Rahner understands that this ability to transcend ourselves has to do with a fact that we are also spiritual beings. But more importantly, our capacity for self-transcendence is possible because of the infinite horizon, identified theologically as "God," in which we are grounded.

One of Rahner's insights with respect to these finite and infinite structures in human beings can be found in his description of "the possibility of sin as a permanent existential."[20] In brief, Rahner affirms human beings as free subjects; we can choose and act freely. As transcendent beings who participate in the infinite, we have the capacity to decide about, shape, and constitute ourselves. This makes us not only free but also responsible, since it is we alone who actualize ourselves. Yet our freedom is located in the finite. The actualization of our freedom can take place only in a particular history and place. In other words, our freedom is conditioned by history and world:

> Man never establishes his own freedom in some absolute sense, in the sense of a freedom which could make complete use of the material which is given to him in his freedom, or could cast it off in an absolute self-sufficiency. . . . In an ultimate and inescapable way, man even as doer and maker is still receiving and being made. What he experiences in himself is always a synthesis: of possibilities presented to his freedom and his free disposition of self, of what is himself and what is the other, of acting and suffering, of knowing and doing, and these elements are synthesized in a unity which cannot be completely and objectively analyzed.[21]

Our freedom, conditioned always by history and world, does not know with absolute certainty how to best synthesize or unite our original freedom and the necessities of the world. This means that a person never knows with absolute certainty whether his exercised freedom really is the freedom that affirms God or the expression of our essential being as God's creature. Therefore, there is always a possibility of sin, according to Rahner, for what he calls a permanent existential "belongs to the whole of a person's earthly life and cannot be eradicated."[22] Like Ricoeur, Rahner sees human freedom at once free and limited.

Fallibility, Justice, and Mercy

Having very briefly thumbed through Ricoeur's Philosophy of the Will and Rahner's idea of human freedom, I want to borrow several ideas from them, as I move our discussion back to the subject of justice and mercy. First, Ricoeur helps to deepen our understanding of human agency by disclosing the interdependent link between freedom and body. Unlike physical or mental determinists such as Hobbes and Freud, Ricoeur shows the irreducible role of freedom within the complex web of physical and psychological needs and desires. Also in contrast to radical existentialists such as Sartre, he demonstrates that genuine human freedom is not something that can completely transcend our bodily and social needs as well as emotions. All of this has a special importance in an age where many view human agency simply either as a product of social construction or as an instance of unmediated interaction of genes. Similarly, Rahner enriches our understanding of human freedom by highlighting its temporal, historical, and social limits.[23] Although not completely bound by these limits, our freedom is not free from the possibility of error, even the acts of radical negation of our own freedom, and that this possibility always exists within each agent.

Related to this is the second insight on the fragility of human agency. It is no secret that both law and ethics presuppose the possibility of human agency. Law punishes those who violate it because it presupposes that people have the freedom of choice not to break the law. Likewise, ethics advises and rebukes those who act immorally because it presupposes that they have the freedom to take a different course of action. Undoubtedly, Ricoeur and Rahner affirm this view of human agency. However, they point out that our primordial freedom is also fragile. Human freedom is fragile in the sense that it is limited and tempered by our finite nature. Just as much as we can freely think, will, and feel, so also our knowledge, character, and emotions are subject to change. As a matter of fact, from childhood to adolescence and from adulthood to old age, our perspective, desire, and emotion do change. In the course of these changes, human beings often act in numerous ways destructive of self and others because, as both Ricoeur and Rahner demonstrate, fallibility or our capability of failing is endemic to human existence itself.

One may argue, however, that this fallibility does not invalidate the fact that human beings still have the freedom to choose their action and life, and that there are different degrees of fault or error. Of course, this point is well taken. As I will argue shortly, this is why I consider measures of justice still necessary to hold people accountable for their action. We must be warned not to reduce the complexity of human agency to an "either-or" logic of doing and not doing. Here we have to be sensitive to many forms or conditions of human life that may strengthen or weaken our ability to choose good. By forms of human life, I mean a plurality of basic goods the availability and the enjoyment of which make human life human. Such goods include family, friends, health, food, shelter, and education, to name only a few. True, we are able to deliberate and choose, but we should not overlook the fact that our thought and choice are also motivated by our needs and desires inherent in our body and sociality. To enlist Iris Murdoch's expression, especially apt here, we are able to choose only within the worlds we see. In this respect, we must acknowledge the facts that neither all individuals enjoy the same level of these basic goods, nor are their capacities for free choice identical.

Put differently, the fragility of human agency is vulnerability. Human freedom is not an uncircumscribed will that is radically free. Our freedom is one that reacts to actions upon us, seeks its meaning within our own social and historical worlds of meaning, and, moreover, is often frustrated by the challenges it faces. Inasmuch as we can impact others by our action, we are affected by conditions and forms of life that are beyond our control. In other words, to some extent human freedom is contingent upon what happens outside of our agency. Ancient Greeks knew best this vulnerable aspect of human existence, which they expressed in their literature on tragedy. Martha Nussbaum, working along similar themes of human fragility in her study of Greek ethics, thus writes that we are not only agents but also, in a sense, plants:

> That I am an agent, but also a plant; that much that I did not make goes towards making me whatever I shall be praised or blamed for being; that I must constantly choose among competing and apparently incommensurable goods and that circumstances may force me to a position in which I cannot help being false to something or doing something wrong; that an event that simply happens to me may, without my consent, alter my life; that it is equally problematic to entrust one's good to friends, lovers, or country and to try to have a good life without them—all these I take to be not just the material of tragedy, but everyday facts of lived practical reason.[24]

Fragility does not excuse someone from the wrongs he or she has committed. But it prods us to put ourselves at least in the shoes of the wrongdoer. Whether fragility is understood in terms of the Ricoeurian concept of fallibility or through the Rahnerian notion of the existential possibility of sin, a structural possibility of evil seems to remain in all of us. When this fallibility is also understood as vulnerability, it means that vulnerability to the contingent availability of basic goods is what we all share as human beings apart from our particular place in the world. This may help us to enlarge our empathy for other human beings, when we see them as vulnerable to this contingency of goods.

Let me now show how this discussion of human fallibility can help shape our views on justice and mercy. That we are fallible is not a normative but a descriptive statement. No one has to commit moral evil because we are fallible, but rather everyone has an inherent capacity for doing so. As our own experience may tell us, we often fail to live up to our moral ideals and values; we seem to grow and mature in our ethical pursuits, but our maturity is never that of perfection. Fallibility should not be a blank check for permitting any or all moral evils.

On the one hand, the idea of fallibility discloses the fact that human beings still have freedom in choosing their action, though limited and contingent. Fallibility designates the occasion for the possibility of evil but does not guarantee it. Justice must hold individuals accountable for their action, for the action, unless coerced by another, belongs only to the agent who willed, moved, and consented to the action. On the other hand, fallibility all too accurately predicts the tragic likelihood that people will commit evils. The society that is governed by the rule of law has a legal obligation to punish those who transgress the law and protect the innocent. Here justice thwarts and limits the consequences of evil, in case human fallibility eventuates into a fallen reality. In this way, fallibility as a structure of human existence grounds justice for no other than the reasons of fallibility.

Mercy also finds its reason of being in fallibility. At one level, mercy, the act of benevolence, is motivated by a thinking and feeling that empathizes with others on the ground of shared fallibility understood as both the structural possibility of evil and the vulnerability of human life. Mercy recognizes that we are all similar, even while being different. The possibility of human error or fault is not an indication of an ontological dualism within the human species but is a genuine mark of the synthetic reality of human being. Our individual pursuit of happiness proves not so much the power of individual autonomy but a common vulnerability to the contingency of basic goods that makes human life human. At another level, mercy affirms our genuine possibility to choose good over against our capability for evil, while at the same time it can enhance our capacity for choosing good by providing basic goods to the vulnerable other. In short, mercy is an act of affirming the human possibility of good, whereas justice remains a kind of remedy for the human possibility of evil. Thus, in my view, each of the two concepts addresses fallibility but in different ways.

I must add, however, that interactions between justice and mercy are also possible. Injustice can activate our empathy for other human beings by reminding us of their fragile and vulnerable conditions, thereby generating respect for them. Likewise, mercy can remind justice that we implement justice not only because our freedom needs accountability or protection but also because freedom has a moral meaning only when it is the freedom for choosing good.

Revisit

Earlier, I problematized Murphy's distinction of justice and mercy as falling along the line between public and private persons on the ground of the nature of justice itself. I also noted his tendency to view mercy as a bargaining concept. While Derrida helpfully differentiates mercy from justice by treating the former as irreducible to the logic of economic exchange, it remained a question whether justice overrun by mercy was acceptable. Therefore, focusing on the problem of human freedom within human experience, I have attempted to show how the idea of fallibility may serve our purpose of justifying and distinguishing justice and mercy. It has been my contention that both justice and mercy have irreducible spheres with distinct purposes and modi operandi, while also each supporting the other's purpose and modus operandi. Thus, I affirm a systematic distinction and relation between the two terms. While a conflict between claims of justice and mercy may be inevitable, we must find a unity between them because this unity is in fact required by the very structure of our existence as the synthesis of finite and infinite. On this account, what may appear as a bargaining or mitigating efficacy of mercy is in fact a strengthening of justice, and what may appear as strict justice is in fact affirming mercy in its respect for the fragile possibility of good. What is needed, then, is not a rejection of one over the other but the understanding of each in relation to the other. By giving human agency its due, we do justice to both mercy and justice.

Notes

1. Machiavelli, *The Prince*, 66.
2. Ibid., 67–70.
3. In this essay, I will use the terms "mercy" and "forgiveness" somewhat loosely to include the latter in the former. I consider forgiveness as an instance of mercy, and for the sake of my argument in this essay, I will use these terms without much distinction, as such distinction is not my main focus here.
4. Murphy and Hampton, *Forgiveness and Mercy*, 162–86.
5. Ibid., 169–72.

KEVIN JUNG

6. Ibid., 175.

7. Ibid., 176.

8. Ibid.

9. Derrida, *On Cosmopolitanism and Forgiveness,* 34.

10. Derrida here responds to Jankelevitch's view that forgiveness requires repentance.

11. Derrida, *On Cosmopolitanism and Forgiveness,* 31–32.

12. Ibid., 32.

13. Ibid., 55.

14. Derrida, "On the Gift," 59.

15. In fairness to Derrida, it is to be noted that he is well aware of this contradiction and rejects this ordinary sense of justice.

16. Ricoeur, *Freedom and Nature,* 8.

17. Ibid., 484.

18. Ricoeur, *Fallible Man,* 140.

19. Ibid., 141.

20. Rahner, *Foundations of Christian Faith,* 104.

21. Ibid., 42–43.

22. Ibid., 104.

23. Ricoeur's subsequent work also develops these themes.

24. Nussbaum, *The Fragility of Goodness,* 5.

Justice and Mercy
The Relation of Societal Norms and Empathic Feeling

PETER J. PARIS

The moral relationship between justice and mercy is analogous to the relationship between a morally good state and a morally good person. That is to say, justice is prior to mercy in the realm of practice. A morally good state is determined by morally good laws, which in turn provide the necessary conditions for the moral development of its citizens and, most important, the practice of justice by both individual citizens and the state. Of course, morally good laws are determined in large part by the moral quality of those who make the laws. In brief, justice pertains to objective standards of fairness that regulate human practices. Clearly the relation between just laws and just practices is circular. Each reflects the other. One cannot have the one apart from the other.

Within the state, justice is the rational dispassionate calculation of the good for all citizens including those who violate the law. In the wider world, justice is the good of all humanity guided in our day by such normative standards as those specified in the United Nations' Universal Declaration of Human Rights. Justice provides the structural conditions that enable humans in general and citizens in particular to grow and flourish so as to actualize their full potentialities.

Since the time of Aristotle, we have known that the morally good person is one whose passions and appetites are ordered by an internal rationality that is harmonious with that which the just laws of a morally good state allow. Accordingly, true friendships between morally good persons are based on the mutual love of each other's character. That love is the basic condition for mercy and its analogue, compassion. Mercy or compassion is empathic feeling for the other. It is based on sympathetic understanding of human weakness. Those who have had the experience of pain, suffering, and other kinds of distress are more likely to have the capacity to put themselves in the other's place and, hence, more capable of mercy than those who have not had such experiences. Like Reinhold Niebuhr, I contend that individual persons generally have a greater capacity for mercy than groups of people. Yet, unlike Niebuhr, I also contend that certain groups of people, often motivated by the inspiration of a particular type of religious insight, can and do undertake acts of mercy by providing habitual nurture and care for the growth and development of many people victimized by enduring cycles of destructive conditions.

Examples of those who practice such acts of mercy are seen in the work of Mother Teresa and others who care for orphans, the homeless, the sick, and the oppressed. All such people do mercy while imagining a more just society wherein the needs of the weak are met. More often than not, however, organizations of mercy do not have the capacity to protest against the structures of injustice as the primary causes of the suffering. Yet, though their acts of mercy produce only limited short-term results, they do not necessarily contradict or take the place of justice. If they were to do either they would be in opposition to justice and hence immoral since justice is surely inclusive of all the moral virtues. Thus, true acts of mercy do not thwart justice even when they cannot work directly for justice. As stated above, mercy refers to the quality of our responses to vulnerable people: the poor, the disabled, the orphans, the strangers, the refugees, or the imprisoned, and others. Mercy and justice are not polar opposites. Embracing and loving mercy implies treating the vulnerable and weak with loving kindness.

Yet, when the conditions for justice do not exist, priority must be given to the aim of establishing those conditions. The civil rights movement of the 1950s and 1960s evidences that endeavor, and the activity of nonviolent resistance illustrated the unity of justice and mercy in its concern for the well-being of both the civil rights activists and their enemies.

Some organizations do the work of mercy while prophetically condemning injustice by demanding structural reform as the necessary condition for justice. Examples of such groups are the Open Door Community in Atlanta, many churches like the Glyde Memorial Church in San Francisco, the Southern Poverty and Law Center in Montgomery, the Exodus Project in East Harlem, the South African Council of Churches during the anti-apartheid movement, to mention only a few. All of these groups unite the practice of justice advocacy with the provision of social services. By doing so they demonstrate their solidarity with the victims of injustice and divide their energies between the provision of emergency care and the struggle for a permanently just solution. The latter aims at the empowerment of the victims to become self-determining moral agents in society rather than dependent entities on the largesse of others.

Murphy Davis, a leader in the Open Door Community in Atlanta, writes the following, which aptly describes the relation of justice and mercy as they are united in the interpersonal experience of solidarity inspired by Christian insight concerning the weak and vulnerable:

> When we walk with our homeless sisters and brothers on the mean streets, we yearn to embrace kindness, we ache for mercy. When we agitate for fairness in the "justice" system, the fire burns in our bones for those who are thrown away into the prison system like so much garbage. When we sit on death row with those who wait year after year, we hunger and thirst for this mercy, we anguish for relief as the minutes tick toward the hour of death by execution. But on the Lenten journey, this anguish can open us to be taught by Jesus to live in active, relentless resistance to the powers that crush and kill the poor and forgotten ones among us.[1]

Clearly, acts of mercy can be exercised in many spheres of activity. Another such sphere is the discretion in the exercise of justice by law enforcement officers. Parenthetically, let me say that the preparation of this essay led to considerable discussion with my son, Peter B. Paris, who is now a criminal defense lawyer in Washington, D.C., after having spent three years as a law enforcement officer in Boston. I am indebted to him for his assistance in helping me to understand the discretionary sphere attending the judgments of law enforcement agencies.[2]

Keeping in mind that mercy should neither contradict the demands of justice nor be a substitute for it, let us look at an example: police officers at the scene of a traffic violation who render their judgment by using their discretion after assessing all the relevant factors in the situation. The officers have the following legal options: (*a*) issue a ticket for the offender to appear in court or plead guilty and pay a fine; (*b*) handcuff the offender and place him/her under arrest; or (*c*) give the offender a written or oral warning. Clearly, all who exercise such discretionary powers are influenced by many subjective considerations attending the offense itself. These include race, gender, economic condition, age, social status, religion, nationality, as well as whether or not this is a first or habitual offense. Depending on the moral development of the officer, one or more of these factors could become the principal determinant either in the exercise of mercy or injustice. Great care must be exercised here since what might be viewed as an act of mercy in one context could be an act of injustice in another context.

In many American states, the sentencing of criminals is at the discretion of judges. Consequently, judges get labeled either lenient or harsh, commonly dubbed either "liberal" or "hanging" judges. In order to avoid the subjectivity of individual judges and the concomitant disparity of sentences, some states like Virginia place the sentencing of criminals in the hand of juries, who in passing judgment render themselves vulnerable to the special pleas of both the victims and the criminal. In either case, however, one invariably finds a wide disparity of sentencing among judges and juries.

As a remedy for both of these situations, the United States Sentencing Commission[3]—a permanent agency in the judicial branch created to monitor sentencing practices in the federal courts—has established a manual of statutory guidelines for sentencing in federal courts. The aim of those guidelines is to provide an objective quantitative judgment that fits every federal criminal offense. Thus the manual seeks to eliminate the subjective discretionary element that inheres in both judges and juries by developing a system that is more honest, uniform, equitable, and proportional in both the sentencing procedures and their results. By severely narrowing the sentencing range attending each category of criminal acts, the federal courts seek a fairer and more uniform result in its sentencing. The adoption of this manual in the Congressional Sentencing Reform Act of April 13, 1987, severely limits the discretion of the sentencing courts by making all criminal offenses liable to the same sentence. Yet the complexity of the sentencing guidelines is seen in deciding between principles guiding real-offense versus charge-offense sentencing; plea agreements; probation and split sentences; and multicount convictions, to mention only a few. In several of those areas, considerable discretion is still operative among prosecutors. Further, it is important to note that the federal guidelines do not satisfy either those who want harsh sentences or those who prefer lenient sentences (see Jonathan Rothchild's essay in this volume). It is clearly a compromise system that solves some problems at the expense of others.

Though the Federal Sentencing Guidelines do not prevent a federal judge from exercising his/her own judgment in such federal cases, the burden is on him or her to justify that judgment in a written rationale specifying the need for departing from the sentencing guidelines. It is important to note, however, that vast numbers of judges and probation officers are opposed to the federal guidelines because they believe the guidelines give too much power to prosecutors and fail to make adequate distinctions among criminal offenses in the same category such as first-time offenses, single or multiple charges in the same case, and so on.

If, as I have claimed, mercy attends the sphere of discretionary judgment, then the federal statutory guidelines aim at eliminating or severely reducing the practice of mercy. The absence of a parole system in federal court eliminates another area of discretionary judgment and thus further erodes the possibility of mercy in sentencing since parole boards decide on the basis of their collective judgment whether or not a convict has been adequately rehabilitated in order to merit release. Though many would like to see more mercy shown in the sentencing practices, and though parole systems were established to make such practices possible, a vast amount of evidence is available to demonstrate that the subjective judgments of parole boards have been "merciful" to some and "unmerciful" to others. In either case, the claims of justice may or may not have been contradicted. Yet, though it is often abused, the parole system is the only means for the retention of hope by providing an incentive for rehabilitation.

Clearly the aim of the sentencing guidelines in federal courts is to standardize all sentencing by providing a uniform rational quantitative sentencing standard. Federal crimes are far fewer in number than other types of crime, and since there are fewer racial and ethnic criminals in federal prisons than in state prisons, this group often receives maximum sentences by judges and/or juries with wide discretionary powers within very limited guidelines. Usually, those limited guidelines merely determine statutory maximum penalties for particular offenses. Although such guidelines comprise important starting points for judges, they provide virtually no guidance whatsoever for sentencing decisions concerning appropriate penalties in particular cases.

Some states, however, have moved closer to the federal sentencing model. Examples of such are those that adopt the so-called "three-strikes-and-you're-out" policy or those that refuse parole to violent felons. Both remove the conditions for mercy in sentencing procedures; by doing so, they destroy the possibility for any future change in the sentence itself. Thus hope perishes, as does the possibility of rehabilitation.

Some contend that the increasing collaboration between local police, the Federal Bureau of Investigation, and the Bureau of Alcohol, Tobacco, Firearms and Explosives portends a gradual displacement of local police jurisdictions by the federal law-enforcement agencies, which introduces another set of problems with respect to municipal, state, and federal jurisdictions. For many, the federal court system of sentencing provides credence to the expression "lock them up and throw away the key."

In my judgment, acts of mercy should occur only after the demands of justice have been met. To do otherwise would promote permissiveness that would be neither merciful nor just. Permissiveness neither corrects the wrongdoer nor restores the original condition that existed prior to the act of wrongdoing. Mercy alone fails to serve the demands of justice either in its deterrent or retributive functions.

Clearly certain criminal actions are so heinous that their perpetrators may rightly be viewed as totally lacking in the capacity to behave properly in civil society. The assumption that such people are curable must be based on adequate scientific and medical evidence. Possible examples of such incurables may be pedophiles, rapists, and serial killers, though further study and research are needed to prove this assessment. In all such extreme cases, acts of mercy must coincide with acts of justice, no more or no less.

After proper diagnosis, all such extreme criminals should be removed from civil society because they have forfeited their civil rights by practices stemming from their mental defect. All such criminals should be treated as mentally deficient and thus a public health risk. They should not be merely stored away in warehouses for the sake of punishment but, rather, treated as incurable until such time as a definitive cure has been adequately demonstrated. Like all diseased persons, they should be treated in a morally just way since the moral quality of our society is reflected in the way it treats its weakest members, including those who are defective in nature. To treat such people in a moral way would evidence the unity of justice and mercy. That unity is expressed in the provision of moral conditions for the moral development of these morally deficient personalities. To do otherwise would diminish the morality of both the criminals and their jailers. Since persons become morally rehabilitated only by developing the habit of doing morally good actions, all criminals should be given the opportunity to develop such habits of moral practice. Such people should be treated with respect by receiving appropriate praise and recognition for their good works and moral deeds. As implied above, many of these people may be required to live indefinitely in surrogate communities apart from civil society. Yet every effort should be made to enable those surrogate communities to become moral communities in both their internal and external relations.

Further, I think that it would be an act of mercy to change our perceptions of criminal justice by moving away from our habitual orientation of merely punishing criminals and begin viewing violent crimes as public health problems that cry out for preventive rather than reactive strategies. Such a viewpoint has been long advocated by Harvard University's Deborah Prothrow-Stith, who has "examined violence as a societal disease that could be prevented through public health strategies."[4] More specifically, she argues that a public health approach to crime would move the society from reactive to preventive measures. Her plan for addressing teenage violent crimes is similar to the way a public health official addresses the problem of teenage smoking—"(a) changing public perceptions, norms and attitudes by changing the way violence is portrayed via the media, television and sporting events. (b) reel-in the kids at risk who are typically absent from school, often suspended and have already had a few brushes with the law. . . . these kids are the ones who are crying out for our attention, money and resources more than ever."[5]

The fear that viewing criminal behavior as stemming from mental deficiency might lead to greater abuse of those so labeled should not be the sole basis for denying such an approach. Admittedly, adequate study and research of the criminal mind requires a necessary allocation of monies and resources. That could be an act of justice and mercy. To do otherwise would only serve to maintain the status quo. The recent release of the one hundredth person from a ten-year stay on death row because of a wrongful conviction should be sufficient evidence that our present system of capital punishment is faulty to the extreme.

Of course, viewing the criminal mind as a public health problem does not imply isolating the criminal from certain social conditions that contribute to the formation of such a mind. Rather, a thorough study of criminal behavior necessitates a study of societal conditions that produce crime as well as the mental condition of the criminal. Preventive remedies must be provided for both.

I am convinced that if more crimes were viewed as public health problems, society would develop a better disposition concerning their treatment. The present prison system is the worst possible environment for rehabilitation because its aim is to punish rather than to rehabilitate; it is neither just nor merciful. Society's reluctance to provide the necessary conditions and resources for effective rehabilitation programs is based on its deep inclination toward vengeance and retaliation.[6] Thus our society spends vast amounts of money that produce no positive return for the society other than the spirit of vengeance. If our moral values were different, we would not prefer spending increasing amounts of money for incarceration rather than for education, child care, and summer enrichment programs. If our moral values were different, we would provide opportunities for those who must be removed from civil society to make substantial contributions to society through educational programs, arts and crafts, music and song, writing and publishing, carpentry, agriculture, and countless other good practices. The expenditure of monies and personnel for such a creative venture would produce good returns since it is well-known that such rehabilitative programs are effective. Such a rehabilitative system would constitute the best possible way of uniting mercy and justice in a genuine criminal justice system. Most important, such a rehabilitative method would rid the society of its present penal system that merely provides a revolving-door situation for short-term offenders, a warehouse condition for long-term criminals, and a waiting system for those on death row. Thus I affirm the call of Angela Davis and others for the birth of a new abolition movement to rid our society of all traces of the present inhumane penal system and its mission of merely punishing offenders by exacting fines, sentencing them to prison for terms of varying length, or executing them either with the electric chair or by lethal injection. In all such cases, punitive measures alone are neither just nor merciful and should be abolished.

Notes

1. Davis, "Walk Humble," 9.
2. I assume full responsibility for any possible errors or misinterpretations contained in my explication of the *Guidelines Manual* and its implications.
3. See *Guidelines Manual,* chap. 1, pt. A, "Introduction and General Application Principles," November 1, 1998, 1–11.
4. See http://www.hsph.harvard.edu/faculty/DeborahProthrow-Stith.html.

5. Shawn O'Leary, "Prevention versus Reactionary Measures: MLK Day Speaker Puts Public Health Spin on Violence Prevention, Focusing on Youth Programs," http://abacus.bates.edu/thestudent/127/11/news/prothrow-stith.html.

6. For an excellent treatise on how Protestant theology has lead our society to adopt a punitive and vindictive criminal justice system rather than one aimed at rehabilitating and healing criminals, victims, and their communities, see Snyder, *The Protestant Ethic and the Spirit of Punishment.*

Criminal Justice and
the Law of Love
Reflections on the Public
Theology of Reinhold Niebuhr

W. CLARK GILPIN

In a penetrating inquiry into the history of modern prison reform, the late Norval Morris, a legal scholar at the University of Chicago, asked us to confront the question of why prison conditions merit a society's most serious consideration. Part of the answer, said Morris, "is to be found in the fact that the criminal justice system exercises the greatest power that a state can legally use against its citizens." Consequently, the treatment of convicted criminals discloses the functioning norms of human decency and fairness, the protections of citizenship, and the restraints on the exercise of force that pervade the society as a whole. Both philosophers and reflective political leaders, Morris continued, "have appreciated that reality and have suggested that the treatment of the convicted criminal is a sound barometer to the civilization of a society."[1] To examine the criminal justice system in order to address a broader ethical question concerning the relation of justice to mercy, as this book does, is one significant way to respond to the challenge that Morris's question poses for American civilization.

This chapter will follow the lead of Norval Morris and focus on prison conditions as a critical location at which to take a "barometric" measurement of social norms and values. It will use a theological barometer. That is, the chapter will adapt the strategy of a 1935 book by the American Protestant theologian Reinhold Niebuhr (1892–1971), entitled *An Interpretation of Christian Ethics,* in order to evaluate the tacit social ethic of prison conditions in America. The specific historical "test case" for this strategy will be the remarkable transformation of the institutions and purposes of imprisonment that occurred in the United States in the years from approximately 1790 to 1860.

The chapter's more general purpose is to explore, through the example of criminal justice, the basic tasks of a public theology. When theologians have occasion to speak on issues facing a complicated social institution such as the criminal justice system, two types of questions arise. One sort of question is about the value of theological language for the interpretation of broad social issues. Is it fruitful to speak theologically, when many participants in the discussion will have scant understanding of the terms and methods of theological reasoning and will frequently assume that it is "in-group" language, ill-suited to the public arena? What can theology contribute to a general analysis of problems in American criminal justice? Does a theologian represent a perspective that is unlikely to be examined by a jurist, sociologist, or police chief but that, nonetheless, illuminates and perhaps fruitfully restates commonly perceived problems and issues? A second type of question turns back toward the theologian and asks whether, or in what way, theological deliberation on social issues is part of the central enterprise of theology itself. Is public theology a necessary feature of theology as a whole? And, for our purposes in this book, do the specific issues surrounding criminal justice provide a productive topic for thinking about the contemporary character and task of public theology?

An Impossible Ethical Ideal

Niebuhr originally delivered what would become *An Interpretation of Christian Ethics* as a public lecture series at Colgate-Rochester Divinity School in 1934. The lectureship was named to honor Walter Rauschenbusch, and, in a brief preface, Niebuhr expressed his hope that the lectures extended and applied the stance of that noted theologian of the Social Gospel, "who was not only the real founder of social Christianity in this country but also its most brilliant and generally satisfying exponent to the present day." In the early 1930s, Niebuhr himself edited a socialist journal, *World Tomorrow,* and, on two occasions, had run for office on the Socialist Party ticket. In 1933, the Protestant systematic theologian Paul Tillich had joined Niebuhr on the faculty of Union Theological Seminary, New York, and the preface concluded by thanking Tillich "for many valuable suggestions in the development of my theme, some of them made specifically and others the by-product of innumerable discussions on the thesis of this book."[2]

However, despite his own direct involvement in politics and his stated appreciation for Rauschenbusch's religiously motivated social criticism, Niebuhr began his book in a way that seemingly made any enterprise of "social Christianity" or public theology extraordinarily difficult, if not positively wrongheaded. He insisted on a sharp divide between a modern social ethic—as it attempted to adjudicate immediately pressing questions of political, economic, and criminal justice—and a religious ethic. "The ethic of Jesus," according to Niebuhr, "does not deal at all with the immediate moral problem of every human life—the problem of arranging some kind of armistice between various contending factions and forces. It has nothing to say about the relativities of politics and economics, nor of the necessary balances of power which exist and must exist in even the most intimate social relationships." Instead, when Christian theology followed the lead of Jesus, it made the "law of love" its central principle, and this was an "impossible ethical ideal." Thus, in the case of criminal justice, "if one were to follow the words of Jesus, 'Let him who is without sin cast the first stone,' without qualification, no criminal could ever be arrested." Elsewhere in the book, Niebuhr expanded this reflection on the words of Jesus (John 8:7) by observing that "an unqualified insistence upon guiltlessness as a prerequisite of the right to punish would invalidate every measure required for the maintenance of social order."[3] In short, political and social ethics could not—or at least should not—be understood as efforts to "apply" the moral insight of Jesus directly to a given situation.

In so stating the matter, Niebuhr appears to have rendered the Christian religion useless to any ethical social policy. His actual purpose was to generate a fruitful paradox. Only by maintaining a sharp—even stark—contrast between social ethics and religious ethics would religion, he thought, gain a significant ethical voice in modern society. "The ethical fruitfulness of various types of religion," Niebuhr wrote, "is determined by the quality of their tension between the historical and the transcendent. This quality is measured by two considerations: The degree to which the transcendent truly transcends every value and achievement of history, so that no relative value of historical achievement may become the basis of moral complacency; and the degree to which the transcendent remains in organic contact with the historical, so that no degree of tension may rob the historical of its significance."[4]

As Niebuhr well knew, this productive tension between transcendence and history had rarely characterized Christianity's social posture. Much more often, Christianity had sought to fashion or to contribute to a cultural synthesis, in which some actual religious, scientific, or political achievement served as the historical norm that consolidated social values. Various efforts to achieve such a synthesis have characterized most of the history of Protestantism in the United States,[5] and Niebuhr's analysis usefully suggested three forms that synthesis has taken. One, which Niebuhr called "Orthodox Christianity," tried "vainly to meet the social perplexities of a complex civilization" by applying to the general society the ethical precepts it had fashioned from authoritative scriptures and traditions in order to guide its own group behavior. Anxious to demonstrate that it did not share this anachronistic ethic, "the liberal church" had taken a second course and devoted itself to demonstrating the compatibility of religious ethics with modern law, medicine, and the social sciences, sometimes falling to the level of "merely clothing the naturalistic philosophy and the utilitarian ethics of modernity with pious phrases." In a third variant, religious presuppositions became untethered from specifically religious practices and institutions, drifting into other social domains, where they tacitly and without critical scrutiny influenced decisions about, to take our case, criminal justice. With respect to this third variant of synthesis, Niebuhr concluded that "the whole of modern secular liberal culture, to which liberal Christianity is unduly bound, is really a devitalized and secularized religion in which the presuppositions of a Christian tradition have been rationalized and read into the processes of history and nature, supposedly discovered by objective science."[6] Features of this threefold typology of synthesis, on which Niebuhr heaped his disfavor, may be seen throughout the history of prison reform in the era from 1790 to 1860, and a brief synopsis of that history makes Niebuhr's own alternative perspective more concrete.

Criminal Justice in Antebellum America

During the past twenty-five years, scholars have greatly expanded our knowledge of the history of imprisonment in Western societies and, in particular, called attention to a dramatic change in the punishment of criminals that occurred toward the close of the eighteenth century and the beginning of the nineteenth.[7] Briefly, with respect to the United States, the penal codes of *colonial* America had been organized around corporal punishment: whipping, public confinement in the stocks, branding, or the death penalty. Consequently, the jail primarily served for temporary detention, while the offender awaited trial and punishment. But in the early republic, theories of punishment began to change rather rapidly, moving away from physical punishment and toward punishment by the deprivation of liberty for a set length of time. During the first half of the nineteenth century, the United States built its first modern prisons, reflecting the newer ideas of punishment, according to which convicted persons served prison sentences of specified duration.

Despite these major changes in the form of punishment, one particularly important continuity persisted from the late colonial period into the nineteenth century: punishment for crime remained thoroughly entangled with economic considerations and distinctions of social class. More strongly put, economics and class established the framework within which justice was understood and administered. Colonial scales of physical punishment, for example, had honored social gradation, such that the most common punishment for a minor offense, whipping, was not permitted in colonial New York for "men of rank." A settled social hierarchy was thought to ground community order, and social outsiders were perceived to be the most likely sources of crime. In the colonial period, this perception had focused on nonresidents of a town or "vagabonds," but, by the middle of the nineteenth century, it applied to recent immigrants who were becoming prison inmates in disproportionately large numbers.

The continuing practice of imprisonment for debt also clearly reflected this linkage among class, economics, and criminal justice. In the years leading up to the Revolution, the plight of American debtors had worsened, with the English financial crisis of 1772 severely affecting colonial commerce and increasing the number of debtors consigned to prison. Historian Gary Nash finds it "one of the ironies of the era" that one of the two largest buildings constructed during the colonial era, the Walnut Street Prison, was widely admired as among the architectural wonders of Philadelphia but was necessitated by jails crowded with hungry city dwellers who stole for a living and tradesmen who had failed to pay debts. The second large Philadelphia construction project of the decade before the Revolution was the Bettering House, an enterprise of the city's Quaker merchants, who formed themselves into an association, the Contributors to the Relief and Employment of the Poor, and built this workhouse for the able-bodied poor.[8]

The states were very slow to alter the colonial debt statutes. In 1816 in New York City, for instance, jails held nearly two thousand imprisoned debtors, with well over half of these confined for debts of less than fifty dollars. The Boston Society for the Relief of the Distressed reported that approximately 3,500 debtors had been imprisoned in Boston between January 1820 and April 1822. Efforts by the Boston Society and similar benevolent organizations helped to turn public opinion, and in 1821 Kentucky led the way in the abolition of imprisonment for debt, with eight more states following suit by 1848.

Throughout these decades religiously motivated individuals and benevolence societies urged better prisons, more humane treatment, and the replacement of physical punishment by extended imprisonment intended to reform the criminal. The earliest and most successful of the prison-reform societies, the Philadelphia Society for Alleviating the Miseries of Public Prisons (1787), involved Philadelphia leaders of varied religious persuasion, including Benjamin Franklin, the Presbyterian patriot and physician Benjamin Rush, Episcopal bishop William White, and the Quakers Roberts and Richard Vaux. In Philadelphia and elsewhere, such reform societies typically combined concern for living conditions, the provision of religious services, the distribution of Bibles, and Sunday schools for both religious instruction and teaching in elementary subjects.

As prison reform developed momentum, the reformers self-consciously wove the purposes of imprisonment into the political, economic, and religious assumptions of the new nation. Just as educators and religious leaders sought to build schools and churches that reflected and supported republican understandings of equal citizenship under the law, so Thomas Eddy of New York worked to revise the inherited criminal codes, which had been built on "monarchical principles" that now seemed ill-suited to "a new country, simple manners, and a popular form of government." Meanwhile, in Philadelphia, Benjamin Rush opposed capital punishment as "the natural offspring of monarchical governments. . . . Kings consider their subjects as their property; no wonder, therefore, they shed their blood with as little emotion as men shed the blood of their sheep or cattle. But the principles of republican government speak a very differ-

W. CLARK GILPIN

ent language. . . . An execution in a republic is like a human sacrifice in religion." [9]

After 1815, religiously motivated humanitarianism combined with rapidly increasing populations to spur construction of new prisons. In New York in 1816, the Auburn Penitentiary utilized a system of individual cells, but each was so small (7 x 3 1/2 feet) that the health of inmates rapidly deteriorated. In 1823, the prison altered its procedures to provide congregate labor during the day and confinement to cells only at night. The reformers believed that the industrial and religious environment of the prisoner could be constructed so as to impose a transformation of character, interior change that made the person self-reliant and self-controlled. Imposed solitude would occasion, it was thought, introspective remorse, and this in turn would reform the prisoner's character. This "Auburn system" became a widely imitated model, not only in the United States but in England and France, and was praised both for its good effects on the inmates' habits of personal industry and its economic efficiency. Foreign visitors not only speculated that Auburn's combination of solitary confinement and collective labor was transforming many convicts into honest and industrious citizens, but they also calculated that income from convict labor might well exceed the expenses of maintaining the prison.

In 1829, the Eastern State Penitentiary outside Philadelphia developed a regimen of prison life that, even more than Auburn, emphasized the belief that institutionalized solitude could awaken conscience and renovate character. Inmates, according to this plan, neither had contact with each other nor were they visited by family and friends. For the duration of their sentences, they would both live and work in solitude, each occupying a separate cell and laboring individually at tasks assigned by the prison authorities. The expected reading for inmates included not news of the outside world but religious materials such as the Bible. Rules of silence, even hoods worn when moving outside their cells, imposed the objective of transformative self-confrontation. These methods conformed to the medical views of Benjamin Rush, who prescribed solitary confinement not only for penal institutions but also for child rearing, as a means to internalize self-control. Although humanitarian impulses had motivated the repudiation of corporal punishment and efforts toward moral reform, observers might well doubt the resulting regimen. When Charles Dickens visited Eastern State Penitentiary in 1842, he regarded the "slow and daily tampering with the mysteries of the brain, to be immeasurably worse than any torture of the body."[10]

Reading of the truly horrific capital punishments meted out against heretics or traitors in the sixteenth and seventeenth centuries, we may well conclude that Dickens's question of better or worse is not self-evident on either side. But for our purposes, it is especially important to note that the prison conditions Dickens observed in the United States had resulted from the convergence or interweaving of economic, political, medical, educational, and religious assumptions about human nature and the psychological underpinnings of social behavior. This "daily tampering with the mysteries of the brain" reflected, in the extreme conditions of imprisonment, a widely held synthesis of ideas about the sources of virtue and the nature of productive citizenship.

The Relevance of an Impossible Ethical Ideal

In deploying "the ethic of Jesus," Niebuhr aimed to gain critical leverage on what we might call "the ethics of social synthesis," illustrated in early nineteenth-century penal theory and practice. Without denying moral motives or some good results to reform efforts such as these, Niebuhr nonetheless thought that their emphasis on the compatibility of educational ideas, codes of personal virtue, and economic prudence left them fatally vulnerable to rationalization that unduly benefited inherited privilege and economic power. If religious ethics had a distinctive role to play in modernity, he argued that this role had to include disrupting any synthesis in which religion too readily sanctioned the status quo.

To suggest the standpoint from which his own argument would proceed, Niebuhr appealed to directional metaphors of depth and height. The distinctive contribution of a religious morality to the general moral life, he proposed, arose because religion was "troubled by the question of the primal 'whence' and the final 'wherefore.'" From this troublesome question, religion pursued "its sense of a dimension of depth" that traced "every force with which it deals to some ultimate origin" and related "every purpose to some ultimate end." In thus "straining after an ultimate coherence," religion employed myth (a term that suggests the influence of his conversations with Tillich) to explore "vertical aspects of reality which transcend the horizontal relationships which science analyzes, charts and records." Mythical language portrayed "the flux of the finite world" as a revelation, in the sense that "every finite event points to something beyond itself in two directions, to a source from which it springs and an end to which it moves." But mythical language also regarded the world as a veil, in the sense that "the human spirit is set in this dimension of depth in such a way that it is able to apprehend, but not to comprehend, the total dimension." Used in this way, Niebuhr thought, mythic religious language was "capable of picturing the world as a realm of coherence and meaning without defying the facts of incoherence." Mythic language of God the creator introduced an absolute dimension of "depth" into the overwhelmingly complex "breadth" of life in the world because "the forms of life are too various and multifarious to be ascribed easily to a single source or related to a single realm of meaning if the source does not transcend all the observable facts and forces, and the realm does not include more than the history of the concrete world."[11] In the pattern of the book as a whole, these metaphors of verticality and depth suggested that religious ethics had the primary purpose of reorienting social ethics. Its aim was not so much to add distinctively Christian ethical principles alongside principles such as justice or compassion but instead to place existing ethical values in a new set of relationships, including new relations to one another.

Niebuhr most clearly distinguished between an ethics of social synthesis and his reorienting religious ethic, which he termed "prophetic religion," in his exegetical remarks on Matthew 5:44–48:

> But I say to you, Love your enemies and pray for those who persecute you, so that you may be sons of your Father who is in heaven; for he makes his sun rise on the evil and on the good, and sends rain on the just and on the unjust. For if you love those who love you, what reward have you? Do not even the tax collectors do the same? And if you salute only your brethren, what more are you doing than others? Do not even the Gentiles do the same? You, therefore, must be perfect, as your heavenly Father is perfect.

Niebuhr found the central moral insight of this text in the idea that, "since God permits the sun to shine upon the evil and the good and sends the rain upon the just and the unjust, we are to love our enemies." The scriptural passage presented the religious imperative to emulate the character of God as the only motive for loving our enemies. It ignored any prudential considerations and set aside social consequences, such as the possibility that the practice of forgiveness might transform enmity into friendship. It fashioned nature's indiscriminate bounty into a symbol for "the supra-moral character of divine grace," which was defined by an impartial, comprehensive, and equal regard for all. The justification for this ethical mandate, Niebuhr asserted, was "put in purely religious and not socio-moral terms. . . . It is oriented by only one vertical religious reference, to the will of God; and the will of God is defined in terms of an all-inclusive love." [12]

Criminal Justice and the Law of Love

By imagining the divine will in terms of "an all-inclusive love" that extended impartial regard to all, Niebuhr sought to orient religious ethics in a way that gave it independence and "uncompromising rigor" with respect to concrete social decisions and values. By orienting itself toward "the unconditioned good which it dimly apprehends as the ground and goal of all contingent values," theological ethics could not, he emphasized, transcend "the partial perspectives of a limited time and space" or surmount the finite constraints that prevented "incarnating, all the higher values which it discerns." But by responding to the pressure "to relate all finite events to causes and consummations beyond themselves," it could serve as a critical, diagnostic theory of the tacit norms governing social relations. [13] Niebuhr summarized this image of the divine governance as "the law of love," and, although his applications of it to criminal justice were brief, they pose three instructive challenges for contemporary public theology.

Niebuhr would have agreed fully with the argument of Norval Morris, with which I began, that the treatment of convicted criminals discloses the standards of civilization that pervade the wider society. For this reason, Niebuhr considered issues of "corrective justice" in tandem with broader social issues of "distributive justice" and proposed that the regulative principle for both was equality. "In the ideal of equality there is an echo of the law of love," understood as the impartial and comprehensive regard by which the necessary conditions of life are available to all—by which the sun and rain benefit just and unjust alike. "In a struggle between those who enjoy inordinate privileges and those who lack the basic essentials of the good life it is fairly clear that a religion which holds love to be the final law of life stultifies itself if it does not support equal justice as a political and economic approximation of the ideal of love." [14]

He recognized that, even in the most equalitarian society, some special rewards and differences of privilege made the performance of various social functions possible and, along with human sinfulness, qualified the actual presence of full equality in any possible society. Nevertheless, equality remained "a principle of criticism under which every scheme of justice stands and a symbol of the principle of love involved in all moral judgments." Clearly, in the case of criminal justice, equality as a principle of criticism challenged the long-standing differences in punishment that resulted from differences in socioeconomic class. At a first—even rudimentary—level, then, public theology in the tradition of Niebuhr employs theological reflection to propose for debate norms and purposes that provide the comprehensive frame of reference for social conduct within a given society. In this case, as a Christian theologian, Niebuhr arrived at the principle of equal justice through a process of theological reflection on mythic thought in the New Testament. But other thinkers, representing other traditions of reasoning, may nonetheless engage his assertion of the ethical primacy of equal justice in a democratic society or deliberate its implications for the criminal justice system.

Second, public theology in the tradition of Niebuhr employs theological reflection to suggest ethical principles that should stand in close relationship to and appropriately modify comprehensive norms such as equal justice. He did not, for instance, relate the ideal of equality to the concept that individuals ought to have independently equal status before the law. Instead, his reflections on equal justice proceeded from human solidarity, the idea of "an unrealizable breadth of obligation of life to life." Here, Niebuhr returned to the story in the Gospel of John of the woman taken in adultery, which I cited earlier: "Let him who is without sin cast the first stone." In this case, however, Niebuhr's point was not about the impossibility of literally following this dictum as an ethical principle. Instead, he took it as the occasion for reflecting on the social interconnections implied by the doctrine of original sin. From this perspective, the criminal and the citizen were more alike than the citizen might wish to think. Crime was implicated in wider social exchanges. Social justice and criminal justice were closely aligned. "The society which punishes criminals," he concluded, "is never so conscious as it might be of the degree to which it is tainted with, and responsible for, the very sins which it abhors and punishes." Realization of this complicity would certainly not lead to cessation of all forms of punishment, but it was "possible to deal with the criminal in terms of this realization and to qualify the spiritual pride of the usually self-righteous guardians of public morals."[15]

These first two strands in Niebuhr's religious ethic, the norm of equal justice and its modification by the idea of human solidarity, are connected to a third point that is significant for the broader purposes of this book. Both equal justice and human solidarity, in my view, led Niebuhr to avoid the concept of "mercy" with respect to criminal justice. As I shall discuss presently, Niebuhr instead used the term "forgiveness." A quick glance at virtually any dictionary will suggest a good reason for this avoidance. In most of its connotations, mercy is forbearance or clemency extended by a person in power to another who has no claim to receive kindness, in a case where severity is merited. The idea of mercy does not rest easily with Niebuhr's commitments to the ideal of equality and human solidarity, and it does little, if anything, "to qualify the spiritual pride of the usually self-righteous guardians of public morals."

This observation leads me to my third and final feature of a public theology in the tradition of Reinhold Niebuhr. This is the persistent claim, found throughout his writings, that many of the most worrisome public problems were, to significant degree, specifically religious problems and therefore required a specifically religious analysis. With respect to punishment of those convicted of crimes, he thought that the purpose of regulating or restraining "the element of vengeance" in punitive justice represented a major challenge to the religious imagination.

In no small measure, social conflict in modern societies had become more brutal, Niebuhr thought, because increasingly rational systems, including religion, "imparted more universal pretensions to partial social interests" by justifying them with appeals "for 'Kultur,' for democracy, for justice, and for every conceivable universal value." Employed in this way, social values, including religious values, heightened inevitable social conflicts by endowing those who waged them with "the fury of self-righteousness."[16] Thus, one important reason to insist, as Niebuhr did, that religion taught an "impossible ethical ideal" was to thwart the appropriation of religious values in ways that aggravated violence in society. To this end, Niebuhr appealed to "the doctrine of forgiveness" as an ethical norm for social conflict in general and for the treatment of the convicted criminal in particular. As with his analysis of equal justice, Niebuhr's appeal to forgiveness, rather than mercy, as a norm for criminal justice sprang from his theological view that the universally pervasive

W. CLARK GILPIN

effects of sin established a fundamental human connection between the prisoner and the free citizen. The "law of love" as exemplified in forgiveness was "the demand that the evil in the other shall be borne without vindictiveness because the evil in the self is known."[17]

Although public theology in the tradition of Niebuhr initially arises because it is religiously "troubled by the question of the primal 'whence' and the final 'wherefore,'" it raises this question of the comprehensive frame of meaning in order to address the common life of a civilization with the intellectual resources distinctively at its disposal. The theologian is by no means, of course, the only citizen concerned with equal justice before the law, with the common humanity of the prisoner, or with the undue intrusion of vindictiveness into the criminal justice system. But, in concert with lawyer, religious activist, or police officer, the public theologian participates in all of these discussions and proposes ethical connections among them. Further, it is the particular responsibility of the public theologian to mount a specifically theological critique of religion itself, insofar as religion rationalizes or justifies social assumptions that undercut equal justice or condone "the fury of self-righteousness." For Niebuhr, these concrete issues of social equity deserved to have theology as a primary intellectual resource: "Human life can have dignity only as it is comprehended and understood in a universe of meaning which transcends human life. It is the life in this ark of prophetic religion, therefore, which must generate the spiritual of any culture of any age in which human vitality is brought under a decent discipline. . . . Nothing short of the knowledge of the true God will save [humans] from the impiety of making themselves god and the cruelty of seeing their fellow men as devils because they are involved in the same pretension."[18]

Notes

1. Morris, *Maconochie's Gentlemen,* 174.
2. Niebuhr, *An Interpretation of Christian Ethics,* preface.
3. Ibid., 39, 229, 47.
4. Ibid., 9.
5. For careful historical analysis of efforts to achieve an "American synthesis" in the period from 1730 to 1865, see Noll, *America's God;* for efforts at cultural synthesis in the period 1865 to 1935, see Hutchison, *The Modernist Impulse in American Protestantism.*
6. Niebuhr, *An Interpretation of Christian Ethics,* 3–5, 10.

7. In this section, I have drawn on Foucault, *Discipline and Punish;* Matthews, *Doing Time;* Morris and Rothman, *The Oxford History of the Prison;* Nash, *The Urban Crucible;* and Tyler, *Freedom's Ferment,* 283–85.

8. Nash, *Urban Crucible,* 317–18, 320, 327, 337.

9. The citations from Eddy and Rush come from David J. Rothman, "Perfecting the Prison: United States, 1789–1865," in Morris and Rothman, *Oxford History of the Prison,* 102–3.

10. Cited in Rothman, "Perfecting the Prison," in ibid., 111.

11. Niebuhr, *Christian Ethics,* 3–7, 65–66.

12. Ibid., 40, 46, 51.

13. Ibid., 42, 66.

14. Ibid., 131; see also 130–31.

15. Ibid., 114, 47, 229.

16. Ibid., 223–24, 235–36.

17. Ibid., 107–11, 223–37.

18. Ibid., 236–37.

Critical Response
to W. Clark Gilpin

WILLIAM C. PLACHER

We live in a country gone mad on sending people to prison. Consider some statistics. From the early twentieth century until the mid-1970s, the United States imprisoned about 110 people for every 100,000 of population. By the mid-1990s, the figure had risen to about 600 per 100,000. Comparable figures to that 600 would be 36 per 100,000 for Japan, from 50 to 120 for the countries of Western Europe, 230 for the famous "police state" of Singapore, and 368 for South Africa at the height of the crisis before the change to majority rule. Putting aside political prisoners or whole races imprisoned in Nazi Germany or the Soviet Gulag and considering just incarcerated "criminals," the United States has had a larger portion of its population in prison or jail in the last few years than any society in history.[1]

Talk about other social issues in the United States today, if honest, leads sooner rather than later to talk about prisons. Take race, for example. One in every three young African American men in the United States is either in jail or prison, on probation or parole, or under pretrial release—in many cities the figure is more than half. More black men are in jail or prison than in college—in California, four times as many. Black males in the United States are locked up at four times the rate of black males under the white regime of South Africa.[2]

In reflecting theologically about issues of criminal justice in the contemporary United States, therefore, we cannot act as if we are simply dealing with universal consequences of human sin; we also face the particular pathology of one country in one period. We do not face a puzzle as to whether any society might find a different and better way of organizing its criminal justice system—at least on the face of things, almost every economically advanced society today has done so.

Even the bleak antebellum American prisons Professor Gilpin describes were at least often designed, however inadequately or unrealistically, for the reform of the criminal. In his famous night in the Concord jail, Thoreau could interact with the neighborhood and even, according to legend, remonstrate with Emerson. There is still a prison in Concord, but it is now out of sight of most people and surrounded by a high wall that prevents anyone seeing in or seeing out. Most Americans may not really want to see what goes on in our prisons. Rehabilitation is pretty much a lost goal. Most addicts and alcoholics do not have treatment programs available to them. Helping people get a high school diploma or learn a trade so that they could get a job on release is perceived as a form of "being soft on criminals." In my state of Indiana, male adolescents often get sent to a facility where they sleep in open dormitories, essentially unpatrolled at night, where the less tough among them are subject to regular rape. High school students in high-crime neighborhoods get signed up for the "Scared Straight" program, in which current prisoners threaten them with sexual assault, so that the threat of rape becomes more or less an official part of our system of deterrence. What results is not only a high psychic cost for prisoners themselves but bad consequences for the rest of us, when they work out their anger on their families or neighbors once they are released.

What then shall we do? Can Christian theology make a serious intellectual contribution to discussions on issues of criminal justice? Clark Gilpin, in his helpful and thoughtful essay, turns to Reinhold Niebuhr for resources for a public theology. He provides, I think, the best imaginable version of a Christian ethic that begins with Niebuhrian premises, but I wonder if his proposals do not still bear some of the faults endemic to their heritage. I'm thinking, as I shall try to make clear later on, at least as much about rhetoric as about substance.

Suppose we begin by asking what the New Testament has to say about prisoners. Radical stuff, it turns out; not close at all to the dominant views of our culture. Jesus defines his mission as proclaiming release to the captives, letting the oppressed go free, and proclaiming the year of the Lord's favor, that Jubilee year every fifty years in which, according to Jewish law, all prisoners would be set at liberty (Luke 4:18–19). He says that we ought to forgive wrong done us not seven times but seventy times seven (Matt. 18:22). If we fail to visit people in jail, he says, it is as if we were failing to visit him (Matt. 25:44–45). Considered in ourselves, we are all sinners, but

Christ has taken on our sin so that, in the light of his salvific work, we are all innocent (2 Cor. 5:21).

Thinking about criminal justice in Jesus's spirit would seem to imply at least that our goals should be protection of the innocent and rehabilitation of those who pose a danger to them, not punishment. Counseling, education, the opportunity to learn a trade, gradual reintegration into the wider society—if we could just get past an obsession with punishment, we could design a system better for criminals and better for the rest of us, since they would be less likely to murder or mug us once they got out. The Gospel surely points us in such directions.

But none of that, Reinhold Niebuhr says. In matters like this we cannot be followers of the Gospel—it's impractical. Indeed, if I have any criticism of Clark Gilpin's interpretation, it would be that he helps Niebuhr out by skipping over the almost obsessive repetition with which Niebuhr insists on the Gospel's impracticality.

Jesus's "impossible ethic" does remind us, Niebuhr admits, that society is in part responsible for the antisocial conduct of some of its members, and "it is possible to deal with the criminal in terms of this realization and to qualify the spiritual pride of the usually self-righteous guardians of public morals."[3] (Our former attorney general comes to mind.)

Those who would follow Jesus can thus keep reminding their fellow citizens, and not least their fellow Christians (more inclined than the national average to favor tougher sentencing and the death penalty), that we ought to work for equal justice as a political and economic approximation of the ideal of love, that none of our fellow human beings is a devil, and that we are all involved in contributing to the conditions that help produce criminal behavior.

That, it seems to me, is the important contribution a Niebuhrian public theology can make to this conversation, and Clark Gilpin has presented it well.

But rhetoric: I worry that Niebuhr's repeated emphasis on the impossibility of following the New Testament's teachings in these matters can make it too easy for Christian realists not to challenge the status quo radically enough. Niebuhr wants to avoid having religion simply sanction the status quo, and Gilpin picks up those important nuances. But Niebuhr assures us so often that we can't really follow Jesus, and that message fits so well with what a great many people in our society want to hear, that I fear even the qualifications will get lost along the way. In a society with a really bad system of criminal justice—and I have already indicated why I think we live in such a society—we need radical challenges to it. Maybe Niebuhr's insistence that Christian approaches to issues like criminal justice can involve modest, realistic reforms is the right message for some times and places, but I'm not sure it's what we need to hear now—at least it's not all we need to hear.

In an earlier essay, Mark Taylor invited us to a theatric of counterterror that would far more radically challenge mainstream American discourse about prisons. I welcome that challenge. Again, my worries would be rhetorical: the understandable anger of those like Taylor who have learned just how awful our prison system is can put off the majority who haven't thought much about these issues. It is a rhetoric that speaks the truth and that fosters ever greater passion among the already committed, but I worry that it does not offer a strategy for rapid growth of a political movement for change. Speaking the truth, however powerfully, is irrelevant if we cannot win enough converts to change the system. Sarah Coakley's eloquent hope for a theatric of love whose rhetorical style would be less at odds with its commitment to nonviolence might also be a recipe for greater political effectiveness.

Another strategy, and one that I think has special value, is for Christians to get local congregations involved in the simple work of visiting prisoners. Gilpin reminded us that such visits, and the concern for prison conditions they generated, represent where religious impact on the American prison system really began. But, at least among "mainline" Protestants, the practice has virtually disappeared. As Will Campbell and James Holloway have written of their own prison work:

> We constantly discover men and women who have been in various types of prisons for decades without *one single visitor* having signed their record card. We have suggested on other occasions that each institutional church adopt three prisoners purely and simply for purposes of visitation—so that at least once each week every man and woman and child behind bars could have one human being with whom he could have community, to whom the prisoner could tell his story. And the visitor his. We have advocated that because we are convinced that this elementary act of charity alone would provide all the prison reform that society could tolerate.[4]

Indeed, I think people who come into contact with our prison system and how it works will very often be radicalized.

What then shall we do?

All of the above, and anything else we can think of. Joining the general conversation in our society, Niebuhrian Christians can remind their fellow citizens that the lines between guilt, complicity, and innocence are, in a world of sinners, fuzzier than we like to think, and work for realistic reforms. Those committed to a theatric of love can challenge our criminal justice system more radically, and maybe get people thinking about just how bad it is. Christians engaged in visiting prisoners will make worthwhile human contacts and likely be inspired to work for either reform or more radical change. These strategies do not seem incompatible, and, with respect to our prison system, any and all might do some good. On these issues, I'm sorry to say, while the question of how to temper justice with mercy is an interesting one, simple justice would be a big improvement over the status quo.[5]

Notes

1. Eric Schlosser, "The Prison-Industrial Complex," *Atlantic Monthly* 282 (December 1998): 52; Currie, *Crime and Punishment in America,* 15.

2. Currie, *Crime and Punishment in America,* 13; Morris, "The Contemporary Prison," in Morris and Rothman, *The Oxford History of the Prison,* 215.

3. Niebuhr, *An Interpretation of Christian Ethics,* 229.

4. Campbell and Holloway, ". . . *and the criminals with him . . . ,*" 148.

5. Some of these comments appeared in different form in my *Jesus the Savior,* 150–56. I continue to be grateful to Scott M. Brannon for conversations that helped me think about these issues.

Postscript

WILLIAM SCHWEIKER

This volume has offered a feast of ideas and concerns about some of the most pressing issues our society now faces. It has given us a glimpse of the human face of suffering and the longing for justice and mercy in a harsh and violent world. The different perspectives have addressed many facets of justice and mercy in the criminal justice system.

How can one possibly and properly conclude such a book? By the nature of the case, anything I write will not be enough. The contributors' ideas, theories, arguments, facts, and figures would all need to be clarified, debated, and tested. What is more, it is not at all clear in an interdisciplinary conversation like this one what perspective or standpoint one could hold to review the event. Like so much in our complex world, it is not obvious what perspective one should adopt in order to interpret and so to glimpse the whole, if it even makes sense to speak of "the whole." As in quantum physics so too in moral and political argument, one's perspective on a phenomenon changes the phenomenon. This is all the more true in morals and politics insofar as one's perspective is part and parcel of one's self-identity and political community. What to do? Should I adopt the academic perspective I know best, that is, theological ethics, realizing that a legal or philosophical or political perspective is also possible? If I were to do so, I would want to explore issues about creation and its goodness as the ground for justice, ideas about a God who actually repents, and complex languages of evil and human viciousness. We have at our disposal an exceedingly rich religious language one could use to explore justice and mercy. But part of the point of this volume is to disallow any one discourse the right to define the terms of reflection. So perhaps I should drop the pretenses of theological ethics to view the "whole." Should I then try some other standpoint to assess this book, realizing that in doing so my own best training will be forsaken? Surely that would not be right.

I do not see any easy way out of the hermeneutical problem. Given that fact, I intend to work interpretively armed with the resources at my disposal. I want to try to catch the issues that swirled around these essays. But I realize that what I offer is one among many possible accounts of the volume. The book must be seen, I submit, as a modest but important attempt to address the vague and often superficial ways in which criminal justice issues are treated in our society. Put simply, the book is dedicated to the task of addressing public issues in a way that is both intellectually rigorous and attentive to the religious and theological issues involved. It is, therefore, a work in public theology.

As we know too well, rarely do basic questions in criminal justice receive informed and careful debate. The political climate after the horrific events of September 11, 2001, has made it increasingly difficult to engage sustained, critical debate about public policy. Even the idea of entering into violent conflict with another nation proved astonishingly difficult to debate within our own country. But a democracy silenced is a democracy dying. In this light, consider the following questions that shaped the essays:

1. What is the warrant for and use of incarceration?

2. How do racial inequalities and the abuse of women in society continue to present challenges for the criminal justice system?

3. What are the rights of the imprisoned and those who have served their sentences?

4. Why and to what end is capital punishment used in this country when there is such a risk of the execution of the innocent in addition to the fact that it hardly functions as a deterrent?

5. What forms of punishment are used, and what are their justifications?

6. What is the relation between economic and cultural forces to issues of criminal justice?

7. In a harsh criminal justice system, are there any "echoes of grace," as Ernie Lewis put it?

If nothing else, the contributors have opened up inquiry into all these topics and have tried to advance understanding and public debate and, thus, to enact and advance the democratic process. In doing so, they have brought major themes to the fore. What are these themes?

First and foremost, it is important to see that despite the disagreements among the contributors on the precise relation of justice and mercy, there is a deep common cause to bend the criminal justice system toward humane purposes. This common cause was argued in various ways. Some contributors argued that human dignity and democratic procedure require and affirm human responsibility, that is, they demand answerability and accountability for actions. Justice is at root a demand that human beings are due respect as moral beings in the world. Yet there is also the demand to respect the social contract, the political bond that ties us as citizens one to the other. We bend a criminal system toward humane ends when we struggle to make it serve not only human dignity but also concord in our social bonds. This requires in the mind of some thinkers a blending of justice and mercy. Other contributors argued that human dignity is found in and through solidarity with the least advantaged, hence acts of mercy do not contravene but establish justice. This affirmation of mercy on behalf of the least advantaged may require deep and important revisions in the very administration of justice, as Marc Mauer argued. Others made still different claims ranging from resistance to all forms of terror to revisions in beliefs about human well-being more generally.

Of course, one can be cynical about any appeal to a humane purpose in public policy and institutions. In the name of hardened political "realism," one can try to banish from political matters all talk about mercy. It is also the case that within the academy such cynicism about humane purposes is fashionable. But I think this common cause to protect and promote human dignity is of signal importance, and it must be grasped as a common thread of these essays.

This thread ties us to others woven here. A second theme is that "justice" and "mercy" are phenomena and concepts that work along two different but intersecting lines. First, justice and mercy designate the right implementation of, and facilitate the interaction between, different social processes and their own logic (say, criminal justice and economy). That is to say, while the criminal justice system and the economy function by their own logic, by specific procedures and expertise, complex societies like ours must provide the means for the interaction of social processes. Ideas like justice and mercy are precisely about these "interactions" insofar as what is "just," for instance, requires attention not only to criminal law but also to economic conditions as well as to cultural, moral, and religious beliefs. Justice and mercy are not the property of one social subsystem, say, the economy or the law or politics. In fact, highly differentiated societies like the United States are internally endangered whenever one subsystem, say, the economy, attempts to monopolize these mediating or bridge ideas. In that case, justice becomes solely a matter of economic distribution.

I might note that this diminishment of basic ideas, like justice and mercy, through the hegemony of one subsystem is the constant threat to pluralistic societies. It is one reason, a correct reason in my judgment, that so many of the authors have been worried about the dominance of economic discourse in public policy about criminal justice. Naturally, economic concerns should factor into our analysis. However, the logic, purposes, means, and authorities of one social subsystem cannot determine the meaning of complex ideas like justice and mercy without a serious diminishment of social existence and social reflection.

Beyond their meaning within social systems, justice and mercy also denote, second, a range of character traits that individuals can and do have within social processes. We naturally speak of a merciful man or a woman of justice. And of course there are a host of moral theories to explain human excellence or virtue. What these theories are trying to explore is the nature of human excellence or virtue and the rightful condition of its predication to an individual and, perhaps, to groups as patterns of action and relations. Theologians and philosophers throughout the ages have noted that justice, including retributive justice, and mercy cross and meet both in the core of moral experience as well as in the interstices of social systems.[1] This is why, for instance, justice and mercy can be seen as human virtues but also as predicates of fair—that is to say, just—social systems or merciful actions within social relations, for example, acts of clemency. Part of the problem, then, in framing the issue is to grasp the interconnections between the experiential and the social "logic," if I can put it like that, of the use of the very terms justice and mercy. Indeed, much confusion arises when we do not clarify whether we are speaking of virtue or social logic or if we assume that ideas about justice and mercy are merely about virtue or merely about social processes.

Now why is it important to be clear about these distinctions? It is important because what we mean by, for example, "retribution" will mean something different if we are talking about an individual experience—hence, the justification or impropriety of feelings of vengeance and hatred with respect to some idea of human excellence—than if we are speaking about the punitive force of the state.[2] It might be the case, and it certainly is the case for Christians, that the hatred of another, even one's enemy, is never warranted insofar as hatred means a denial of the moral worth of someone created by God. But this is not to say that a Christian might nevertheless see the justification of punitive force within a social system or for the defense of a nation against unjust aggression.[3] Likewise, it is the case, by and large, that liberal political systems, like those in the United States, have been much more concerned with the working of a social system than with private life and so have forgone attention to our experiences of justice and mercy, leaving these to the private, nonpolitical lives of its citizens. And too much of modern Christian practice has focused on feelings and attitudes of individuals rather than on the working of the social order. In other words, we need to be clear about the diverse "logic" of justice and mercy (experiential and social) if we are to avoid conceptual confusion and a false polarization between individual and political existence. One large theme of the volume, then, has been to clarify these diverse rationales.

This brings us to another common theme, that is, the effort to clarify and validate the most basic concepts of thinking—ideas like "justice" itself or what we mean by a moral agent. Yet none of the essays seems to have really addressed these matters of a first principle head on. To be sure, how thinkers used these basic concepts was clear enough. But questions of first principles remain somewhat on the horizon of this book, for good or for ill.

Complexity, however, abounds on this point. Not only have we seen the discussion of justice and mercy factored through the different "logic" of social systems and personal experience and character. It is important to grasp that we have also seen these matters of first principle, these basic ideas, used within different cognitive frameworks. Therefore, not only has the phenomenon under consideration (social systems, personal existence) but also the cognitive frameworks deployed differed among essays. The main cognitive frameworks used to consider justice and mercy have been the legal, on the one hand, and the moral/religious, on the other hand. Even then, various "methods" of reflection and argument have been used within the same cognitive frameworks, ranging from social theory and anthropology to hermeneutics, description, and pure advocacy. The theologians, for instance, have used different methods among themselves, but so have the legal scholars, ethicists, and political thinkers among us. It may be the penchant of academics to fuss about issues of method and theory, but at some point in the future these matters of first principle, cognitive frameworks, and method will arise and must be addressed. In a political situation that stridently avoids all consideration of basic concepts and "first principles," it may be the special task of intellectuals to press such matters and to show the practical importance of doing so. I believe this to be true and therefore to be one task that remains constantly before us. In any case, a major theme of this book calls for the deployment of a variety of cognitive frameworks and specific methods to explore justice and mercy precisely because these human phenomena are so complex that they resist reduction to one or the other.

Another common theme was the authors' reliance on the complexity of justice and mercy in order to make their case. For instance, some scholars (Peter Paris, for example) saw justice primarily as a predicate of a social system or social action, whereas forgiveness and/or mercy were considered matters of individual human experience. The question then becomes, Is personal experience ever admissible within the system of justice and on what condition without thereby upending justice? These authors invoked diverse logic (social/experiential) and different methods of reflection in order to make their case. Other thinkers (for instance, my own essay) tried to parse the relation of justice and mercy along different lines, more in terms of a system of justice and what constitutes the ground and good of that system. Still others—I think of Mark Taylor—were less interested in these matters and more concerned to counter what is perceived as terrorist forces in the name of justice for those terrorized by a system.

My point here is that the historical distinction between justice and mercy as predicates of personal experience and character, on the one hand, and their use in speaking of social actions and systems, on the other hand, provided an easy way for some of the essays to approach this problem from a variety of frameworks and methods. But as with matters of "first principles" so with accounts of justice and mercy: more work needs to be done. Matters of justice and mercy are differentiated not just in terms of (1) personal action and character and (2) social action and system. Their meaning is also determined by the increasingly internal differentiation of our society. As I noted before, high modern, reflexive societies are internally differentiated among various subsystems (law, economics, media, education, politics) that operate according to their own logic, values, and norms.[4] But various institutions of civil society and powerful social and ideological movements must also be explored. Justice and mercy not only work at the interface of social subsystems and personal character and action, they also adhere to the domain of civil society and social movements.

Several of the essays—I think of Mark Taylor's—were clear about this level of differentiation in our society. But none of the contributors, I submit, tackled what highly differentiated societies really mean for thinking about justice and mercy. Are these ideas used in the same way in each subsystem, every institution, all social movements? Do we have to trace the shifts in meaning between social subsystems, movements, and individual lives? I suggest that we might want to begin to think about justice and mercy as bridge ideas or contact points between the various subsystems, institutions, and movements that constitute complex societies. What justice and mercy provide are ways to trace the interaction among and within subsystems, institutions, and movements. They facilitate and carry communication that is necessary for complex social orders even to function. The importance of this point for our topic is that it might help us address more carefully the interaction between the criminal justice system and other facets of society that, come what may, will affect justice—for example, the dynamics of race, gender, and religious association.

This brings us to the last—but in many respects the first—theme I want to note, namely, the entanglement between religious claims, specifically those from the Jewish and Christian traditions, and matters of justice and mercy within highly differentiated societies. It is of course fashionable and constitutionally necessary to maintain a separation of church and state. It is not at all clear that a system of justice or even the concept of mercy requires any specifically religious support. Indeed, if we look around the world, we see the danger of insisting that justice and mercy depend on an institutionalized religion. Yet a book like this one exposes the ways in which some of our fundamental ideas, values, and conflicts spin around claims found in these ancient religious traditions.

If one were to try to remove the massive civilizational force of these religions from our most basic and fundamental conceptions, it is not clear—at least to me—that we would in any way remain the same. Of course, we must realize that in many ways an experiment with that "removal" is under way not only in the contemporary West but also elsewhere in the world. But as a volume like this shows, it is not obvious that this removal would or could be successful. I am suggesting here a different perspective on the question of religion and society than is usually raised. I am not asking how something called "religion" interacts with something called "society." I have already noted that our contemporary social world is so highly differentiated that it is hardly useful to imagine it as a blocklike reality. But the same complexity is also found in every living religion. "The" Christian or "the" Jewish or "the" Buddhist tradition or some other "Religion" is at best a high abstraction with limited heuristic value. What we must explore instead is the wild and wooly history of effects, for good and for ill, of convictions on basic cultural outlooks and social processes. That is to say, we need to trace out how "religious" convictions can inform, empower, distort, and even transform complex social realities.[5] On one level, this is simply a matter of intellectual honesty about powerful forces driving social existence. On another level, it is an attempt to release and direct humanizing forces within the domain of political life. In this respect, those contributors who were attentive to the "religious" dimension of this book's topic were in common cause with the first major theme I noted above, namely, how to turn social forces, including religious traditions, to humane ends. So these have been some major themes of this book and even some directions for further inquiry.

Once we recall and assess the essays, it becomes crystal clear that major themes and particular issues within the present criminal justice system in this country are deeply intertwined. Two things follow from this insight. First, it will be important for those interested in matters of criminal justice to ask if the connection between general themes that characterizes reflection on highly differentiated societies and specific issues of criminal justice is a contingent fact of the United States' system or if the same links can be found within the systems of justice in other nations. This prompts one to imagine a line of research that would be genuinely comparative. That kind of inquiry would explore and assess one nation's system of justice in light of others. Of course, the work of comparison raises its own methodological and conceptual challenges; it, too, dips into matters of first principle. But so far as I can see, in an increasingly global environ-

WILLIAM SCHWEIKER

ment and also the spread of legal procedures worldwide, some kind of comparative work is in order. Presumably such work is already under way, for instance, in the fashioning of the Charter of Fundamental Rights by the European Union and in the activity of the International Criminal Court.

Second, what has emerged from our analysis is a picture of how deeply intertwined processes of criminal justice are with wider and deeply problematic cultural forces—questions of race, economic self-understanding, gender, and the like. Without explicitly saying so, this volume has provided a cultural analysis of the criminal justice system and the need for revisions in cultural forces. Too often the interaction between cultural forces and systemic social processes is hardly seen, let alone evaluated. But more than that, attention to cultural dynamics helps us to grasp the important ways in which beliefs and values and ideas—about justice, mercy, and human dignity—are mediated in the justice system.

Having run against the grain in confronting the ways in which religious convictions permeated basic legal and political ideas, and in displaying the cultural mediation of beliefs in the criminal justice system in both positive and negative ways, this volume has also, in almost every essay, moved between thought and advocacy. Of course it is popular now, and maybe a little shopworn, to insist on the relation between knowledge and human interest or the necessary relation of theory and praxis or of the political context and consequences of discourse. The days of scientific tidiness are gone. So why mention the point? And why conclude with it? Is it just the predictable coda we have come to expect in our overpoliticized "sites" of action and discourse? I think not. The point is that in a society that is increasingly differentiated, in a social world that too easily and too often relegates debates of the most pressing kind to vague and superficial treatment, and yet in a society in which there is deep longing for human life to flourish in some measure, one must dedicate oneself to the recognition of the link between theory and practice.

Intellectuals have a responsibility, after all. Only the cynical and morally callous can deny this responsibility, and they do so at great peril. This is not to say that words and thoughts and arguments alone will transfigure the social world. Alone, they surely will not. Yet this is to say that without argument and thoughts and clarity of concepts, other forces too often blind and too easily manipulated will have their way with us and with the weakest among us. Would it be too much to end our work together to acknowledge that fact? I think not. Let us embolden our resolve to do what we can to address these human longings and in that way, perhaps most concretely, do justice to mercy.

Notes

1. It has long been debated whether or not and to what extent moral predicates like "mercy" can really be assigned to human collectives. The validity of that predication rests on the analogy a thinker draws between person and community. It is not necessary to address this problem here.

2. See Murphy and Hampton, *Forgiveness and Mercy*.

3. This distinction between the attitude of a believer toward others and the justification of the use of force within specific situations under defined criteria is basic to conceptions of "just war" within most of the world's religious and moral traditions.

4. For recent accounts of these developments, see Niklas Luhmann, *Social Systems*, and Jürgen Habermas, *Theory of Communicative Action*.

5. I note here that another matter of "first principle" that could not be addressed in these essays is the meaning of the idea of "religion." I doubt that after thousands of years of debate on the question, one volume could have settled the matter even if we had addressed it! But my suggestion is that there is some wisdom in exploring in more detail the actual working of beliefs and values (convictions) within social processes, whether or not one calls those convictions "religious."

Bibliography

Abu-Jamal, Mumia. *Live from Death Row*. Reading, Mass.: Addison-Wesley, 1995.

Adamson, Christopher R. "Wrath and Redemption: Protestant Theology and Penal Practice in the Early American Practice." *Criminal Justice History: An International Annual* 13 (1992): 75–111.

Alschuler, Albert W. "The Failure of Sentencing Guidelines: A Plea for Less Aggregation." *University of Chicago Law Review* 58, no. 4 (1991): 901–51.

———. *Law without Values: The Life, Work, and Legacy of Justice Holmes*. Chicago: University of Chicago Press, 2000.

Amnesty International. *Broken Bodies, Shattered Minds: Torture and Ill-treatment of Women*. New York: Amnesty International, 2001.

———. *United States of America: Rights for All*. London: Amnesty International, 1998.

Arendt, Hannah. *The Human Condition*. Chicago: University of Chicago Press, 1968.

Auerbach, Eric. *Mimesis: The Representation of Reality in Western Literature*. Princeton: Princeton University Press, 1953.

Augustine, Saint, Bishop of Hippo. *Concerning the City of God against the Pagans*. Translated by Henry Bettenson. New York: Penguin Classics, 1972.

Banaszak, Lee Ann. *Why Movements Succeed or Fail: Opportunity, Culture, and the Struggle for Woman Suffrage*. Princeton: Princeton University Press, 1996.

Bane, Mary Jo, Brent Coffin, and Ronald Thiemann, eds. *Who Will Provide? The Changing Role of Religion in American Social Welfare*. Boulder, Colo.: Westview Press, 2000.

Banner, Stuart. *The Death Penalty: An American History*. Cambridge: Harvard University Press, 2002.

Becker, Gary. *The Economic Approach to Human Behavior*. Chicago: University of Chicago Press, 1976.

Beckett, Katherine. *Making Crime Pay*. Oxford: Oxford University Press, 1997.

Bentham, Jeremy, and John Stuart Mill. *The Utilitarians*. Castine, Me.: Dolphin Books, 1961.

Biggar, Nigel, ed. *Burying the Past: Making Peace and Doing Justice after Civil Conflict*. Washington, D.C.: Georgetown University Press, 2001.

Blumenthal, David R. *Facing the Abusing God: A Theology of Protest*. Louisville, Ky.: Westminster/John Knox, 1993.

Braithwaite, John. *Crime, Shame, and Reintegration*. Cambridge: Cambridge University Press, 1989.

————. "Restorative Justice: Assessing Optimistic and Pessimistic Accounts." *Crime and Justice* 25 (1999): 1–127.

Brock, Rita Nakashima, and Susan Brooks Thistlethwaite. *Casting Stones: Prostitution and Liberation in Asia and the United States.* Minneapolis: Fortress Press, 1996.

Brown, Lyn Mikel, and Carol Gilligan. *Meeting at the Crossroads: Women's Psychology and Girls' Development.* Cambridge: Harvard University Press, 1992.

Browne, Angela. *When Battered Women Kill.* New York: Free Press, 1987.

Calvin, John. *Institutes of the Christian Religion.* Edited by John T. McNeill. Translated by Ford Lewis Battles. Philadelphia: Westminster Press, 1960.

Campbell, Will D. and James Holloway. *". . . and the criminals with him . . . "* New York: Paulist Press, 1973.

Carey, Roane, and Jonathan Shainin, eds. *The Other Israel: Voices of Refusal and Dissent.* New York: New Press, 2002.

Certeau, Michel de. *The Practice of Everyday Life.* Translated by Steven Rendall. Berkeley and Los Angeles: University of California Press, 1984.

Chang, Nancy. *The Silencing of Political Dissent: How the Patriot Act Undermines the Constitution.* New York: Open Media Pamphlet Series, 2001.

Chiricos, Ted, Kelly Welch, and Marc Gertz. "Racial Typification of Crime and Support for Punitive Measures." *Criminology* 42, no. 2 (2004): 359–89.

Clarkson, Chris, and Rod Morgan, eds. *The Politics of Sentencing Reform.* Oxford: Clarendon Press, 1995.

Coakley, J. F. *Christ without Absolutes: A Study of the Christology of Ernst Troeltsch.* Oxford: Oxford University Press, 1988.

————. "Jesus's Messianic Entry into Jerusalem: Jn 12.12–19 par." *Journal of Theological Studies* 46 (1995): 461–82.

————. *Powers and Submissions: Spirituality, Philosophy, and Gender.* Oxford: Blackwell, 2002.

Crenshaw, Marsha. *Terrorism in Context.* Harrisburg: Pennsylvania State University Press, 1995.

Crossan, John Dominic. *The Birth of Christianity: Discovering What Happened in the Years Immediately after the Execution of Jesus.* San Francisco: Harper San Francisco, 1998.

Currie, Elliot. *Crime and Punishment in America.* New York: Holt, 1998.

Dan-Cohen, Meir. "Decision Rules and Conduct Rules: On Acoustic Separation in Criminal Law." *Harvard Law Review* 97 (1984): 625–77.

Daughen, Joseph R., and Peter Binzen. *The Cop Who Would Be King: Mayor Frank Rizzo.* Boston: Little, Brown, 1979.

Davis, Murphy. "Walk Humble: A Lenten Journey." *Hospitality: The Open Door Newletter* 21, no. 3 (2002): 7–9.

Derrida, Jacques. *The Gift of Death.* Translated by David Willis. Chicago: University of Chicago Press, 1995.

———. *Given Time.* Translated by Peggy Kamuf. Chicago: University of Chicago Press, 1992.

———. *On Cosmopolitanism and Forgiveness.* New York: Routledge, 2001.

———. "On the Gift." In *God, the Gift, and Postmodernism,* edited by Michael J. Scanlon. Bloomington: Indiana University Press, 1999.

Donziger, Stephen. *The Real War on Crime: Report of the National Criminal Justice Commission.* New York: Harper Perennial, 1996.

Douglass, Frederick. *The Life and Writings of Frederick Douglass, Reconstruction and After.* Edited by Philip Foner. Vol. 4. New York: International, 1975.

Doyle, Michael. *Empires.* Ithaca: Cornell University Press, 1986.

Ellis, Marc H. *Revolutionary Forgiveness: Essays on Judaism, Christianity, and the Future of Religious Life.* Waco, Tex.: Baylor University Press, 2000.

Erickson, Victoria Lee, and Michelle Lim Jones, eds. *Surviving Terror: Hope and Justice in a World of Violence.* Grand Rapids, Mich.: Brazos Press, 2002.

Farsoun, Samih K., with Christina E. Zacharia. *Palestine and the Palestinians.* Boulder, Colo.: Westview Press, 1997.

Feitlowitz, Marguerite. *A Lexicon of Terror: Argentina and the Legacies of Torture.* New York: Oxford University Press, 1998.

Finkelhor, David, with Gerald T. Hotaling and Kersti Yllo. *Stopping Family Violence: Research Priorities for the Coming Decade.* Newbury Park, Calif.: Sage, 1988.

Fishbane, Michael. *Biblical Myth and Rabbinic Mythmaking.* Oxford: Oxford University Press, 2003.

Foucault, Michel. *Discipline and Punish: The Birth of the Prison.* Translated by Alan Sheridan. New York: Knopf, 1995.

Fredriksen, Paula. *Jesus of Nazareth, King of the Jews: A Jewish Life and the Emergence of Christianity.* New York: Knopf, 1999.

Gaita, Raymond. *A Common Humanity: Thinking about Love and Truth and Justice.* New York: Routledge, 1998.

Gamwell, Franklin I. *The Meaning of Religious Freedom: Modern Politics and the Democratic Resolution.* Albany: State University of New York Press, 1995.

Gandhi, Mahatma. *Gandhi on Non-Violence: A Selection from the Writings of Mahatma Gandhi.* Edited by Thomas Merton. New York: New Directions, 1964.

Geertz, Clifford. *Negara: The Theatre State in Nineteenth-Century Bali.* Princeton: Princeton University Press, 1980.

Gelles, Richard J., and Claire Pedrick Cornell. *Intimate Violence in Families.* Beverly Hills, Calif.: Sage, 1985.

Gilligan, James. *Violence: Reflections on a National Epidemic.* New York: Vintage, 1996.

Gilly, Adolfo. *Chiapas: La razon ardiente: Ensayo sobre la rebellion del mundo encantado.* Mexico, D.F.: Ediciones era, 1997.

Gleijesis, Peter. *Conflicting Missions: Havana, Washington, and Africa, 1959–2002.* Chapel Hill: University of North Carolina Press, 2002.

Glover, Jonathan. *Humanity: A Moral History of the Twentieth Century.* New Haven: Yale University Press, 1999.

Goldsmith, Timothy H., and William F. Zimmerman. *Biology, Evolution, and Human Nature.* Hoboken, N.J.: Wiley, 2000.

Green, Stephen. *Taking Sides: America's Secret Relations with a Militant Israel.* New York: Morrow, 1984.

Greene, Felix. *The Enemy: Notes on Imperialism and Revolution.* London: Cape, 1970.

Grelle, Bruce, and David Krueger, eds. *Christianity and Capitalism: Perspectives on Religion, Liberalism, and the Economy.* Chicago: Center for the Scientific Study of Religion, 1986.

Gustafson, James M. *An Examined Faith: The Grace of Self-Doubt.* Minneapolis: Fortress Press, 2003.

Hardt, Michael, and Antonio Negri. *Empire.* Cambridge: Harvard University Press, 2000.

Hauerwas, Stanley. *Christian Existence Today: Essays on Church, World, and Living In-Between.* Durham: Labyrinth Press, 1988.

Hegel, G. W. F. *Early Theological Writings.* Translated by T. M. Knox and with an introduction and fragments translated by Richard Kroner. Chicago: University of Chicago Press, 1948.

Hengel, Martin. *Crucifixion in the Ancient World and the Folly of the Message of the Cross.* Philadelphia: Fortress Press, 1977.

Herman, Judith Lewis. *Trauma and Recovery.* New York: Basic Books, 1992.

Heyd, David, ed. *Toleration: An Elusive Virtue.* Princeton: Princeton University Press, 1996.

Hiltermann, Joost R. *Behind the Intifada: Labor and Women's Movements in the Occupied Territories.* Princeton: Princeton University Press, 1991.

Hirsch, Andrew von. *Doing Justice: The Choice of Punishments.* New York: Hill and Wang, 1976.

Hobbes, Thomas. *Leviathan.* Edited by C. B. Macpherson. Baltimore: Penguin, 1968.

Horseley, Richard A. *Jesus and the Spiral of Violence: Popular Jewish Resistance in Roman Palestine.* San Francisco: Harper and Row, 1987.

Horseley, Richard A., and Neil Asher Silberman. *The Message of the Kingdom.* New York: Grosset/Putnam, 1997.

Hutchinson, William R. *The Modernist Impulse in American Protestantism.* Cambridge: Harvard University Press, 1976.

Jacobs, David, and Jason T. Carmichael. "The Political Sociology of the Death Penalty: A Pooled Time Series Analysis." *American Sociological Review* 67 (2002): 109–31.

Jacques, Genevieve. *Beyond Impunity: An Ecumenical Approach to Truth, Justice, and Reconciliation.* New York: World Council of Churches, 2000.

Johnson, Chalmers. *Blowback: The Costs and Consequences of America Empire.* New York: Holt, 2000.

Juergensmeyer, Mark. *Terror in the Mind of God: The Global Rise of Religious Violence.* Berkeley and Los Angeles: University of California Press, 2000.

Kaplan, Robert. *Warrior Politics: Why Leadership Demands a Pagan Ethos.* New York: Random House, 2002.

Keil, Thomas J., and Gennaro F. Vito. "Race and the Death Penalty in Kentucky Murder Trials: 1976–1991." *American Journal of Criminal Justice* 20, no. 1 (1995): 17–36.

Kornbluh, Peter, ed. *The Pinochet Files: A Declassified Dossier on Atrocity and Accountability.* A National Security Archive Book. New York: New Press, 2003.

Kozol, Jonathan. *Amazing Grace: The Lives of Children and the Conscience of a Nation.* New York: Crown, 1985.

Levinas, Emmanuel. *Levinas Reader.* Edited by Seán Hand. Oxford: Basil Blackwell, 1989.

———. *Otherwise Than Being or Beyond Essence.* Pittsburgh: Duquesne University Press, 2000.

Lindbeck, George. *The Nature of Doctrine.* Philadelphia: Westminster Press, 1984.

Livezey, Lois Gehr. "Human Rights and Gender Justice: The Case of Domestic Violence," *Process Studies* 33, no. 2 (2004): 217–40.

———. "Sex and Power Politics: A Theological Reflection." *Working Together* 19, no. 2 (1999): 114–30.

Lonergan, Bernard. *Insight.* New York: Longman, 1958.

Lovin, Robin. *Reinhold Niebuhr and Christian Realism.* Cambridge: Cambridge University Press, 1995.

Luther, Martin. *Martin Luther: Selections from His Writings.* Edited by John Dillenberger. Garden City, N.Y.: Anchor Books, 1961.

Machiavelli, Niccolò. *The Prince.* Translated by Harvey C. Mansfield. Chicago: University of Chicago Press, 1998.

MacIntyre, Alasdair. *Three Rival Versions of Moral Enquiry: Encyclopedia, Genealogy, and Tradition.* Notre Dame: Notre Dame University Press, 1990.

Maclin, Tracey. "Race and the Fourth Amendment." *Vanderbilt Law Review* 51 (1998): 333–93.

Matthews, Roger. *Doing Time: An Introduction to the Sociology of Imprisonment.* New York: Palgrave, 1999.

Mauer, Marc. "Developments in the Law—Race and the Criminal Process." *Harvard Law Review* 110, no. 7 (1988) 1473–641.

———. *The Race to Incarcerate and Invisible Punishment: The Collateral Consequences of Mass Imprisonment.* New York: New Press, 1999.

Meilaender, Gilbert, and William Werpehowski, eds. *The Oxford Handbook of Theological Ethics.* Oxford: Oxford University Press, 2005.

Melucci, Alberto. *Challenging Codes: Collective Action in the Information Age.* Cambridge: Cambridge University Press, 1997.

Milbank, John. *Theology and Social Theory.* Oxford: Blackwell, 1990.

Miller, Jerome G. *Search and Destroy: African-American Males in the Criminal Justice System.* New York: Cambridge University Press, 1996.

Milosz, Czeslaw. *To Begin Where I Am: Selected Essays.* Edited and with an introduction by B. Carpenter and M. G. Levine. New York: Farrar, Straus, and Giroux, 2001.

Morris, Norval. *The Future of Imprisonment.* Chicago: University of Chicago Press, 1975.

——. *Maconochie's Gentlemen: The Story of Norfolk Island and the Roots of Modern Prison Reform.* New York: Oxford University Press, 2002.

Morris, Norval, and David Rothman, eds. *The Oxford History of the Prison: The Practice of Punishment in Western Society.* New York: Oxford University Press, 1995.

Morris, Norval, and Michael Tonry. *Between Prison and Probation: Intermediate Punishments in a Rational Sentencing System.* Oxford: Oxford University Press, 1990.

Morton, Nelle. *The Journey Is Home.* Boston: Beacon Press, 1985.

Murphy, Jeffrie, ed., *Punishment and Rehabilitation.* 2nd ed. Belmont, Calif.: Wadsworth, 1985.

——. *Retribution, Justice and Therapy: Essays in the Philosophy of Law.* Boston: Reidel, 1979.

Murphy, Jeffrie, and Jean Hampton. *Forgiveness and Mercy.* New York: Cambridge University Press, 1988.

Musto, David F. *The American Disease: Origins of Narcotic Control.* 3rd ed. New York: Oxford University Press, 1999.

Myers, Ched. *Binding the Strong Man: A Political Reading of Mark's Story of Jesus.* Maryknoll, N.Y.: Orbis Books, 1997.

Nash, Gary. *The Urban Crucible: Social Change, Public Consciousness, and the Origins of the American Revolution.* Cambridge: Harvard University Press, 1979.

Niebuhr, Reinhold. *An Interpretation of Christian Ethics.* New York: Harper, 1935.

——. *Moral Man and Immoral Society.* Introduction by Langdon Gilkey. Library of Theological Ethics. Louisville, Ky.: Westminster/John Knox Press, 2001.

——. *The Nature and Destiny of Man.* Vol. 2. New York: Scribner's, 1949.

Noll, Mark A. *America's God: From Jonathan Edwards to Abraham Lincoln.* New York: Oxford University Press, 2002.

Nussbaum, Martha C. *The Fragility of Goodness: Luck and Ethics in Greek Tragedy and Philosophy.* New York: Cambridge University Press, 2001.

——. "The Professor of Parody." *New Republic,* February 22, 1999, 37–45.

———. *Sex and Social Justice.* Oxford: Oxford University Press, 1999.

O'Donovan, Oliver. *The Desire of the Nations: Rediscovering the Roots of Political Theology.* Cambridge: Cambridge University Press, 1996.

Osiel, Mark J. *Obeying Orders.* New York: Transaction, 1999.

Paper, Robert. *Dying to Win: The Strategic Logic of Suicide Terrorism.* New York: Random House, 2005.

Parenti, Christian. *Lockdown America: Policing and Prisons in the Age of Crisis.* New York: Verso Books, 1999.

Park, Andrew Sung, and Susan L. Nelson, eds. *The Other Side of Sin.* Albany: State University of New York, 2001.

Perry, Michael J. *The Idea of Human Rights: Four Inquiries.* Oxford: Oxford University Press, 1998.

———. "The Morality of Human Rights: A Nonreligious Ground?" In "The Foundations of Law," special issue, *Emory Law Journal* 54 (2005): 97–150.

Placher, William. *Jesus the Savior.* Louisville, Ky.: Westminster/ John Knox, 2001.

Pohl, Christine. *Making Room: Recovering Hospitality as a Christian Tradition.* Grand Rapids: Eerdmans, 1999.

Poling, James Newton. *The Abuse of Power: A Theological Problem* Nashville: Abingdon Press, 1991.

Rahner, Karl. *Foundations of Christian Faith: An Introduction to the Idea of Christianity.* New York: Crossroad, 1966.

Ramsey, Paul. *Basic Christian Ethics.* Chicago: University of Chicago Press, 1978.

———. *The Essential Paul Ramsey: A Collection.* Edited by William Werpehowski and Stephen D. Crocco. New Haven: Yale University Press, 1994.

Rawls, John. *Political Liberalism.* New York: Columbia University Press, 1993.

Reinarman, Harry, and Craig Levine, eds. *Crack in America: Demon Drugs and Social Justice.* Berkeley and Los Angeles: University of California Press, 1997.

Richie, Beth. *Compelled to Crime: The Gender Entrapment of Battered Black Women.* New York: Routledge, 1996.

Ricoeur, Paul. *Fallible Man.* New York: Fordham University Press, 1986.

———. *Freedom and Nature: The Voluntary and the Involuntary.* Evanston: Northwestern University Press, 1966.

———. *The Just.* Translated by David Pellauer. Chicago: University of Chicago Press, 2000.

Romero, Oscar. *Voice of the Voiceless: The Four Pastoral Letters and Other Statements.* Translated by Michael J. Walsh. Maryknoll, N.Y.: Orbis Books, 2004.

Rothchild, Jonathan. "Ethics, Law, Economics: Legal Regulation of Corporate Responsibility." *Journal of the Society of Christian Ethics* 25, no. 1 (2005): 123–46.

Rothman, David. *The Discovery of the Asylum: Social Order and Disorder in the New Republic.* Boston: Little, Brown, 1990.

Rotman, Edgardo. *Beyond Punishment: A New View of the Rehabilitation of Criminal Offenders.* Contributions in Criminology and Penology Number 26. New York: Greenwood Press, 1990.

Ruether, Rosemary Radford, and Marc H. Ellis, eds. *Beyond Occupation: American Jewish, Christian, and Palestinian Voices for Peace.* Boston: Beacon Press, 1990.

Sabo, Don, Terry Kupers, and Willie London. *Prison Masculinities.* Philadelphia: Temple University Press, 2001.

Said, Edward. *Power, Politics, and Culture: Interviews with Edward W. Said.* New York: Pantheon, 2001.

Scheffer, David J. "Delusions about Leadership, Terrorism, and War." *American Journal of International Law* 97 (2003): 209–15.

———. "The Future of Atrocity Law." *Suffolk Transnational Law Review* 25 (2002): 389–432.

———. "Genocide and Atrocity Crimes." *Genocide Studies and Prevention* 1, no. 3 (December 2006): 229–50.

———. "Review Essay." *American Journal of International Law* 95 (2001): 970–77.

Schweiker, William, ed. *The Blackwell Companion to Religious Ethics.* Oxford: Blackwell, 2005.

———. *Mimetic Reflections: A Study in Hermeneutics Theology, and Ethics.* New York: Fordham University Press, 1990.

———. *Power, Value, and Conviction: Theological Ethics in the Postmodern Age.* Cleveland: Pilgrim Press, 1998.

———. *Responsibility and Christian Ethics.* Cambridge: Cambridge University Press, 1995.

———. *Theological Ethics and Global Dynamics: In the Time of Many Worlds.* Oxford: Blackwell, 2004.

Schweiker, William, Michael Johnson, and Kevin Jung, eds. *Humanity before God: Contemporary Faces of Jewish, Christian and Islamic Ethics.* Minneapolis: Fortress Press, 2006.

Selznick, Philip. *The Moral Commonwealth: Social Theory and the Promise of Community.* Berkeley and Los Angeles: University of California Press, 1992.

Shriver, Donald. *An Ethic for Enemies: Forgiveness in Politics.* Oxford: Oxford University Press, 1995.

Skotnicki, Andrew. *Religion and the Development of the American Penal System.* Lanham, Md.: University Press of America, 2000.

Smith, Christian. *Disruptive Religion: The Face of Faith in Social Movement Activism.* New York: Routledge, 1996.

Snyder, T. Richard. *The Protestant Ethic and the Spirit of Punishment.* Grand Rapids: Eerdmans, 2001.

Sobrino, Jon. *Christology at the Crossroads: A Latin American Approach.* Maryknoll, N.Y.: Orbis Books, 1976.

Sophocles. *Antigone.* Translated and with an introduction by David Grene. In *Sophocles I,* in *The Complete Greek Tragedies,* edited by David Grene and Richmond Lattimore. 2nd ed. Chicago: University of Chicago Press, 1991.

Spohn, Cassia. "Thirty Years of Sentencing Reform: The Quest for a Racially Neutral Sentencing Process." *Criminal Justice 2000: Policies, Processes and Decisions of the Criminal Justice System* 3 (2000): 427–501.

Stackhouse, Max D., and Peter J. Paris, eds. *God and Globalization.* Vol. 1, *Religion and the Powers of the Common Life.* Harrisburg, Pa.: Trinity Press International, 2000.

Stark, Rodney. *The Rise of Christianity: A Sociologist Reconsiders History.* Princeton: Princeton University Press, 1996.

Stephson, Amy. *Gender Bias Crimes: A Legislative Resource Manual.* Seattle: Northwest Coalition against Malicious Harassment, 1994.

Stith, Kate, and Jose Cabranes. *Fear of Judging: Sentencing Guidelines in the Federal Courts.* Chicago: University of Chicago Press, 1998.

Tanner, Kathryn. *The Politics of God: Christian Theologies and Social Justice.* Minneapolis: Fortress Press, 1992.

Tarrow, Sidney. *Power in Movement: Social Movements and Contentious Politics.* 2nd ed. New York: Cambridge University Press, 1998.

Taylor, Charles. *Sources of the Self: The Making of Modern Identity.* Cambridge: Harvard University Press, 1989.

Taylor, Mark C. *Critical Terms for Religious Studies.* Chicago: University of Chicago Press, 1998.

Taylor, Mark Lewis. "The Executed God: The Way of the Cross in Lockdown America." *Princeton Seminary Bulletin* 21, no. 3 (2000): 301–23.

———. *The Executed God: The Way of the Cross in Lockdown America.* Minneapolis: Fortress Press, 2001.

———. *Religion, Politics, and the Christian Right: Post-9/11 Powers and American Empire.* Minneapolis: Fortress Press, 2005.

Tillich, Paul. *Christianity and the Encounter with World Religion.* New York: Columbia University Press, 1963.

Tilly, Charles. *From Mobilization to Revolution.* Reading, Mass.: Addison-Wesley, 1987.

Todorov, Tzvetan. *Imperfect Garden: The Legacy of Humanism.* Translated by Carol Cosman. Princeton: Princeton University Press, 2002.

Tombs, David. "Crucifixion, State Terror, and Sexual Abuse." *Union Seminary Quarterly Review* 53 (1999): 89–109.

Tonry, Michael, ed. *Ethnicity, Crime, and Immigration: Comparative and Cross-National Perspectives.* Chicago: University of Chicago Press, 1997.

———. *Penal Reform in Overcrowded Times.* Oxford: Oxford University Press, 2001.

———. *Sentencing Matters.* Oxford: Oxford University Press, 1996.

Touster, Saul. *The Treatment of Jewish Survivors of the Holocaust, 1945–1948: Dilemmas of Law, Care, and Bureaucracy.* The 1999 Guberman Lecture on

Law and Social Policy. Boston: Heller School for Advanced Studies in Social Welfare, Brandeis University, 2000.

Tracy, David. *The Analogical Imagination: Christian Theology and the Culture of Pluralism.* New York: Crossroad, 1981.

———. *Plurality and Ambiguity: Hermeneutics, Religion, and Hope.* San Francisco: Harper and Row, 1986.

Troeltsch, Ernst. *Religion in History.* Edited by James Luther Adams and Walter F. Bense. Minneapolis: Fortress Press, 1991.

Trombley, Stephen. *The Execution Protocol: Inside America's Capital Punishment Industry.* New York: Crown, 1992.

Tyler, Alice Felt. *Freedom's Ferment: Phases of American Social History from the Colonial Period to the Outbreak of the Civil War.* 1944. Reprint, New York: Harper, 1962.

United States Conference of Catholic Bishops. *Responsibility, Rehabilitation, and Restoration.* Washington, D.C.: USCCB Publishing, 2001.

United States Sentencing Commission. *Federal Sentencing Guidelines Manual.* Washington, D.C.: United States Sentencing Commission, 2001.

Volf, Miroslav. *Exclusion and Embrace: A Theological Exploration of Identity, Otherness, and Reconciliation.* Nashville: Abingdon Press, 1996.

Wainwright, Hilary. *Arguments for a New Left: Answering the Free Market Right.* London: Blackwell, 1996.

Waite, Robert. "From Penitentiary to Reformatory: Alexander Maconochie, Walter Crofton, Zebulon Brockway, and the Road to Prison Reform—New South Wales, Ireland, and Elmira, New York 1840–70." *Criminal Justice History: An International Annual* 12 (1991): 85–101.

Weinreb, Lloyd. *Leading Constitutional Cases on Criminal Justice.* 1996 Edition. Westbury, N.Y.: Foundation Press, 1996.

West, Traci C. *Wounds of the Spirit: Black Women, Violence, and Resistance Ethics.* New York: New York University Press, 1999.

Whitehead, Alfred North. *Science and the Modern World.* Cambridge: Cambridge University Press, 1932.

Whittaker, David J. *The Terrorism Reader.* New York: Routledge, 2001.

Wink, Walter. *Engaging the Powers: Discernment and Resistance in a World of Domination.* Minneapolis: Fortress Press, 1992.

Wolterstorff, Nicholas. *Until Justice and Peace Embrace.* Grand Rapids: Eerdmans, 1983.

Wooden, Kenneth. *Weeping in the Playtime of Others: America's Incarcerated Children.* New York: McGraw-Hill, 1976.

Young, Iris Marion. *Justice and the Politics of Difference.* Princeton: Princeton University Press, 1990.

Zehr, Howard. *Changing Lenses: A New Focus on Crime and Justice.* Scottdale, Pa.: Herald Press, 1995.

Zimring, Franklin. *The Contradictions of American Capital Punishment.* Oxford: Oxford University Press, 2003.

Zimring, Franklin, and Gordon Hawkins. *Incapacitation: Penal Confinement and the Restraint of Crime.* Oxford: Oxford University Press, 1995.

Zimring, Franklin, Gordon Hawkins, and Sam Kamin. *Punishment and Democracy: Three Strikes and You're Out in California.* Oxford: Oxford University Press, 2001.

Zinn, Howard. *A People's History of the United States.* 20th anniversary ed. New York: HarperCollins, 2000.

Contributors

ALBERT W. ALSCHULER is Professor of Law at Northwestern University and Julius Kreeger Professor of Law and Criminology Emeritus at the University of Chicago. He has been a law clerk to Justice Walter V. Schaefer of the Illinois Supreme Court, a special assistant to the assistant attorney general in charge of the Criminal Division of the U.S. Justice Department, and a professor of law at the University of Texas, the University of Colorado, and the University of Pennsylvania. Mr. Alschuler has written on many topics including plea bargaining, sentencing reform, civil procedure, jury selection, legal history, legal ethics, William Blackstone, Oliver Wendell Holmes, and American legal theory.

MATTHEW MYER BOULTON is Assistant Professor of Ministry Studies at Harvard Divinity School. His research interests include public theology, biblical studies, ritual and cultural studies, and the arts. His most recent work is *God against Religion: Rethinking Christian Theology through Worship* (2007).

SARAH COAKLEY is the Norris-Hulse Professor of Divinity at the University of Cambridge. A systematic theologian and philosopher of religion, she has wide interdisciplinary interests, including recent research and teaching at the intersection of theology and law. Her published works include *Christ without Absolutes: A Study of the Christology of Ernst Troeltsch*; *Powers and Submissions: Spirituality, Philosophy, and Gender*; *Religion and the Body* (editor); *Re-Thinking Gregory of Nyssa* (editor); and *Pain and Its Transformations: The Interface of Biology and Culture* (co-editor). She is at work on a four-volume systematic theology, the first volume of which will appear as *God, Sexuality, and the Self: An Essay "On the Trinity."*

W. CLARK GILPIN is Margaret E. Burton Professor of the History of Christianity and of Theology at the University of Chicago Divinity School. Professor Gilpin is a historian of American Christianity whose research and writing have focused on Puritanism and on the relation between religion and education in American culture. He has published a biography of Roger Williams and *A Preface to Theology*, which examines American theological scholarship in terms of its historic responsibilities to a threefold public in the churches, the academic community, and civil society.

KEVIN JUNG is Assistant Professor of Christian Ethics at Wake Forest University Divinity School. He is the coeditor of *Humanity before God: Contemporary*

Faces of Jewish, Christian, and Islamic Ethics (2006). Jung works in the areas of moral philosophy and religious and social thought with particular interests in ethical theories and problems.

ERNIE LEWIS has been Public Advocate for the Commonwealth of Kentucky since 1996. He has been with Department of Public Advocacy since 1977, serving as an appellate lawyer and head of the Department's trial services efforts. He received the Kentucky Bar Association's "Lawyer of the Year" award in 2000. Lewis has been a faculty member of the National Criminal Defense College in Macon, Georgia, since 1985 and is a charter board member of the Kentucky Association of Criminal Defense Lawyers. He has represented capital clients at trial, appeal, and state and federal postconviction.

DAVID LITTLE is the T. J. Dermot Dunphy Professor of the Practice in Religion, Ethnicity, and International Conflict at Harvard Divinity School, and Director of Initiatives in Religion and Public Life. Until 1999, he was senior scholar in religion, ethics, and human rights at the United States Institute of Peace in Washington, D.C. From 1996 to 1998, he was a member of the U.S. State Department Advisory Committee on Religious Freedom Abroad. He has written in the areas of moral philosophy, moral theology, history of ethics, and the sociology of religion, with a special interest in comparative ethics, human rights, religious liberty, and ethics and international affairs.

LOIS GEHR LIVEZEY is Professor of Christian Social Ethics at McCormick Theological Seminary, Emerita. An ordained elder in the Presbyterian Church (USA), she served on the Committee on Social Witness Policy Task Force on "Why and How the Church Makes Social Policy and Social Witness." She has published several articles and book reviews focusing on the church's response in the areas of family ethics, feminist ethics, and sexual and family violence.

MARC MAUER is the Executive Director of the Sentencing Project, a nonprofit organization engaged in research and advocacy on criminal justice policy. Mr. Mauer has written extensively and testified before Congress and other legislative bodies. His critically acclaimed book *Race to Incarcerate* was named a semifinalist for the Robert F. Kennedy Book Award, and he is the coeditor of *Invisible Punishment,* a collection of essays examining the social costs of incarceration. Mr. Mauer is the recipient of the Donald Cressey Award for contributions to criminal justice research and the Alfred Lindesmith Award for drug policy scholarship.

PETER J. PARIS is the Elmer G. Homrighausen Professor of Christian Social Ethics at Princeton Theological Seminary. Professor Paris has written many books on various issues of social ethics, notably *The Social Teaching of the Black Churches and the Spirituality of African Peoples: The Search for a Common Moral*

Discourse. He has previously been president of the Society for the Study of Black Religion and vice president of the Society for Values in Higher Education. He is also a past president of both the American Academy of Religion and the Society of Christian Ethics. Professor Paris is also the senior editor of the New York University series Religion, Race, and Ethnicity and serves on the editorial boards of several journals.

WILLIAM C. PLACHER is the Charles D. and Elizabeth S. LaFollette Distinguished Professor in the Humanities at Wabash College in Crawfordsville, Indiana. His books include *A History of Christian Theology; Unapologetic Theology; Narratives of a Vulnerable God; The Domestication of Transcendence;* and *Jesus the Savior.* He has served the Presbyterian Church (USA) as a member of the committees that wrote *A Brief Statement of Faith* and the church's new catechisms, and he has been a Senior Fellow at the Martin Marty Center for the Advanced Study of Religion at the Divinity School of the University of Chicago.

JONATHAN ROTHCHILD is Assistant Professor of Theological Studies at Loyola Marymount University. His research interests include the intersections of theological ethics, moral philosophy, legal theory, and sociopolitical structures. His work has appeared in the *Journal of the Society of Christian Ethics.*

DAVID SCHEFFER is the Mayer, Brown, Rowe, and Maw/Robert A. Helman Professor of Law and Director, Center for International Human Rights, at Northwestern University School of Law. Previously he was a Senior Fellow of the U.S. Institute of Peace. From 1997 to 2001, he was U.S. Ambassador at Large for War Crimes Issues, and from 1993 to 1996, he was Senior Adviser and Counsel to the U.S. Permanent Representative to the United Nations, Dr. Madeleine Albright.

WILLIAM SCHWEIKER is Professor of Theological Ethics in the Divinity School of the University of Chicago. Professor Schweiker is the author of numerous articles on theological ethics and hermeneutical philosophy. His most recent books include *Responsibility and Christian Ethics; Power, Value and Conviction: Theological Ethics for the Postmodern Age; Theological Ethics and Global Dynamics: In the Time of Many Worlds;* and *The Blackwell Companion to Religious Ethics* (editor). Professor Schweiker is also the series editor for the Library of Theological Ethics and Internationale Theologie.

MARK LEWIS TAYLOR is Professor of Theology and Culture at Princeton Theological Seminary. Dr. Taylor's special interest in culture and theology is reflected in both his life and his work. Since 1987, he has studied regularly in Guatemala and in Chiapas, Mexico, where he analyzes the cultural and political dynamics of the churches as they move closer to a contextualized Mayan theology that also facilitates resistance to military repression. An ordained minister in the Presbyterian Church (USA), he is also the coordinator of Academics for Mumia

Abu-Jamal, Inc. (AMAJ) and a New Jersey organizer for Save-Our-Children Coalition against Police Brutality. He has written many books on cultural and political theology, including *The Executed God: The Way of the Cross in Lockdown America* (2001). His most recent book is *Religion, Politics, and the Christian Right: Post-9/11 Powers and American Empire* (2005).

Index

justice, purposes of: deterrence, 11, 55, 63, 65, 69, 80, 84, 246; economic approach, 90; public health problem, 228; rehabilitation, 6–7, 11, 41, 61, 63–72, 78–80, 83–85, 109, 112, 118, 129, 226–27, 229, 246–47; restitution, 52, 81, 206; restoration 6–9, 34, 60, 64, 79, 81–84, 91, 112–15, 117–19, 133–40, 196, 199; retribution, 11, 77, 94, 123, 133–34, 136–37, 140–41, 144, 190, 199, 254–55
juvenile justice, 40

Kant, Immanuel, 69–70, 86–87, 213
Kaplan, Robert, 110–12
Kentucky Racial Profiling Act, 56–59
King, Martin Luther, Jr., 182
Koon v. *United States,* 75, 77, 89

Lemkim, Raphael, 107
love, 4, 11, 184, 186–87, 193, 202, 222; divine, 156, 240; of enemies, 43–44; —, in Matthew 5:38–39, 50; —, in Matthew 5:44–48, 239; law of love, 231–40; the love commandment, in Leviticus 19:18, Deuteronomy 6:5, Mark 12:28–31, 41–42; —, in Deuteronomy 6:5, Leviticus 18:5, Leviticus 19:18, Luke 10:28, 50, 133, 130, 137–38, 139, 141, 143, 240; nonretaliatory, 159; related to mercy and justice (Micah 6:8), 142
Luther, Martin, 78, 192–93, 196

mandatory sentencing, 6, 34–38, 42
margin: being marginal/marginalized, 58, 137, 141, 157; outsider (Exodus 23:9), 4, 8, 129–30, 132–36, 139, 140–43, 235. *See also* covenant, God's fidelity to
marijuana policy (drug policy), 20, 22, 276
mass media, 29, 152
McCleskey v. *Kemp,* 56

mercy: as lament for victims-survivors, 4–6, 12–13, 16; —, in Psalm 55:1, 45; meaning of, 184–86, 207–11, 227, 242–43; private mercy, 97–99; responsible mercy, 197–201; as transformative of mourning (Psalm 30), 47. *See also* transgressive care
Milbank, John, 178
Mistretta v. *United States,* 87
mitigation, 87–88, 92, 95
Morris, Norval, 65, 81, 231, 240
Murphy, Jeffrie, 70–71, 78, 86–87, 202, 205, 207–9, 212, 220

Niebuhr, Reinhold, 11–12, 44, 193, 223, 231–43, 246–49
Nussbaum, Martha, 175, 248

Osiel, Mark, 105

Paul, Saint: and anti-imperial praxis, 155; and cross, 155–56; on God's righteousness and mercy, 187
Penry v. *Texas,* 55
Pennsylvania Penitentiary System, 66, 67, 68. *See also* antebellum America, rise of prison systems in
Prothrow-Stith, Deborah, 228
public health problem. *See under* justice
public theology, 11–12, 146, 148–51, 231–33, 240–42, 246–47, 252, 274

Quakers, 65, 67, 85, 236

race and racism, 5, 15–28, 37, 51, 56–58, 171, 245
racial disparity. *See* disparity
Rahner, Karl, 11, 215–18
Rauschenbusch, Walter, 232–33
realism: classical realist positions, 192–93
reciprocity, 4, 7, 65, 94

Studies in Religion and Culture